PRAISE FOR *PURPOSE*

"At this time, when the credibility of American CEOs has been drowned by greed, here is a roadmap for future leaders in whose wisdom the fate of the world rests. The notes and bibliography alone are worth a read—buy this book!"
—Robert A. G. Monks, co-author of Corporate Governance

"For the pharmaceutical industry, purpose is central. Mourkogiannis makes clear how we can use purpose to draw on the passion of our people to save and improve lives."
—Dr. Daniel Vasella, CEO, Novartis

"Mourkogiannis has it right: the organizations with a moral purpose are the long-term winners because they are motivated by something more powerful than money."
—Chris Hohn, Chairman of The Children's Investment Fund

"Mourkogiannis can make things happen, because he really knows how business works."
—Professor Dr. Wolfgang Reitzle, CEO, Linde AG

"Mourkogiannis glides beautifully on the razor's edge of where we are in the current reality of the business world today. Purpose is the future practice that is here now. You will find insight that will help you become more aware and centered on the realities of practicing in today's global business environment."
—Louis Carter, President and CEO, Best Practice Institute

"Building on vast experience, Mourkogiannis analyzes what drives action and adds a new dimension to leadership. A truly inspirational piece of work."
—Thomas Thune Andersen, CEO, Maersk Oil and Partner, A.P. Moller Maersk

"An overriding sense of purpose is hard to achieve, and hard to change once achieved, but potentially transformational in its implications, as Nikos Mourkogiannis's book so persuasively demonstrates."
—*Pankaj Ghemawat, Professor, Harvard Business School*

"Across a broad array of industries and businesses, Nikos Mourkogiannis has made a substantial impact; he has an inquisitive mind with exceptional mental agility. He has turned many companies, in loss-making circumstances, into winners in this field. In *Purpose* he reveals many of the processes that have brought his clients success."
—*Sir Jackie Stewart*

"Mourkogiannis reinvents strategy by anchoring it to purpose. Strategy that has no purpose is merely tactics; true transformation of an organization depends upon the principles described in Mourkogiannis's book."
—*Dr. Reto Francioni, CEO, Deutsche Borse*

"Through his vast global business experience, Nikos Mourkogiannis offers fascinating stories and insights on the role of purpose in business success. This book will inspire CEOs, aspiring CEOs, and students of business everywhere."
—*Donald T. Phillips, author of* Lincoln on Leadership *and* On the Wing of Speed

"Nikos is the genuine Philosopher Consultant—with him you gain completely new insights."
—*Sir John Parker, Chairman, P&O and National Grid*

PURPOSE

THE STARTING POINT
OF GREAT COMPANIES

Nikos Mourkogiannis

Foreword by Roger Fisher

First published in 2006 by
PALGRAVE MACMILLAN™
175 Fifth Avenue, New York, N.Y. 10010 and
Houndmills, Basingstoke, Hampshire, England RG21 6XS.
Companies and representatives throughout the world.

PALGRAVE MACMILLAN is the global academic imprint of the Palgrave
Macmillan division of St. Martin's Press, LLC and of Palgrave Macmillan Ltd.
Macmillan® is a registered trademark in the United States, United Kingdom
and other countries. Palgrave is a registered trademark in the European Union
and other countries.

ISBN-13: 978-1-4039-7581-2
ISBN-10: 1-4039-7581-7

Library of Congress Cataloging-in-Publication Data

Mourkogiannis, Nikos.
    Purpose : the starting point of great companies / Nikos Mourkogiannis.
        p. cm.
    Includes bibliographical references and index.
    ISBN 1-4039-7581-7
    1. Business planning.   2. Leadership.   I. Title.
HD30.28.M686   2006
658.4'01-dc22

                                                                    2006049494

A catalogue record of the book is available from the British Library.

Design by Letra Libre

First edition: October 2006
10 9 8 7 6 5 4 3 2 1
Printed in the United States of America.

To Waleed Alexander Iskandar (1967–2001)

My beloved friend and colleague,
Whose altruism brought
Purpose to our lives

CONTENTS

ACKNOWLEDGMENTS

I focused on Purpose after many years of studying Leadership.

Leadership is the one conversational topic that has followed me throughout my life. Around our family table there seemed to be no discussion except what would have happened if people, famous and otherwise, had acted differently. We often started by revisiting the family war stories. But soon the stories came to involve other people that my father had met; Churchill, de Gaulle and Eisenhower were his favorites. My mother, who was from Macedonia, had only one cherished historical reference: Alexander the Great.

As I grew up, I came to know and admire two people who were significant leaders. Professor Michael Stassinopoulos, who was also a judge, one day declared null and void a decision by the then dictator of Greece. I know for a fact that Professor Stassinopoulos did not do it to become anyone's hero. He was just doing his job, interpreting the law. In the process, however, he triggered the first moral awakening against the dictatorship in my country. Eventually, in 1974, he became the Republic's first President. Professor Adamantios Pepelassis, an accomplished economist, went out of his way to find promising Greek students, myself included, and helped them pursue graduate studies in America. If it were not for him, I would not have gone to Harvard.

While at Harvard, I often traveled to Greece to work for Evangelos Averoff and Christoforos Stratos, statesmen who taught me by example that one enters the public domain only to make a contribution.

My first acknowledgments, therefore, are to my parents and to my Greek mentors.

The first person who made me think about purpose as an intellectual topic was Professor James Buchanan, who was later to receive a Nobel Prize in Economics. Professor Buchanan, who kindly asked me to be his research assistant at Virginia Polytechnic Institute, was totally preoccupied with questions of purpose, not only with the purpose of government, but also with other questions: "What is *not* the purpose of government?" "What is the purpose of private enterprise?" "What is *not* the purpose of private enterprise?"

Like many people of my generation, I spent a significant part of my time fighting the Cold War, or trying to find ideas to settle it. During this period I came to know Professor Roger Fisher at Harvard, with whom I worked for over six years. Roger's exciting purpose has been "Getting to Yes." Negotiation is his preferred strategy.

If Roger trained me to look for the answers, there were five professors of the Harvard Graduate School of Arts and Sciences who equipped me with the facility to research fundamental questions. Karl Deutsch asked the question, "What is nationalism?" Stanley Hoffman and Guido Goldman asked, "What is peace and what is war?" Sidney Verba asked, "What is different about American voters?" And Richard Musgrave asked, "What is economy and what is society?"

It was not until the Cold War ended that I came to focus on the purpose of the business firm. As a strategy consultant, I learned a lot about leadership and moral purpose from my clients. Madame Suna Kiraç taught me the most. She was the daughter of Vehbi Koç, the most successful entrepreneur and businessman in Turkey. Of Koç's four children, it was she who kept the clan together. I observed for years how she "walked the talk" of any ideal her father had preached, while at the same time transforming the conglomerate that her father had built into a regional competitor with the purpose of being Turkey's national champion.

Eight years ago I realized I wanted to focus on issues of leadership and purpose with the same singlemindedness that others had focused on strategy. For a while I thought this could be accommodated under the roof of a strategy firm. I enjoyed enormously my lengthy discussions with Mark Fuller, Bruce Allyn and other Monitor Group colleagues. Those conversations helped me to realize that I could not write a book about leadership while my work had me focused on strategy.

I took a year off and went to my house on the Isle of Wight in England where I read, thought and wrote. During this critical time, four people sustained me: Charles Seaford, who was indefatigable in research, contribution of ideas and the compilation of the bibliography on which this book rests; Richard Rawlinson, a tower of strength, who engaged me in an endless debate over the ideas; and Lord Jacob Rothschild and Sir Jackie Stewart, leaders of unique accomplishments, who continually encouraged me.

It was not until I met Art Kleiner, who helped me write an article for *strategy+business*, that my ideas crystallized. At this same time several of my Panthea colleagues contributed their own perspectives and thoughts, for which I am deeply grateful: Max Weston, Lilian King, Bill Acker, Khoi Tu, Sam Gilpin and Chiku Sinha.

It seemed that my ideas for a book could become a reality when Sal Bianco and Randy Rothenberg of Booz Allen Hamilton read a draft. Randy became its champion, introducing me to my agent, Jim Levine, who guided me through the labyrinth of publishing houses. When I met Airie Stuart at Palgrave Macmillan, I immediately sensed that she was the right editor for my book. She understood the content and related to it with passion. Jesse Kornbluth helped me polish the manuscript into a book.

My 12 years at Monitor Group taught me a lot about business and strategy, for which I am very grateful. But it was my 10 years at General Dynamics that taught me about management and allowed me to see leadership in action. I am very grateful to the people at General Dynamics who allowed me to think outside of the box: David Lewis, George Sawyer, Robert Duesenberg, Jim Mellor, Nick Chabraja, Dain Hancock, Vernon Lee, Ralph Heath, John Tibbs and Henry Gomez, to cite only a few.

A lot of gratitude is due to Booz Allen Hamilton for the support the firm has extended to this book in the past year. Shumeet Banerji realized the potential of the ideas. Dan Lewis started the ball rolling. Dennis Doughty, Klaus Mattern, Steve Wheeler and Lloyd Howell extended the support of the organization. Adrienne Crowther and

Jonathan Gage mobilized the network. John Harris generously gave of his time in introducing the ideas of the book to CEOs in both North America and Europe.

And then it was Panthea and its incredible team, as well as the clients of Panthea, who encouraged me and helped me every step of the way. Special thanks are due to Deutsche Bank, Arab Bank, Tesco and Braun for giving me an opportunity to write about their Purpose.

My wife, Janet, encouraged me to take the most difficult step of all: to leave a secure and highly remunerative position to spend a year researching and writing this book. Our daughter, Ceci, was a source of inspiration as she herself relentlessly pursued excellence in academics, music and horsemanship. My brother Alex dealt with the family affairs, allowing me to concentrate on more lofty endeavors. And none of this could have been possible without the probings of Dr. Bruce Lloyd; as the Ancient Greeks would say, "One has to know oneself before entering the public domain."

FOREWORD

by Roger Fisher

Thirty years ago, Karl Deutsch, distinguished social scientist and then chairman of the American Academy of Arts and Sciences, introduced me to one of his teaching assistants, Nikos Mourkogiannis. Deutsch would joke that the only one of his previous assistants with as heavy an accent had been Henry Kissinger. The comparison was apt in a more substantive way as well. Like Kissinger, Nikos was a young man of remarkable intelligence who sought to play a role in the major issues of the day.

Initially, Nikos worked with me to develop the curriculum for a course on negotiation that I then began to teach at Harvard. This was the beginning of several years of fruitful creative collaboration, in which he played a vital role in establishing the Harvard Law School's Program on Negotiation and refining the principles that I explored in my book *Getting to Yes*. But Nikos's true passion went beyond negotiation: It was leadership, and leadership in action, that he truly cared about. He wanted to take the Program's ideas about negotiation and put them to work in the world. To this end, he looked for ways to apply the tools we developed at Harvard to the ongoing conflict between Greece and Turkey over Cyprus. On his behalf, I invited political leaders to come and formulate possible solutions to the problem.

He also made important contributions to the Program's work on the Camp David negotiations.

Since then, Nikos's career has taken him away from academic and political circles and into the world of business via positions of responsibility in companies such as General Dynamics, Monitor Group, and now Panthea. But his life story has given him a perspective different from that of most CEOs and consultants. He has never lost sight of his desire to make positive contributions to the world around him. Having seen the effects of atrocities committed in the name of communism and nationalism in his native Greece, Nikos speaks with authority on the power of ideas to motivate people, for good or for ill. The book you are holding now is his exploration of this aspect of human nature, and the indispensable role it plays in successful leadership. It is informed by his wide reading and the insights that come from more than thirty years of first-hand experience—and reflection.

From the war on terror to human rights to domestic politics, we inhabit a world that, perhaps now more than ever, is defined by competing values and ideas. Yet somehow this basic insight is too often lost on corporate leaders, who constitute one of the world's most influential communities. Business is often mistakenly thought of as a dispassionate, value-free pursuit, reducible to quarterly earnings reports and valuations of brand equity. But just as there are no atheists in a foxhole, there are no automatons bound by the laws of finance found in a company's executive offices. There is a fundamental human need for guiding ideals that give meaning to our actions. Here Nikos refers to them as Purpose, which he correctly identifies as one of the most potent tools for managing an organization. Great leaders are those who can articulate a company's vision and inspire their employees to work toward its realization, bound together with a shared Purpose.

Over the last several years we have seen in Enron, Tyco, and others of their ilk the consequences of abandoning Purpose (or having none to begin with). Through the principles described in this book, Nikos not only shows how to avoid the practical problems that accompany corporate scandal. More importantly, he demolishes the popular conception of business as rapacious and inherently amoral.

Here business joins politics, science, and, yes, religion as one of the great avenues for bettering the world and the lives of everyday men and women. It is my hope that Nikos's book will help to dismantle the false dichotomy of financial success versus social good. It will be an essential resource for today's business leaders and for the next generation as they face the fresh challenges of this new century.

PART I

WHAT IS PURPOSE?

CHAPTER ONE

INTRODUCING PURPOSE

"One must be something, in order to do something."
—Johann Wolfgang von Goethe

Other children had fairy tales at bedtime. I had the nightmare story of my family. And from the time I was six or seven, that story was what I thought about as I drifted off to sleep—the story of the day the Communists came to our farm in Greece. They wanted my father, but my father was long gone; he'd left to fight the Communists. So the Communists made do with the women.

There were 54 women in our village that day. The Communists demanded that they denounce my father. They refused—all of them. So the Communists shot them all. Two women survived, only because there were so many bodies that the wounded could hide under the pile.

I offer this story not for shock value, but because concrete stories are usually more powerful teachers than abstract ideas. Indeed, stories are the way we learn, from childhood fairy tales to the biographies we devour. This is not to say that I recommend extreme tragedy as the best way to learn the importance of Purpose. There are less cruel ways. But one thing about tragedy is that it never—even on a good day—quite leaves you.

As a result, because of the tragedy that befell my family, I have never been in danger of forgetting the centrality of Purpose for any enterprise—because, even though my family was destroyed that day, their deaths added to the horrific body count that ultimately toppled the Communists. The women in my family died to help freedom prevail in their country.

Serious stories make for serious boys. I was 12 when I first read Thucydides and thrilled to the Funeral Oration that Pericles gave for the Athenian dead in 490 B.C. For those who have forgotten their Greek history, the background of this speech was the long-running war between Athens and Sparta. They were not just rival cities but rival cultures: "liberal" Athens and "conservative" Sparta. Their yearly battles were often inconclusive—Spartan troops regularly assaulted Athens, ran out of supplies and retreated. But the year before Pericles' speech, Sparta had been uncommonly successful. The Spartans had won a decisive battle against Athens, inflicting significant casualties, among them some of the most noble and highly regarded people in the Athenian city-state. Morale in Athens was low.

And then Pericles spoke. His words were the model for Abraham Lincoln's second inaugural address and for Winston Churchill's "Battle of Britain" speeches—I not only read the Funeral Oration speech over and over, I fell in love with it. By the time I was a teenager, I had copied it out twice. Eventually, I memorized it.

What about this speech appealed to me? This passage: "For the whole earth is the tomb of famous men; not only are they commemorated by columns and inscriptions in their own country, but in foreign lands there dwells also an unwritten memorial of them, graven not on stone but in the hearts of men." Which is to say: True fame comes from goodness and high purpose, and true fame is immortality.

As a boy, I believed that my dead family members—their names forever unknown, even in their own country—were nonetheless immortal. I wanted to be their equal, to be somebody who changed the world for the better. To do that, I concluded, I would not only have to be somebody important, I would have to stand for something—I would need to find a Purpose worth living for, and, if necessary, dying for.

✺

Just about everything that has happened in my life since I made that teenage resolution has proved to me that Purpose is crucial for all truly successful enterprises. Let others play with "strategy" and "tactics" and "management." Purpose is the game of champions. Only strong-minded men and women—adults with powerful intellects and real character and spines of steel—are suited for it.

Purpose is a function of character, and character is something we mostly notice by its absence. The news these days is filled with stories about the absence of character: Enron; Arthur Andersen; Worldcom. And that is just in the realm of business. The headlines tell us, almost on a daily basis, about the gap between rhetoric and reality in government and warfare. Even sports—with contests that take place, unscripted, in real time—have been tainted by scandal.

Behind every tainted enterprise, we like to think, is someone who simply forgot that the law applied to him. So he cut corners. He bent the rules. He didn't consider himself to be a criminal—he was just being "aggressive" and "entrepreneurial." And in the personal lives of those caught in scandal, we see more of the same self-justifying explanations. It wasn't as if they were immoral; they were good spouses, involved parents, concerned citizens.

What is troubling about the faces we see going in and out of courthouses is that they look so like ours. Could they be us? Yes, if we find ourselves "going along" with behavior that we know to be dodgy. No, if we are people of Purpose.

What is Purpose? Why is Purpose so important? Is something so seemingly esoteric really essential to effective leadership?

After all, there are plenty of success stories, in business and government alike, in which the overwhelming purpose of the leaders has been to make as much money as possible, or to be recognized as star achievers. There are many successful enterprises in which the purpose is no more than a confection, providing a little boost to morale when needed, but only peripheral to the central dynamic of maximizing profit or pursuing some other kind of tangible success.

Given these undeniable facts, why shouldn't we attribute success to, say, the personal characteristics of an individual leader (like a CEO or government head), or the workings of the top team?

Because Purpose is bigger than ambition or greed.

Purpose is bigger than tactics. Tactics represent the "how," the means by which leaders pursue their goals.

Purpose is bigger than strategy. At best, strategy is short-term Purpose, a step-by-step path toward optimal results. Enron had strategy—indeed, it had many strategies. But strategies are about means; they cannot be an end in themselves. An end is a reason. Enron lacked a reason—it lacked Purpose.

Purpose is crucial because of its scope and ubiquity. It is large, much larger than any other element in a business formula. And much more involving. It is a choice to pursue your destiny—the ultimate destination for yourself and the organization you lead. Though it represents a choice you make as a leader—a leader of yourself and others—it is not the kind of choice that you make all at once, or entirely through a rational or analytical process. A successful Purpose will incorporate a deeply felt awareness of yourself, your circumstances, and your potential calling: what the world might be asking you to do. It draws equally upon your emotional self-knowledge and intellectual thought—it calls upon everything you are, everything you've experienced, everything you believe.

Purpose is your moral DNA. It's what you believe without having to think. It's the answer you give when you're asked for the right—as opposed to the factually correct—answer.

☙

Purpose is crucial to a firm's success for three reasons.

First, Purpose is the primary source of achievement. Most stories about wealth creation and success are far easier to understand when we recognize the part that Purpose has played.

Second, Purpose reveals the underlying dynamics of any human activity, the most fundamental issues involving motivation and behavior, in either a community or an organization. It's the core energy, the element that fuels everything else, big and small.

Third, Purpose is all that successful leaders want to talk about—although they do not usually use the word itself. They care about it because of what they see every day: The executives they value most are all driven by Purpose, and the executives they worry about most are not.

I appreciate that Purpose is not commonly understood to be an animating idea. In Business 101, it's not just overlooked, it's completely ignored. All the focus is on economics: Public companies make products or perform services that create profits for their shareholders; private companies exist to support their owners; non-profits create value for the funds they are given. Money, money, money.

And in the real world of business and public affairs, Purpose gets only a little more respect. Recommending business books for the *Wall Street Journal*, Gil Schwartz, chief of public relations at CBS, has this to say about a book that guts the importance of Purpose in human affairs—Niccolo Machiavelli's *The Prince:*

> *Masquerading as a philosophical treatise in support of a strong senior executive, this book is actually a road map for ruthless narcissists—the kind that does very well because their primary concern at all times is Numero Uno. Machiavelli discovered a central truth that leads to business success: Moral concerns have very little utility in the day-to-day conduct of successful management. No, it's not a nice book. It advises all kinds of pre-emptive murder and destruction of one's enemies and, when necessary, of one's friends. But an embrace of its world view has been at the center of virtually all executive success since the beginning of time. What Machiavelli did was to make the tactics of the big guys available to anybody who cared to consider them. A firm grasp of his tenets creates a business etiquette that is at once cool, polite, thoughtful, strategic and brutal.*

One sentence jumps out: "Moral concerns have very little utility in the day-to-day conduct of successful management." But in reality, this is not the case: Moral concerns in fact have immense utility. And so my book represents an answer to that kind of knife-at-the-ready, quarterly-results-are-all, get-a-corner-office-at-any-cost thinking. I acknowledge that an executive can rise quickly to the top by brilliant gamesmanship—but at some point you have to do the job. And you just might have to do the job when business turns bad and there's a terrible crisis and your people are looking to you for leadership like baby birds in a nest awaiting their mother's return with food. What help is Machiavelli then? When there's no one left to knife, and there's nothing you stand for, won't the knives be pointed at you?

⁂

Ralph Waldo Emerson said that "business is divine activity." That is what I have come to believe—that people who aim high are the ones who go high. I believe that Purpose turns out to be the quality that CEOs most need in order to do their jobs well. Purpose is what they look for in the executives they select to succeed them. Purpose is the difference between good and great, between honorable success and legendary performance, between fifteen minutes of fame and a legacy.

We may read in the papers about whistle-blowers who do the right thing—and get crushed. Or major executives who say no to immoral schemes, and are ejected from the executive floor. Purpose is no guarantee of success, in itself. But it is a prerequisite—at least for success in the long term. The road to the top requires a clear, consistent understanding of the reasons for our decisions and actions. And the rewards of keeping to the institution's highest values, while adjusting strategy along the way, are reflected in title, power and money. The acclaim of millions, the bust in the hall—the big rewards—don't go to the hustlers. They go to the heroes, to the leaders with Purpose.

I believe that Purpose—not money, not status—is what people most want from work. Make no mistake: They want compensation; some want an ego-affirming title. Even more, though, they want their lives to mean something, they want their lives to have a reason. In the Middle Ages, craftsmen worked—with no thought of personal recognition—on cathedrals that even their grandchildren would not live to see completed. That didn't bother them; in fact, it kept them going. For what is more important than doing God's work? Bach, at the bottom of his compositions, wrote SDG—Soli deo Gloria, "to God alone the glory." In the composer's view, he was simply the messenger. You don't have to be religious, or an artist, to want a Purpose in your life. It's simply a matter of seeing the meaninglessness of modern material culture. Once you've received that message, Purpose may matter a great deal to you.

⁂

My views of Purpose are not abstract. They come from my experience. When I graduated from Athens Law School, I was the valedictorian. It should have been a great day. Instead, I was weeping—in sorrow and anger. The sorrow was for my country. The Turkish Army had staged a second invasion; many Greeks were dead. The anger was for members of my graduating class—two policemen who had, during the regime of the Colonels, "invited" me to the police station to be "questioned." In my valedictory speech, seeing them there in the same room, I wondered if I should say anything about that incident. Should I let it go? Sorrow ruled. I held my rage.

By the time I enrolled at Harvard that fall, I was even more disturbed. There had been more violence in Cyprus; it was difficult to concentrate on graduate courses in Economics. By my second year, I was in crisis. I told a professor: "All these theories are fine, but I need theory that can become practice and make a better world—I have to do something to help my country." He sent me to see Roger Fisher, a professor at Harvard Law who was exploring new strategies of negotiation. This was exactly what I was looking for. I worked with Professor Fisher's team on developing Harvard's first course in Negotiation. (I also joined the campaign to get the U.S. Congress to impose an arms embargo on Turkey. This was not terribly wise—foreigners are not allowed by law to participate in American politics. I risked deportation. But I had to do something to help Greece.)

Professor Fisher's course in Negotiation eventually became the third most-attended course at Harvard and was introduced to many

American professional schools. I taught this course for several years, in the process helping Professor Fisher develop the ideas that led to the best-selling book *Getting to Yes*. In 1978, I was part of the team that devised the "Single Negotiating Text," a technique used by Secretary of State Cyrus Vance to establish peace between Israel and Egypt in the Camp David Accords. Three years later, I was appointed senior advisor to the Harvard Negotiation Project.

But I was attracted to the world outside academia. In 1982, I joined Westinghouse as Manager of Business Development for Europe and the Middle East. I coined the word "offsets" and put together the first "offset" programs in support of Westinghouse's defense division, which was a major supplier of the F–16 aircraft. Yes, I wanted to move peace forward, to be present at the signing of treaties. But these were the 1980s, and the Soviets were rattling their sabers—and you can't negotiate with anyone who's brandishing a weapon. I went into the American defense industry very consciously, the better to defend Greece against the Communists. I had, you might say, taken on my father's struggle.

I have been accused of being the person who masterminded the "commercial sale" of F–16s to Greece at the beginning of the 1980s. I plead guilty. Until the first sale of F–16s to Greece, commercial sales of military aircraft were unheard of. It was necessary to have the concept of "commercial sales" in order to enable those first 40 F–16s to go to Greece when the American and Greek governments were experiencing a period of extremely frosty relations, effectively not talking to each other. My purpose was not just to contain the Soviets, but also to pre-empt the Turks from taking advantage of a period of Greek military weakness and political isolation. It was this purpose, definitely not the salary I received as the employee of a defense contractor, that made me work day and night for years, thinking far outside the box and with dogged determination.

Even though the sale of the F–16s was immensely popular with all the centrists in Greece, one group was opposed to it, even more than the Communists were. The Greek extreme right blamed me for pushing the sale through, because it helped a Socialist government, headed by Andreas Papandreou, to prolong its stay in power. But given my purpose, I made it my duty to disregard all considerations of power politics and money.

From Westinghouse I moved on to General Dynamics, where, in 1984, I was named its youngest Director of Programs. Five years later, I resigned. The Berlin Wall had fallen. Communism as we knew it had come to an end. I flew to Greece to see my father. He was old and, everyone said, failing. But he was clearly pleased to hear the news about the Soviets' fall. And, with eyes shining, he had a question for me: "Now . . . what about the Chinese?"

❧

But I had fulfilled my obligation to my father. Indeed, I was ready for a personal "peace dividend." I asked General Dynamics to send me to Harvard Business School for two years so that I could continue to explore my obsession: the relationship between Purpose and achievement. It was, I saw, one thing to defeat evil, another to do good. Dimly, I could see the outline of a new career—bringing ideas into action. Not just accomplishing day-to-day results but actually making a better world, by making companies more effective and more fully realized in their Purposes.

I was in my late thirties when I went to Harvard Business School. After graduating in 1992, I joined Monitor Company, a strategy consulting firm founded by Harvard Business School professors Mike Porter and Mark Fuller. And as I worked with companies and helped them address their problems, I began to see something that no one else was really talking about—their problems tended to stem from a lack of idealism. Making companies more effective was too abstract a goal. To make better companies, one must start with developing better leaders. I had a chance to test this approach between 1994 and 1996, when I was head of Global Recruiting at Monitor; as I interviewed and hired hundreds of new MBAs and graduates, I checked out their values and ambitions.

The bottom line about recruiting is, it's mostly dependent on internal morale. The Harvard MBAs would call people from the preceding classes who were already at our firm. The testimony of our employees had much more impact than all the presentations and social events we would put together to attract the best. (This was especially true of foreign students, who had their own tightly knit networks, and who I was particularly interested to attract because I saw how vital they would be to a mid-sized firm with international ambitions.)

Later, as head of Eurasia for Monitor, I was more involved with clients. I led the growth of the firm in countries such as Turkey, UAE, Russia, Greece, Germany, France and Israel. Waleed Iskandar—the colleague to whom this book is dedicated—and others who joined me expected as their reward very careful attention to their individualized needs for professional development and the functioning of a joyous and mutually supportive community. This gave me my first inkling into something that would become my motto at Panthea: "The best way to grow a firm is to grow its people." Monitor indeed experienced phenomenal growth in Eurasia. I remain very proud of the achievements of the team.

Later, as chairman and CEO of Monitor Europe, Eurasia, Africa and the Middle East, I had to cope with the dot com revolution, which caused the greatest upheaval in the history of the consulting industry. Times had changed; we could not offer traditional rewards and compete with the dot coms. We were on the defensive. History had taught me that the best way to lift morale in an aggressive war is to invoke ideology, but the best way to sustain morale in a defensive war is through patriotism. So with Waleed's help, I appealed to the loyalty of our younger employees in the community. We did not lose a single account in Europe. And our ranks grew as senior and junior hires from other firms noticed both our newly minted equity program and our revitalized programs for training consultants.

In 2004, I resigned from Monitor to do the reading and thinking that led me to write this book. These ideas were also instrumental in my decision to join Panthea (Greek for "many gods"), a firm that consults with companies on strategic leadership issues. Conceptually, we try to combine a broad overview of the many sources of organizational effectiveness with the deep impact that leaders can have, within

and outside their organizations. This tends to involve us in comprehensive initiatives, working primarily with CEOs and on large issues
that require changes in strategy, in leadership direction, and in organizational capability.

Along the way, I have had to confront a variety of attitudes, in
myself and others, that make it difficult to see the value of Purpose
clearly. One is the idolization of "character" as the source of success.
"In moments of crisis," the business guru Warren Bennis has said,
"style dissolves into character." But for those who believe that their
ability to handle a crisis depends only on their own character, style
will dissolve into panic whenever a serious crisis threatens their self-
esteem. An understanding of Purpose makes it easier to follow the
ancient learning ritual—fail and try again, fail and try again, and ultimately succeed.

Another attitude I had to confront, again and again, was magical
thinking. Many people, consciously or not, grow up looking to someone greater than themselves—a father or mother figure with perceived magic powers—to step in and solve major problems. This is
the concept of the CEO as Moses, if not as God Himself. He or she is
all-knowing and charismatic, and will be seen as legitimate as long as
the masquerade holds. But when the charismatic CEO fails, many
people assume that there is something wrong, even duplicitous, about
the individual. They don't understand that any individual without a
clear Purpose would fail in that position.

The more I saw the absence of Purpose, the more I knew that values mattered, and not just to me. The modern world may not know
how to phrase the question, but it wants its own realistic recipe for
Purpose. Competition has done us a lot of good in the last half-cen-
tury, but one question remains inadequately addressed: "What are we
competing *for?*" Leaders all over the world are now increasingly motivated to deal with that question. Some of them feel that it is part of
their mandate. There is an increasing, albeit unspoken, preoccupa-
tion with doing the right thing. In the last few years in particular—in
my dialogues with the chairmen and CEOs that I respect, and in reports of critical issues on the front pages of daily newspapers—I can
see the thought frontier moving from an obsession with "How do we

get the results we want?" back to "What is to be done?" and "Why does it have to be done?"

So I thought again about Thucydides, the first to write about the "man and the plan"—that is, the relationship between leadership and strategy. His purpose, he said at the time, was to teach. Historians have used that statement to claim that he was the father of historical writing. But no writer writes just for posterity. Thucydides was also writing for the leaders of his generation. He was the first to write systematically about the importance of Purpose in leadership decisions. The strategies he described, the orations and the campaigns were all part of his curriculum in Leadership studies.

This thought gave me an anchor: The domain that I would serve would be Leadership. Not in history, but in business, the field I knew best—business leadership, from the vantage point of philosophy. At Panthea, we help CEOs excavate their moral codes and apply those beliefs, where possible, to their businesses. In this way, they not only find a personal source of strength, they find a way of inspiring their colleagues and getting everyone's eyes on the real prize: The contribution that they make, to wealth and humanity alike, from yoking Purpose together with their own innate energy, creativity, talent and resources.

As I've said, ideas are powerful but stories are more powerful. So I went back to my library, this time to read about the pioneers of American business—men who seized the opportunities of unfettered, unregulated capitalism to shape their companies and their century as well. Even allowing for the differences between their time and ours, it was obvious that these men were not gods in the temple of charisma; today they might never be appointed CEOs. But they were visionaries, and not just in their businesses—they had Purpose. Indeed, the common thread that linked these great figures of the twentieth century was Purpose.

I believe that today's business leaders—and tomorrow's—can be inspired by stories of Purpose. Thus, I have not limited my stories to past success, but also to some leaders—such as Warren Buffett of Berkshire Hathaway, Lord John Browne of BP, Steve Jobs of Apple Computer and others—who are very active today. My intent in including them is not to lionize them as individuals, but rather to show how an explicit sense of Purpose has enabled them to attain their visible and well-known accomplishments.

✌

It is my hope that this book finds a number of audiences.

First, of course, it is for the CEOs and leaders of today's organizations. These men and women will be in their late forties and fifties, when what Erik Erikson called "the crisis of generativity" manifests itself. They have worked hard and achieved much; now they are looking for meaning. They want their lives to matter, and the obvious way to do that is to make their companies and organizations great. And not just during the remaining years of their stewardship—they want to leave their successors poised to rule the future. That will require instituting more than good business practices and developing executives the right way. At the end of the day, that will require articulating the company's Purpose with clarity and eloquence, and making sure that message reaches every employee and every critical outside constituency, be they unions, the press, local and national government, or—most important of all—customers.

Second, this book is for executives who aspire to become CEOs. There are volumes galore that will give them strategic advice and shiny new ways to get attention and "manage up." But to my mind, there is no other book that shows them that the real way to get ahead is to stand for something—to explicitly and consciously develop values that will coalesce into the kind of Purpose that businesses can follow to succeed in today's world.

Happily for all of us, I believe that this 25-to-45-year-old audience hungers for Purpose. A colleague writes: "My generation has spent a decade enhancing our own employability—becoming increasingly skilled mercenaries interested in getting paid and promoted, changing firms or building new ones in the chase for 'success.' It hasn't been very satisfying. We no longer have loyalty to a firm, we're lonely from being journeymen, we're disillusioned by pure material gain. Purpose matters because it makes work meaningful and integrates it into my life; it enables me to feel pride in what I do and liberates me to do it better. And it gives me a mantra: 'Do the right thing and do well.'" He has it exactly right.

Finally, this book is for business students and those who are contemplating business careers but are hesitant for any number of reasons. In our time, many people clearly hunger for worthy challenges and for the opportunity to produce achievements that endure. In my own career, I have learned, as leaders do, that the Purpose-driven climb to the top is as satisfying as the view from the mountain top. It is a great thing to receive great rewards for hard work. It is a greater thing to do so in a way that ripples out into the world, inspiring others and helping them, in their turn, set a meaningful example for those who follow.

༄

This is what I hope you will take away from this book.

Purpose is preparation for doing what is right and what is worthwhile. As such it creates a sense of obligation. But this obligation is not a weight or a drag in any way—it's a way of knowing what you can and can't do. Because Purpose provides certainty, it also provides confidence. All of that comes together to contribute to a firm's competitive advantage. "Do the right thing and do well"—a new way of saying "Do well by doing good."

Interpretation is up to the individual. And indeed, people define "goodness" in personal ways. "Purpose" elicits the same subjective response. In the chapters that follow, I will focus on four specific Purposes—four moral ideas that appeal to our deepest instincts and that can inspire a business or enterprise to long-term success in today's world. A Purpose's effectiveness depends both on its relevance to the problems that leaders face today, and on its connection to the shared culture of humanity. It must draw on philosophical ideas that have stood the test of time. Not all ideas are born equal.

There are many more moral ideas that we could consider, but these four are fully realized moral traditions in our culture, and they are also equipped to form the basis for a competitive Purpose in today's commercial society. These Purposes revolve around four conceptions of what is right and worthwhile; they involve pursuit of Discovery (the *new*), Excellence (the *intrinsically beautiful*), Altruism (the *helpful*) and Heroism (the *effective*).

Each idea provides an ultimate justification for an action. The discoverer seeks action that is freely chosen for the sake of advancing into new places. The pursuer of excellence seeks action that constitutes innate fulfilment for its own sake (and thus "beautiful" or "elegant"). The altruist seeks action that increases happiness. And the hero seeks action that demonstrates achievement.

In each of these four ways, those who act with Purpose distinguish themselves from other mortals. The ideas behind these principles were best articulated by four great philosophers: Søren Kierkegaard, Aristotle, David Hume and Friedrich Nietzsche.

These ideas, and the wars between them, drive action in all walks of life, including business. In this respect business is not different from politics, or culture or any other public activity. Accordingly, these ideas represent neither a constraint on business (an obligation that becomes a cost item or reduces profits) nor an enabler of business success (a tool for making profits). Instead, these ideas, when understood and articulated, drive the business forward.

Six key points about Purpose:
- It is based on well-established moral ideas. To build a business that lasts, one does well to draw on ideas that have lasted.
- It advances both competitiveness and morality: Purpose is in an area of overlap between the two.
- It relates people to plans and it relates leaders to their colleagues.
- It cannot be chosen quickly or on an ad hoc basis; it has to be discovered, and this may take time and trial and error.
- It is a matter of a firm's life or death. Its presence can transform a firm and its loss can destroy an institution. As a result, it is worth more money than anything else.
- Finally, it is a paradox. It will boost profits—but will only do so if it is pursued for its own sake. It will boost morale, build the brand, help in assessing the strategy—but it can never be just a

tool. It is this duality that makes Purpose difficult to harness—
and hence so valuable.

WHO HAS IT?

There is always a story of Purpose underlying the identity of significant business leaders. It may not always be the same story that the
outside world perceives, but it is there to be seen when you look
closely at the leader and the impact of his or her organization. Consider, for example, the stories of four leaders and the organizations
they founded, all of which continue to sustain success long after their
deaths: Henry Ford (and the Ford Motor Company), Thomas J.
Watson, Sr. (and IBM), Sam Walton (and Wal-Mart), and Siegmund
Warburg (and the S. G. Warburg investment bank, headquartered in
London). What is interesting in their stories is not just their motivation; while all four men became wealthy, their Purposes transcended
making money. More significantly, in each case their personal, moral
and commercial Purposes supported each other: The same actions
served all of their goals.

Ford set out to end the "frightful rule of folly and chance," to use
Nietzsche's words, in the form of a powerful new machine called the
motor vehicle. This *heroism* led him to develop the Model T—the
one car he believed the world wanted and needed. Warburg more
than once bet his own career and the reputation of his firm in order
to win a takeover battle. He emerged victorious very often, and always the hero of the iconoclasts. Warburg's *heroism* was also closely
linked with Nietzsche—the only difference between him and Ford
was that he knew it and he spoke about it. Watson set out to find
things "beyond our present conception." His emphasis on *discovery*,
even when times were bad, meant IBM grew when times were good.
Walton set out to serve his customers in a way that would exalt and
inspire their lives. Among his employees he instilled the ethic that
they, like him, would treat customers "better than sales people in
other stores did." This ingrained *altruism* led to an incredibly tightly
managed organization—one that could always negotiate the best

prices, deliver goods rapidly across long distances, and remain flexible and responsive.

Of course, outsiders may not always credit Sam Walton with altruism; they may attribute more self-interest to Wal-Mart than to other organizations. They may also have good reason for feeling this way. But this does not affect the degree to which an ideal of service drove Sam Walton and his employees during his lifetime, and made possible Wal-Mart's success.

Nor is the impact of Purpose visible only in business stories from the past. Today, well-known leaders in the private sector can be found who embody each of these Purposes. Warren Buffett has always explicitly pursued *excellence*—as he once wrote, he considers himself an artist, and investment his "canvas." This has led him to a highly rational, measured investment style in a very small organization (Berkshire Hathaway) that has allowed him to benefit from Wall Street's less refined competition. Like Henry Ford before him, Bill Gates is an avatar of heroism; his corporate Purpose, from the beginning, has been tied to a will to achieve on a scale beyond that of any other company. Richard Branson, the creative spirit behind the Virgin Group of companies, embodies discovery in each of his enterprises: a means or technique that will allow him to understand the world better, and thus offer a distinctive new service. And Herb Kelleher's Southwest Airlines was altruistic in its intent from the beginning: to make airline travel inexpensive and comfortable for the sake of the customers who flew with them. David Neeleman, founder of JetBlue, took that altruistic concept one step further and successfully competed with Southwest on its own Purposeful turf.

Some companies change Purpose at the moment of CEO transition: Jack Welch's heroism has been supplanted by Jeffrey Immelt's Purpose of discovery at GE. This is an appropriate change given the company's role in shepherding the next wave of industrial infrastructure. Some leaders carry the same Purpose from one company to the next: Steve Jobs has been a living symbol of excellence at Apple, NeXt, Pixar and Apple again, and he will undoubtedly bring the same Purpose to Disney. And some leaders may well switch Purposes during the course of their own careers, as Lord John Browne of BP has done. Through most of the 1990s, like its archrival ExxonMobil, BP was a company with a highly heroic Purpose; but in championing the environmental cause and taking up a role as the most proactive oil company in facing climate change, no matter where that decision may lead it, BP has adopted a mantle of discovery instead.

Every time a company changes Purpose, there is a transformation involved. When the leaders understand this shift in Purpose and are explicitly prepared to talk and think about it, then the transformation is likely to succeed. When they don't, the transformation is likely to stall, backfire or short-circuit.

Finally, it is not just famous entrepreneurs or large corporations who display Purpose. Anyone who leads a modern enterprise, large or small, public or private, can discover a Purpose and manage it so that it contributes to competitive advantage.

&

How can leaders use Purpose to create advantage? Leaders do not simply invent a Purpose; they discover it, while at the same time developing a strategy and ensuring that Purpose and strategy support each other. This requires that they listen to themselves and their colleagues, and are sensitive to their moral ideas, as well as being aware of the commercial opportunities offered by the firm's strengths.

Then they must establish a Community of Purpose in their organizations, offering themselves as prototypes, and they must negotiate the individual tasks and goals that will convert the resulting sense of Purpose into action. They must keep the Purpose under review—ensuring, through the negotiations of tasks, that it remains right for the firm and for the people in it. And they must also ensure that there are systems and mechanisms in place that maintain the momentum.

An effective Purpose will not simply translate into goals. It will also stimulate and guide actions in the firm that are not specified in this formal way, illuminating and guiding day-to-day interactions with customers and colleagues. The Purpose gives the array of these actions coherence, not just at any given moment, but over time, and thus helps ensure that the firm does achieve a genuine specialization, a genuine difference from its competitors. In this way it makes superior profits possible.

Purpose also reduces risk aversion and fear, and helps innovators see beyond current convention. It underpins trust between individuals both within and beyond the firm, as well as making individuals more sensitive to each other's requirements. In these ways Purpose stimulates the two key forms of action that contribute to the strengths of the firm and thus competitive advantage—innovation and the formation of relationships. These forms of action constantly refresh the firm's strengths, creating an enduring advantage that is not dependent on the fate of this or that strategic position.

⤲

It is very unusual for senior executives to diagnose their problems in terms of Purpose. Normally the symptoms will seem to point to something else, something less profound. Here are some telltale situations that indicate that something is lacking in the realm of Purpose:

1. There appears to be a morale problem in the company—things are flat, there's a shortage of energy, no buzz. Often this flatness is accompanied by a feeling among employees that the top management cannot or will not "walk the talk"—that they do not really believe what they say.
2. There are calls for a new strategy. Sometimes this means there is a need for a completely new direction, sometimes just a need for reassurance, a rediscovery of the foundations of the current strategy.
3. There are problems implementing the strategy. The segments to be targeted have been identified, the action plans developed—but action, or at least the right action, does not follow.
4. There are reputational problems that just will not go away. However much the chief executive declares integrity as a core value and despite the best efforts of the PR department,

newspapers continue to report a series of scandals—even minor ones seem newsworthy.

5. There is a window of opportunity for a new direction—for example a new chairman or chief executive has been appointed, and this creates an expectation that the company will rediscover its way, or get back to its roots, or find a new sense of itself.

6. There is a major structural change—typically a merger or acquisition—that forces a re-examination of the company's strategy and its employees' sense of direction and identity.

Do these situations sound familiar? They should; these days, it seems that most companies are afflicted with problems involving Purpose in one way or another. In which case, what follows should be of interest even to those who thought they had seen the last of philosophy when they staggered out of their required humanities course in their freshman year of college. Because Purpose is the way to succeed. And when you get down to ultimate motivation, no sane person enters business to fail.

CHAPTER TWO

THE REAL VALUE OF PURPOSE

I f you ask people anywhere in the world to name an American soft drink, why do they always say "Coke?"

It's not the taste. It's not the advertising. It's the power of the brand—a power built upon the brand's Purpose.

That Purpose went international during World War II, when CEO Robert Woodruff promised to put a bottle of Coke in the hands of every American soldier. The U.S. government built almost one hundred Coke bottling plants overseas, which enabled Coca-Cola to supply American soldiers with 95 percent of the soft drinks they consumed during the war. And when the war ended, Coca-Cola had the makings of a global business, courtesy of the U.S. government.

Coke used that opportunity brilliantly. In the most distant villages, where no one had any profound association of the United States, people equated Coke with America. To drink Coke was to taste freedom. For a price almost anyone could afford, citizens of repressive dictatorships could—for a few moments—feel what it was like to be free.

The Purpose of Coke was thus to provide freedom in a bottle.

And a powerful Purpose it was. Talk all you want about Ronald Reagan bringing down the Berlin Wall, there were other factors. Blue jeans. Rock music. The Catholic Church. And Coke. Indeed, as the Wall was crumbling, the Coca-Cola Company was shipping truck-loads of Coke to Eastern Europe.

Strategies must be re-examined every few years. If a company is lucky, Purpose is forever—or, at least for two or three decades. And that seemed to be the case with Coca-Cola in the 1980s and 1990s. Freedom was spreading around the world, and Coke was always there, a celebration of that freedom, a kind of pop champagne.

Cut to 2003, and America's invasion of Iraq. The president's ad-visers spoke of U.S. troops being welcomed with flowers; one can imagine Coca-Cola bottlers loading cases of soft drinks bound for Basra and Baghdad. But then everything went wrong. America's civil-ian leaders failed to prepare for an insurrection. America's traditional allies sat on their hands. Civil war followed. The liberators were de-scribed as imperialists, invaders, colonialists.

That harsh assessment has persisted ever since. And, around the world, hostility to America has been extended to products that symbol-ize the United States. What does Coke represent now? As a global brand, it's the pause that refreshes—that is, the pause that refreshes op-pressors. Freedom? For a taste of that, many people—even if repelled by insurgency and terrorism—will drink anything *but* sodas associated with the United States. And, in Europe, other companies have begun to believe that Coke's market share just might be vulnerable.

Can Coca-Cola find a new marketing strategy to address this changed perception? I think not. Such a strategy would be of the mo-ment and on the fly—a hostage to ongoing political and military de-velopments. Coke could not hope to find a message powerful and seductive enough to change negative perceptions for very long by adopting a new marketing strategy.

Coke has had a long run with its global Purpose. Now it is time for a new one.

Consider: Back when Coke became a global brand, one of its selling points was that it was safe to drink. In places where the local water might be risky, Coke was a beverage you could trust—it didn't make you sick.

Now, in many places, water is once again an issue. This time, it's not just purity, it's also scarcity. What Coke needs to do abroad is what it's already doing in America—wean consumers off sugar-based drinks, sell them "healthy" beverages instead, and, if necessary, address local issues of shortages and purity.

Coke, in short, needs to make its Purpose a socially redeeming one: alleviating thirst around the world.

If you wanted to make this case to the CEO of Coca-Cola, you would argue for the importance of Purpose by repeating its key advantage: Not all companies have a Purpose—but enduringly successful ones do.

Purpose makes employees feel their work is worthwhile and so maintains morale and energy levels. If effectively managed, it also guides their work, leading them to do things that create competitive advantage for the company.

Sam Walton turned serving the customer into a Purpose for his associates at Wal-Mart. By tapping into their natural good feelings toward fellow human beings, he made them feel that what they were doing was worthwhile. He led them to treat customers in a friendly and helpful way, which built customer loyalty and thus advantage. And he could do this because these were his feelings—and because he communicated them at every turn.

Or consider JetBlue, one of the rare airlines in America that are fun to fly. The individual televisions are part of the reason. So are the roomy leather seats and generous legroom. But the real difference between JetBlue and other carriers is that the employees actually seem to enjoy their jobs—they actually like serving you. And so, at the end of a flight, when they ask you to help them tidy up the plane so it can take-off again more rapidly, you're happy to pitch in. Where does that attitude come from? It comes from the CEO and founder, David Neeleman, who is not above quietly boarding a plane, donning a steward's apron, and announcing, "Hi, I'm Dave, the CEO of JetBlue. I'm here to serve you this evening, and I'm looking forward to meeting each of you before we land." It's a simple formula: The CEO has a reason beyond business for running his company in a certain way, and he communicates that reason, and his employees accept it, believe it and follow it.

The value in establishing a Purpose and tapping employees' hunger for that Purpose has long been recognized. Henry Ford was sued by his own shareholders in 1914 for breach of fiduciary responsibility. On the witness stand, he argued in effect that businesses run solely for shareholder profit would ultimately make less money than businesses run for Purpose. When Philip Selznick wrote in 1957 about the differences between "organizations" (which were "technical instruments judged on engineering premises") and "institutions" (which were "the receptacles of group idealism"), he made it clear that the role of leaders was to turn organizations into institutions.[1] In 1981 Richard Pascale and Anthony Athos identified "vision" as a key component distinguishing successful Japanese management from unsuccessful American management.[2]

Thirteen years later, Jerry Porras and Jim Collins reported that strong underlying values, and purposes going beyond profit, were a distinguishing feature of some large U.S. companies that had long outperformed their peers.[3] Purpose "reflects the importance people attach to the company's work," as the authors put it, and they quote Dave Packard as a typical leader of such outperforming companies: "Profitability . . . is a means to more important ends. People get together in a company [in order to] accomplish something collectively that they could not accomplish separately . . . they make a contribution to society." More recently, in 2002, Richard Ellsworth argued that top management's purpose needs to be serving customers, not maximizing profit, if it is to achieve long-term competitive advantage.[4] Paradoxically, shareholders are best served by those who do not care too much about them.

But renunciation of worldly affairs, while it may be a good purpose for a monastery, is not in itself a viable purpose for business. Managers that want a company to last should build it on ideas that have lasted. Among these are offering great products, giving good service and focusing on the customer.

In their influential book *Built to Last*, Porras and Collins tell us that the content of the ideas animating a corporation matters little compared to how hard they are pushed by management.[5] I disagree. The content of a purpose matters. It is true that an institution that draws a tight boundary between its members and the rest of the world can effectively brainwash those members into believing anything. This is the technique of some religious groups; perhaps some exceptional companies have a comparable hold on their employees' attitudes. But in an era when the average length of employment with one company is 4.5 years,[6] employees don't stay around long enough for cult-like allegiance to become standard business practice.

A successful Purpose both drives a company forward and helps build sustainable competitive advantage. In the hands of an effective leader, Purpose becomes the engine of a company, the source of its energy. And you can tell, by a loss of energy, whenever there has been a lessening of Purpose. Such lassitude often happens after a major change—a change in the strategic environment, or a change in ownership, or a reorganization. These may precipitate some kind of crisis, and for a time the energy generated by the crisis keeps the company going. But when the company is emerging from its crisis, it enters the real danger zone. If it does not reconnect to its Purpose at this stage, it simply stops moving forward. Things do not happen. The old systems and incentives no longer summon up employees' creativity and energies. Teams no longer fire off each other and people either fall back on routine or lose direction because they're not sure what to do.

The result is an upsurge in anxiety, demoralized employees, lower productivity, top management disproportionately preoccupied with reassuring outside constituencies, painful efforts to restructure the firm, frustration with vain efforts to revive it, the eventual split of the top team and ultimately the decline of the firm or unfavorable absorption by another. As a client said to me years ago, "Bankruptcy is not so painful because it is an event. It is the decline that I dread because then the pain lasts for ever."

Purpose is more important now than it has ever been. Those companies that are genuinely "receptacles of group idealism," to use Selznick's phrase, stand out sharply against a background of corporate greed, scandal and moral uncertainty. In 2004 a survey conducted by the UK Committee on Standards in Public Life ranked directors of large companies among the "least trusted"—barely above tabloid journalists and real estate agents but below MPs.[7] A survey in the United States in 2002 found that only 26 percent of the public believe companies are straightforward and honest in their dealings[8] while a World Economic Forum report in 2003 showed a significant decline in levels of trust in companies over the previous two years in almost all countries where data was available.[9] By many accounts, the mistrust of corporations has become even more pronounced since then. The triumphant capitalism of the late nineties is over.

But interest in Purpose is growing. And it's more than a passing fashion or a reaction to the ethical problems of the new millennium. Uncertainty breeds a desire for something to believe in, a code of behavior that's immune to fads. And when uncertainty takes the form of frequent layoffs and ever-changing executive teams, there's even more demand for Purpose. The point was made by Goran Lindahl, former chief executive of ABB, the Swiss-Swedish Industrial Giant: "In the end managers are not loyal to a particular boss or even to a company but to a set of values they believe in and find satisfying."[10]

In an era of change, the hope is that shared Purpose will provide an anchor, something to hold on to, which will make insecurity more tolerable. It will do in the twenty-first century what job loyalty was meant to do in the twentieth. And in an era of innovation, Purpose will justify the risks associated with innovation, which would not normally be acceptable to executives focused on short-term profits.[11]

Purpose works wonderfully as rhetoric. Who's against it? No one. But an effective Purpose has to involve more than rhetoric. It has to drive strategy, and help shape the choices managers make. Even more importantly, it has to motivate employees and underpin the dynamics of the company's teams, including its top team. If Purpose is to play such a vital role, it must have a moral dimension.

In the dictionary, morality and ethics are synonyms; both concern the question of distinguishing right from wrong behavior. But in practice, they have come to mean different things. Today, ethics generally refers to day-by-day guidelines: People mostly think of "ethics" in its breach. Corporate behavior, for example, is often pointed out as "unethical," but few people have thought much about the nature of "ethical" behavior, by corporations or anyone else. By contrast, "morality" has come to refer to the standards of good behavior. A moral code is a means of distinguishing conduct that is acceptable from conduct that is not. Since different people around the world have very different standards of morality, it is difficult to argue that any one standard of morality is absolutely right; and I do not make that argument in this book. But I do argue that some standards of morality are more effective than others, particularly as sources of understanding about Purpose for corporate or organizational success.

The most effective standards of morality, when it comes to Purpose, are internally consistent. They do not contradict themselves. They are also relevant; they speak to the decisions that leaders are trying to make right now. And they agree with our sensibilities; they appeal to our ideas about what is right and what is worthwhile. As such they create a sense of obligation.

Please note that "moral" does not necessarily mean "altruistic." There are many moral ideas that have nothing to do with "serving others," or even with "doing unto others as you would have them do unto you." A moral idea is one that concerns itself with the value of some types of human activity over others. A moral Purpose is one that adopts a valued end result for human activity, over a person's lifetime or the lifetime of an organization. Ultimately, only a Purpose governed by morality can drive a firm's competitive advantage, for the simple reason that success is ultimately a moral matter: It stems from the continued discipline of making decisions that favor some actions regularly, and not others.

Morality is personal. And there are many personal reasons why an individual leader might develop a particular purpose for a business, firm or organization. The four Purposes at the heart of this book are not the only possible purposes one might choose—as we'll see, there are many others. But these four are by far the most likely to engender success. Different people, of course, are likely to be attracted to different Purposes, and they will be drawn to environments reflecting those Purposes. See which of these descriptions apply to you.

DISCOVERY: ADVENTURE'S CHALLENGE

Discovery put men on the moon, America on the map and the dot coms in business. It involves a love of the new and the innovative, and it animates many technological businesses. At Sony, the "joy of technological innovation" was explicitly stated by its founder as one of the reasons for the company's existence,[12] and innovation has consistently driven 3M.

Many of the dot com entrepreneurs were driven by intellectual curiosity; they believed they were reinventing their industries, economics and indeed themselves. There were no constraints: As an employee or inventor, what you did was your own decision. You created yourself in every choice you made. Those who remained hamstrung by traditional economics or ways of doing things were not only foolish, but even immoral in their refusal to face the wide range of options open to them. The dot com entrepreneurs genuinely believed in a moral imperative to transform the world though discovery.

This type of Purpose and morality is rooted in the intuition that life is a kind of adventure. We are free and should not be bound by convention. When we live authentically, we are constantly seeking out and creating the new. But this does not mean constantly changing course. Precisely because we are creating something, precisely because we have chosen the course we have embarked on freely, we are committed to pursue that course consistently. The best reason for staying with an action is that we have freely chosen it.

This is the intuition of the existentialist, which was first articulated by Søren Kierkegaard in Denmark in the early nineteenth century. Individuals must take responsibility for their choices and cannot hide behind convention or rules. In the last analysis each individual has to make their own choices, *if only to decide which rules to accept.*

Kierkegaard makes this point using the biblical story of the sacrifice of Isaac:

> When Abraham hears the voice of the angel telling him to sacrifice his son Isaac, he obeys; but he may realize afterwards that it was in fact his choice to take the voice to be a genuine message from God. There could never be any proof that it was genuine. Therefore, believing that the voice was the voice of an angel was his own act, and thus sacrificing his son in obedience to it was his own act too. No one but he was responsible.[13]

This emphasis on our complete freedom of choice *and* our resulting commitment to the consequences of our choices recurs again and again in the writings of existentialist philosophers. It emphasizes the importance of the individual and applauds his constant attempt to break out of conventional ways of doing things. We must "think of each situation afresh," proclaimed Jean-Paul Sartre, "and try and see . . . what ought to be done for the best. . . . We must really decide for ourselves . . . remembering we could decide anything."[14]

Tom Watson of IBM would have agreed with this idea: "THINK" was the slogan that he plastered up all around the company's offices. He recognized that he could not hide behind convention, and he would have to live with the consequences of his decisions—which took the company to the edge of bankruptcy on more than one occasion.

Discovery is a difficult principle to live by because humans tend to want to identify with something else, another group, say, or corporate body. They have a tendency to accept external rules governing behavior and thought. The existentialists recognize this: Sartre writes that the freedom resulting from limitless discovery is unbearable, precisely because we are no longer in a position to say, "I couldn't help it."[15] Discovery requires a constant openness, which brings pain as well as joy. Nonetheless, for those who accept this Purpose, there is a morality that transcends the pain, and a keen appreciation for the accompanying freedom and power. In each choice we make, we have the potential for discovering a new world.

EXCELLENCE:
VIRTUE'S FULFILLMENT

Excellence built the great cathedrals of Europe and today's most successful professional and creative businesses. It implies standards, like those of an artist, defined by the craft itself rather than by the customers; it creates a picture of a never-ending struggle to achieve ever-higher standards. Medieval craftsmen spent as much time carving angels that would be invisible to spectators on the ground as they did on the cathedral's more prominent ornaments, because God would see them too. Excellent businesses prefer to turn away customers rather than compromise their quality standards. Publishing businesses such as *The Economist*, although theoretically interested in the greatest possible profit, are in practice strongly driven by a passion for truth and intellectual integrity.

Not that the pursuit of excellence and profit maximization need conflict: Warren Buffett, who we will consider in detail later, is one of the best examples in modern business of both.

This type of Purpose is rooted in the belief that excellent performance in our role in life represents the supreme good. If you care about excellence, you are automatically part of a community; someone outside of yourself must exist to judge your contribution. If excellence is your priority, you should cultivate your character in such a way that you can flourish in your community.

Aristotle articulated this thought in Athens in the fourth century B.C. His audience was young men who were to become citizens, and the ideals of citizenship and of the "polis" or city-state to which citizens belonged were real and powerful.

In his scheme, the ultimate end of human activity is "eudaimonia," which is sometimes translated as "happiness," but is perhaps closer to "fulfillment," "flourishing" or "success." Implicit in this idea is the view that man has a function, with eudaimonia as the fulfillment of that function. But we do not achieve fulfillment simply by aiming for it; instead we must cultivate the "virtues." These are not abstractions of good behavior; rather they are traits of character, which lead us to behave in a way that contributes to our success.

Aristotle has been called the eternal optimist. In his scheme success and virtue are closely entwined, in contrast to the situation common in the modern world where we often draw a sharp distinction between ends and means. For Aristotle, the end (success) cannot be understood in the absence of the means (virtue). To my mind, Warren Buffett is perhaps the most powerful example in modern business of this aspect of Aristotelian morality.

Aristotle identified the following as relevant for the Athens of his day: Courage, Temperance, Liberality, Magnificence, Pride, Good Temper, Friendliness, Truthfulness, Wittiness,[16] Shame, Justice, Honor. In our time, we might choose others; the particular virtues matter less, under the Purpose of excellence, than the commitment to try to reach them.

To every virtue there are usually two vices, corresponding to too much and too little of the virtue in question. In contrast to the vicious man, the virtuous man adopts a reasonable and measured course of action. This is the Aristotelian balance, the "golden mean," which leads an individual and an organization to an excellent life.

ALTRUISM: EMPATHY'S JUSTIFICATION

Altruism lies behind major political movements, charities and a whole range of businesses that exist primarily to serve their customers. In these organizations, altruism may take the form of personal service beyond formal obligation (as at Nordstrom), delivering products at affordable prices (Sam Walton's Wal-Mart) or using technology and ideas to improve, or save, lives (Hewlett-Packard and even Hallmark Cards). A good proportion of small business is animated by this benevolent ethic.

In these examples, altruism is directed at the customer, but it does not have to be. For Anita Roddick of the Body Shop, and other leaders of so called new age businesses, altruism and customer benefit are distinct. In her case the altruism is directed at animals, and to some extent her staff. As she put it, rather brutally, "How do you ennoble the spirit when you are selling something as inconsequential as a cosmetic cream?" The answer is by following certain principles, but the company's most famous principle (not selling cosmetics tested on animals) is quite unconnected with what Body Shop employees do day to day or with standards of customer service.[17] Another, more traditional, variation on altruism is paternalism toward staff. A good example is the leading British retailer Marks and Spencer (at least in its heyday) whose Jewish founders established a tradition that staff were to be treated as "part of the family." Service businesses often "care" about the staff, which will in turn care for customers—an approach summed up by Federal Express as "People-Service-Profit."

Altruism, as described by Scottish philosopher David Hume in the eighteenth century, is less a principle than an emotion. He argued that we care about others' well-being as well as our own—indeed we maximize our own happiness only by taking into account the happiness of others, trading off our selfish pleasures against those generated by our moral instinct to care about others. The ultimate reason for an action is thus that it increases happiness.[18]

More formally Hume argued that the will is driven, in the last analysis, by the prospect of pain or pleasure. In addition we have a natural sympathy with other humans that results in our emotions being triggered when we contemplate harm or good coming to them: "It is from the prospect of pain or pleasure that the aversion or propensity arises towards any object," an aversion or propensity that drives action; it follows that "reason alone can never produce any action." But "morals . . . have an influence on . . . actions [so] it follows that they cannot be derived from reason."[19] The pleasure and pain we get from contemplating virtue and vice is closely dependent on this natural human sympathy or compassion:

> If any man from a cold insensibility or narrow selfishness of temper is unaffected with the images of human happiness or misery, he must be equally indifferent to the images of vice and virtue; as on the other hand, it is always found that a warm concern for the interests of our species is attended with a delicate feeling of all moral distinctions, a strong resentment of injury done to men, a lively approbation of their welfare.

Sam Walton was a highly competitive, tough businessman, but this kind of fellow feeling shines through his own account of his motivations:

> Also I think those associates in our company who believe in our ideals and our goals and get with the program have felt some spiritual satisfaction—in the psychological rather than the religious sense—out of the whole experience. . . . Many of them decide they want to go to college, or to manage a store, or take what they've learned and start their own business, or do a good job and take pride in that. Wal-Mart has helped their pocketbooks and their self-esteem. There are certainly some union folks and some middlemen out there who wouldn't agree with me, but I believe that millions of people are better off today than they would have been if Wal-Mart had never existed. So I am just awfully proud of the whole deal, and I feel good about how I chose to expend my energies in this life.[20]

Sam Walton, in other words, was the Hume of American business. His company was powerful and effective precisely because customers recognized that caring about them was the core Purpose of the company.

Later philosophers, notably Adam Smith, Jeremy Bentham and John Stuart Mill, built on these ideas, eventually producing "Utilitarianism." This is the view that the right action in any situation is what brings about the greatest possible happiness (or absence of unhappiness) to the greatest number of people—a more widely known philosophy than Hume's. It is important in our story because this is the moral system often used to justify capitalism, markets and profit maximization: These are all said to be good because they maximize wealth, which, in turn, maximizes happiness.

HEROISM: POWER'S EFFECTIVENESS

Heroism resulted in the Roman Empire, Wimbledon champions Serena and Venus Williams and many of the most spectacular growth companies, from Standard Oil to Microsoft. Bill Gates' plan to put his operating system into every desktop was just such an obsession. It is not the "winning" or the specific goals themselves that tap into broader human aspirations, but the ambition, daring or heroism evident in those goals.

Henry Ford was by far the most famous industrial hero of his day. At first sight, his ambition to "democratize the automobile" and his introduction of the $5 day for his workers might indicate a strongly altruistic Purpose, a desire to bring happiness to customers and workers alike. But this is an illusion. The specific social and economic goals he pursued at different times were quite inconsistent—these goals were less important to him than his ambition to use the Ford Motor Company as his "machine." Ends and means were curiously reversed; the outputs were the means to his ultimate end, exercising his will to improve the world.

Heroic Purposes such as Ford's gain their force from the Nietzschean intuition that only some people are truly free and have the capacity to lead. If you are one of these people, you realize you must exercise your willpower and your influence. If you are not, you realize you should follow those who are capable of leadership.

Writing in Germany in the late nineteenth century, Nietzsche was repelled by what he perceived to be the mediocrity of the democratic age—he longed for rule by an aristocracy of great men. "The [French] Revolution made Napoleon possible," he wrote. "That is its justification. We ought to desire the anarchical collapse of the whole of our civilization if such a reward were to be its result." [21] For him, Christianity and compassion should be shunned: They tame great men like Napoleon, and may tempt us to think there is no fundamental difference in value between the elite and the masses. These ideas have resulted in a "dwarfed, almost ludicrous species . . . something sickly, mediocre, the European of the present day."

Courage, pride and firmness are raw materials of the Nietzchean leader, but the necessary level of these characteristics is found in relatively few human beings. These men are the leaders who can command those without the necessary character. It is easy to see how this moral theory could be used to justify the extremes of fascism. But in less violent forms, adulation of willpower and command also justified the bureaucratic structures emerging as Nietzsche was writing.

SUMMARY

Four possible sources of energy for the company, four sets of moral ideas that can underpin Purpose—and each includes beliefs about the ultimate moral basis for an action. Each set of ideas is associated with a particular philosopher and is exemplified in action in different companies. Each company expresses the idea in its own way: No two excellent companies are alike; nor will companies manifest heroism, discovery or altruism in the same way. But every great company has come to its greatness by drawing on one of these philosophical traditions (consciously or not) and applying it with integrity. This is summarized in the following table.

Table 2.1

Moral Purpose	Type of Morality	Moral Basis for an Action	Philosopher	Company
Discovery	"The New"	I have freely chosen it	Søren Kierkegaard	IBM, Sony, Intel, Virgin
Excellence	"The Good"	It constitutes fulfillment	Aristotle	Berkshire Hathaway, *The Economist*, Apple, BMW
Altruism	"The Helpful"	It increases happiness	David Hume	Wal-Mart, Hewlett-Packard, Nordstrom
Heroism	"The Effective"	It demonstrates achievement	Friedrich Nietzsche	S.G. Warburg, Microsoft, Ford, ExxonMobil (and its predecessor, Standard Oil)

LESS RELEVANT MORAL IDEAS

There are other moral ideas that are less likely to be useful to most modern competitive companies, but which have animated organizations in the past and to some extent still do. You need to understand them for the simple reason that you will need to confront them. I summarize some of them here.

Patriotism differs from the four varieties of Purpose we have just described because it is often defensive. It is often evoked by the need to defend an existing community, rather than a desire to conquer or expand into new ones. In the 1830s the Prussian General and military theorist Karl von Clausewitz argued that the only purpose of an army was to serve the sovereign. World War II proved him half right; the German and Russian armies fought for their respective *ideologies* when they were winning, but fell back on traditional *patriotism* when they were losing and fighting for survival. Patriotism is the instinct for group survival that all organizations have in reserve.

Sometimes the defense of the nation can energize a company. At Toyota after World War II, helping to rebuild Japan was of primary importance. The Mondragon businesses, a group of collectively owned companies in the Basque region of Spain, are successful at least partly because they are emblems of Basque identity. In Korea, Hyundai has taken the lead on re-unification. However, while this kind of nationalism still exists, especially in the United States and Korea, it is unlikely to drive most businesses active in the global economy.

Universalism is the spirit behind the national postal networks, the old AT&T, Britain's National Health Service, most railway services, and the World Wide Web. It is rooted in the ideas of the European Enlightenment, most forcefully articulated by the philosopher Immanuel Kant. Writing a little later than Hume, at the end of the eighteenth century, Kant had the same project as Hume: to find a basis for moral duty independent of the Church. But instead of emotion, he alighted on reason. Whereas Hume believed "morals cannot be derived from reason," Kant believed they were founded on reason, and that like mathematics they had universal applicability. His prescriptions can be summed up in two rules: "Act only on the maxim which you can will as a law for all rational beings," and "Act so as to treat rational beings always as ends in themselves and never as means only."

Kant remains one of the most influential moral philosophers. His morality corresponds with a widely held view that there is some universal and underlying basis for duties, independent of any person's emotions or desires; his line of thinking continues to count as a major influence on politics. Universalism has successfully underpinned the public institutions and infrastructure of the West. But it is difficult to know how to apply these rules in competitive businesses, which—in contrast to public institutions and monopolies—are constantly looking to segment their markets and differentiate themselves from competitors in order to establish advantage.

Religion lies behind the idea of a calling or vocation, which has had much influence in business. Martin Luther first preached this in the sixteenth century, urging Christians to work hard in the role God had appointed for them. John Calvin built on his ideas, and preached that worldly success was evidence of divine favor, of being a member of the elect predestined for eternal life. Not surprisingly, this gave great impetus to those wishing to prove that they were part of the elect; according to Max Weber, this is how the religiously driven work ethic was born.[22] Since the Industrial Revolution, Christianity and the work ethic have marched less closely in step, though Christian charity animated nineteenth-century Quaker businesses like that of English chocolate maker Joseph Rowntree. Even today there are businesses such as ServiceMaster in the United States, whose motto is "To honor God in all we do."[23] There are also Islamic-led businesses with a significant religious presence, while the Parsi ethic animates businesses such as the Tata group based in India.[24]

The law—our final variety of Purpose—is exemplified in one particular form of religion. In the fifth century A.D., as the Vandals were destroying the Roman civilization he had grown up in, St. Augustine of Hippo argued eloquently for the moral supremacy of a new institution, namely the Catholic Church. However appalling material conditions might be, there was hope for those who accepted this new, spiritually invincible authority, and the divine *law* that it enforced.

The ideal set out by Augustine held sway in Europe for over one thousand years. It was reinforced by the monastic movement launched by St. Benedict; the spiritual purity of St. Francis and the mendicant orders; and the philosophy of Thomas Aquinas and others, who married authoritarianism and support for the Pope with Aristotelian principles. Eventually the corruption of the papacy at the end of the Middle Ages and the Scientific Revolution of the seventeenth century undermined the authority of divine law. Now, while many people continue to obey and believe, few outside the Church hierarchy itself recognize authority or precedent as a moral imperative.[25]

PURPOSE AND THE WAR OF IDEAS

At the most fundamental level, competition between companies is at least in part a competition between different moral ideas. Successful ideas generate successful companies; unsuccessful ideas generate failures. To understand company success and failure we should look at this underlying competition between ideas, not just at its surface manifestations.

This competition takes place in the market. That is where companies win or lose their everyday battles for customers, staff, suppliers and capital. No commercial organization can succeed without winning these battles.

Those in the thick of the fighting naturally think in terms of winning *tactics*—a little more value added for customers here, a new mix of incentives for staff there, and so on. Senior management have been trained to think in terms of *strategy*, the medium- and long-term choices they can make about establishing an ongoing competitive position for their company. Some have thought at length about *leadership*, finding ways to maximize their influence on outcomes, and to make that influence reflect their priorities more accurately. All of these levels of conflict are inevitably shaped by the company's Purpose—whether or not that Purpose is explicit.

In large companies, there are always many strategic options that managers can support. Provided the strategic options managers face are at least compatible with what they know, the most reliable basis for their choice of one option over another is not yet more analysis. For this is unlikely to narrow the options significantly. Instead, executives tend to gravitate to the options that they believe the organization will act on effectively. This in turn depends on the level of emotional support the strategy attracts from the chief executive, other executives and, to a lesser extent, employees generally.[26] Where effective action depends on the morale of a small group only, this emotional support can be rooted in personal ambition or a group dynamic. But where the morale of a wider group is critical, strategy needs to fit the Purpose—that is, leaders will be effective to the extent that they can articulate an effective Purpose and align their strategy with it.

Over the medium to long term, morale in a large company is more influenced by the strength of its Purpose than the strength of its leader. Charismatic leaders like Sam Walton are effective precisely because they are communicating Purpose; leaders who try to inspire by sheer force of character have at best a short-term impact.[27] By contrast, well-known companies like 3M maintain high morale over the long term without resorting to charisma. It is the Purpose, not simply the leader, that attracts, retains and motivates the best staff. Leaders are effective to the extent that they express effective Purpose.

But not all Purposes are equally effective. While it may be both morally right and sensible to choose a strategy that fits the Purpose, this does not guarantee success. Henry Ford found before World War I that his Purpose—using mass production to make cars available to many people inexpensively, without variation in color or style—fit the market environment perfectly. The strategy based on his Purpose created competitive advantage. After the war, this Purpose no longer fit the market environment. Different customers wanted different colors and styles. Ford's heroic Purpose of creating a market was less persuasive than General Motors' altruistic Purpose of providing service to its customers, and Ford was overtaken by GM.

There is a level, then, at which the competition between large companies is not between strategies and leaders, but between more or less effective Purposes and the moral ideas that underlie them. Apple and Microsoft, for example, are not just competing on price and convenience. Underlying their superficial differences are two quite different sets of ideas about what matters in the world: great design versus effectiveness. Apple aims for perfection: Its iPod goes far beyond what anyone else thought a music player could be, and its iMac computers—with the computing power in the monitor rather than in an empty box with twisted wires—are nothing short of astonishing. Microsoft, in contrast, does not seek perfection. As a result, engineers and programmers who dream of creating beautiful, breakthrough products gravitate to Apple. Those who dream of being the dominant player find Microsoft a more attractive home.

Morale may be high at both Microsoft and Apple. Both visions of a digital company are valid. At Apple, however, it is possible to feel like an artist—or a David. That is less possible at Microsoft, where Goliath dwells. Either way, those images provide a moral foundation for each brand. And that moral foundation is, in each case, a significant corporate asset.

The same applies to the 1930s competition between Ford and General Motors, which can be seen at the tactical level as a race between individual models for customer dollars. Or it can be seen as a contest between different strategies and styles of leadership—the single brand versus the multibrand, dominant leader versus collegial leadership. The prize, in that case, was lifelong brand loyalty. But it can best be seen as a battle between two sets of moral ideas: Ford's Nietzschean vision, which gave him an advantage in the early years, and the more customer-focused, Humean ethic at GM, which gave that company a long-term advantage.

There has been an evolution in the way people think about competition. Once, it was thought that the winner was the company with the most tangible assets—the quality of plant or the location of outlets. Then winning was thought to be driven by intangible assets such as brands, patents, internal systems and the quality of people. All of these factors determined the effectiveness of tangible assets. Now it is ideas—I would say, primarily moral ideas—that are thought to determine the effectiveness of people and of intangible assets. What is to be pursued? The new, the excellent, the helpful or the effective?

In arguing that the most fundamental competition between companies is between competing moral ideas, we are only removing an artificial distinction between business and other human activities. In politics, the arts, science and everyday life, there is a constant war of ideas in which individuals are continually engaged. These skirmishes are not simply intellectual. The most common question about the current war in Iraq, for example, is why the United States and United Kingdom initiated the invasion. Assuming there was a moral Purpose, what was it? Was the reason grounded in heroism—to exercise dominance over the oil supply and the Middle East, and thereby crush the threat of terrorism? Was it altruism—to help the people of Iraq escape the rule of a tyrant? Was it discovery—to find out what a modern army could do and how to promote democracy in a new environment? Or was there a Purpose of excellence involved, aimed at deterrence, by demonstrating the quality with which the Americans and British could engage in war?

In peace as well as war, political winners tend to be those groups who can evoke a clear, consistent Purpose that attracts followers. That is why it is more important in elections for politicians to be seen as having "character"—the ability to embody and project sets of moral ideas—than to be clever. Cleverness, unless it is grounded in a clear and explicit Purpose, will simply be seen as trying to evade the need for making hard decisions.

In business, similar skirmishes are taking place. What counts as the new or excellent or the helpful or the effective is constantly debated. The character of business and business leaders is constantly questioned. Competence is no longer enough, if it ever was, to guarantee either legitimacy or success. The war of ideas, in short, is as relevant in the marketplace as it is in any other sphere of human endeavor.

CHAPTER THREE

WHAT PURPOSE IS NOT

Koç is a venerable Turkish conglomerate that represents perhaps 4 percent of the country's economy. Its owners are highly responsible, ethical and committed to each of their businesses.

Several years ago Koç had a textile division that had been losing money. I conducted a study that indicated that efforts to prop it up would be fruitless—this division had no competitive advantage. The study showed that this business couldn't win. Indeed, Koç probably couldn't even find a buyer for the factory.

Eight hundred workers. Eight hundred families. That's what the owners were thinking of when I presented my recommendation to consider just the real estate—because that was the only value of this division.

The family that owns Koç has a serious business focus. But this particular factory had sentimental value—it was one of the first opened by their father, half a century ago. When I gathered the family together and told them the bad news, some of them wept. Their first solution: never see me again. So much for the image of capitalists as cold and unfeeling.

In half a century, though, things change. The great Zen master Shunryu Suzuki was once asked to summarize Buddhism in a sentence. The audience laughed at the impossibility of that challenge. But Suzuki had a ready answer. "Easy," he said. "Everything changes." What is true for Buddhists is true for others as well. To adapt to the new situation Koç's owners would have to sacrifice some of their loyalties, but they would have to do it in a way that was thoughtful, large-spirited and courageous.

In the end, they closed the factory. But they insisted that we find jobs for the workers. To be sure, that slowed down the process and led to some discomfort and added cost. But it demonstrated, both to their customers and employers, that the Koç family was as good as their word. And I continued to consult for Koç for some time.

In retrospect I realize that we—like so many others involved in business—were dealing with Purpose, even though we didn't recognize it at the time. What we were doing was adapting Koç's heroic Purpose in a new business era. Purpose is very different from many of the business concepts with which it is often associated. It is not a responsibility of any kind. It is not a "mission," "vision" or "value"—at least not the kind that can be codified in a "mission, vision and value" statement. It is not a reason for doing something. Nor is it a tool, a vehicle for maximizing profit, a form of brand identity or a constraint (like a regulatory policy).

It is none of those things because, at heart, Purpose is a call to action. But in order to hear that call and respond to it, we need to understand the distractions that get in the way of a serious discussion of an organization's Purpose.

And in many companies, that starts with the most persuasive distraction: the maximization of profit.

PURPOSE VERSUS PROFITS

Economists such as Milton Friedman have argued that profit maximization should *itself* be the purpose of a company.[1] There is no question that every company has to achieve profits to survive and prosper, but this doesn't suggest a *moral* duty to *maximize* profits.

Two arguments attempting to prove that profit maximization is the only duty of company directors are sometimes put forward. The first is that maximizing profits is the surest way of maximizing happiness in the world, and of course general happiness is a good thing. The trouble is, maximizing profits does not always maximize happiness. In any case, if happiness is the real goal, then maximizing profits is only a rule of thumb, not a moral duty.

The second argument suggests that profit maximization is the company's only ethical duty because of the legal fiduciary duty that directors have to shareholders. (This is only applicable in the United States; in the UK and elsewhere, directors hold a more compelling legal fiduciary duty to the company as a whole. Even so, in the UK and elsewhere it is still widely felt that managers have a duty to maximize profits.) This is also a weak argument. While profit maximization is indeed a duty, no one has ever shown that this is or should be the directors' *only* duty.

PURPOSE VERSUS GOVERNANCE AND LONG-TERM THINKING

Other advocates in the realm of corporate governance have argued that the Purpose of a company should automatically come down to *balancing the demands of stakeholders or constituencies.* In real life, this is already the way companies are managed. Corporate directors have to balance demands in the short run—from customers, workers, shareholders, community and so on—or they will find themselves out of business or in jail.

Companies that go beyond this minimum are often just adopting a long-term perspective: If we screw the customers, workers or public now, they will get us in the end. Or, to look at the bright side: If we are good to our stakeholders, workers and customers will stay with us and the public will respect us. We will build good relationships, and in doing so we will be creating an intangible asset.

Long-term thinking is not the same as Purpose, but it may reflect one. A classic example of the value of Purpose to long-term thinking is the Tylenol case at Johnson & Johnson. Several deaths were caused in 1982 after someone tampered with packages of the drug. The tampering was clearly not the company's fault and was confined to a very small number of outlets, but management decided to withdraw the product anyway. A few months later, it was reissued in a tamper-proof container. The company took a financial hit in the short term, and Wall Street thought the Tylenol brand was dead, but management made the decision in the (correct) belief that it would maximize profits in the long term, strengthening the company's brand and its reputation for looking after its customers.

Such decisions are often purely pragmatic. Did the Tylenol decision reflect a Purpose or was it simply about profit maximization? It is difficult to know the answer for sure, but there are indications. Johnson & Johnson has a "Credo," first written in 1946, that specifies its obligations to stakeholders. Perhaps it does encapsulate a genuine Purpose. Ralph Larsen, the former CEO, has claimed that he and his colleagues "would hold [the values embodied in the Credo] even if they became a competitive *dis*advantage."[2] This suggests genuine Purpose.[3]

PURPOSE VERSUS FIRM PRINCIPLES

Firm principles are useful because it is often difficult to make Tylenol-type decisions unless the ethical principles involved are internalized; only then are the individual decisions made in ways that protect the long-term value of the brand. Johnson & Johnson, after the Tylenol crisis, took steps to make its Credo and ethical considerations part of everyday decision making. Similarly, in the late 1970s, the Cummins Engine Company began a training program to help managers introduce an ethical dimension into their decision making.[4]

The danger is that ethical principles are not sufficiently robust to influence the really difficult decisions—the ones that matter. As Tom Chappell, of Tom's of Maine, has written, "At the first sign of crisis, you will begin managing more about the bottom line than the mission."[5] But if the principles follow from an active Purpose, they will be central to what the business is all about and therefore be *most* evident when difficult decisions need to be taken.

For those companies without Purpose, there will often be a great deal of agonizing about the ethical dilemmas facing a company. Possibly there will be a dependence on standards or methods presented by outside constituencies, including governments and NGOs, or even on consultants or academics. The danger is that in outsourcing ethical judgment because it is so difficult and its basis so uncertain, the leaders are actually abandoning it.

PURPOSE VERSUS CODES OF PRACTICE

If following a Purpose is not the same thing as following ethical principals or seeking ethical advice, it is also not the same as following *a code of "ethics," "practice," "governance"* or *"approved behaviors."* These codes, common in large companies, are not designed to make things happen but to prevent or restrain action that might lead to liabilities, like bribes, or sexual harassment. The role of these codes is therefore opposite to that of Purpose. The codes constrain, while Purpose inspires.

Citigroup, for example, recently struggled to re-establish a reputation for ethical behavior after a series of scandals; it pushed an ethical code throughout the company. If Citigroup had a Purpose that aligned its strategy and the moral ideas of its employees, it would be in a better position to rebuild its reputation.

PURPOSE VERSUS REPUTATION

Purpose is not simply *a tool for improving your reputation.* Unfortunately this is still how many large companies think of it in practice, if they think of Purpose at all. They know they have to go beyond satisfying the material interests of stakeholders and either attract customers or avoid liabilities by establishing an image as a "good citizen" or "responsible company." The resulting policy is often called *corporate social responsibility* or *good citizenship*, but the goal is only an improved reputation, not a more ingrained mission.

Sometimes this is defensive, as when Nike was forced to listen to customers' concerns about its subcontractors' labor practices. This kind of reactive posture does not constitute a Purpose. At other times it is a more positive mixture of brand development and genuine ethical concern, as when Starbucks adopted ethical guidelines on sourcing coffee, or The Co-operative Bank in the UK started to turn down "unethical" customers (and increased its market share as a result). Global, multiproduct companies like Nestlé and Procter & Gamble have also recognized that their brand equities depend on improving their social and environmental performance.

The target for this kind of responsibility is not just customers, it is also staff. Niall Fitzgerald, former chairman of Unilever, has pointed out that social responsibility is good business because "we need a constant flow of talented people . . . [who] ask themselves if this is an organization whose values they share."[6] Ethics are more important than ever before to a company's reputation with customers, investors, potential recruits and indeed its own staff.

And yet, doesn't a statement like Fitzgerald's make you feel a bit uneasy? No doubt he and his colleagues are sincere on a personal level, but what will happen when the values they proclaim conflict with the underlying dynamic of the business? In any company, if the primary reason for an ethical stance is to attract good people, then that stance will not necessarily survive a crisis. Some industry sectors, like auto dealerships, have struggled with this dilemma for years; they attempt to build a reputation for ethical behavior, but their business model depends on trying to squeeze the greatest price possible from every customer through persuasion and obfuscation.

If a company's reputation-building efforts appear to be somehow separate from its business model, then you suspect they are primarily a corrective to its naturally amoral or immoral inclinations—a medicine to relieve the symptoms but not a cure for the basic disease. The approach is at bottom defensive. Purpose is not the same as having a reputation as *an ethical leader in your industry.* Nor is it simply having a reputation for *integrity,* or for that matter reporting your earnings honestly. It is widely believed that investors' lack of confidence in what companies say has contributed to the recent, post-Enron stock market doldrums. But in reality, the underlying cause of lack of confidence is corporate behavior grounded in a lack of Purpose. Companies such as Enron and Tyco were striking for their Purposelessness, being merely opportunistic. And if you have no Purpose, you are far more likely to cheat.

PURPOSE VERSUS PHILANTHROPY

The phrase "social responsibility" may also refer to even more peripheral reputation-building efforts, such as *philanthropic* or *charitable activities*. These may be a source of energy and can be used to help build the firm's sense of community and morale, which is valuable. For this reason, these activities are particularly popular in management consultancies, which often donate staff time to solve problems of poverty, development and so on. Sometimes they may be linked thematically to the company's business: Nokia sells mobile phones to young people and for this reason invests in youth development projects. But peripheral activities are by definition not connected to the driving intention of a company; they are not part of its Purpose.

This is the case even when the philanthropy is used for strategic purposes. In a 2002 article, Michael Porter and Mark Kramer suggest that corporate philanthropy can improve the firm's competitive context.[7] That is, philanthropy can shape the environment to maximize the firm's advantages. When companies such as Hewlett-Packard and Microsoft take steps to bridge the "digital divide" by donating computers to schools in low-income neighborhoods, they are both creating more connected communities and building more potentially profitable markets. This approach represents a clever and creative way for managers to reconcile conflicting commercial and ethical pressures. But this is not the same as tapping into Purpose in order to guide or inspire strategy.

PURPOSE VERSUS BRAND

Finally, many organizational leaders see their reputation as akin to a corporate identity or brand—the vehicle by which people in the world at large recognize them. To be sure, a corporate identity or brand conveys something permanent about a company, and forms a focus for the allegiance of employees and the respect of outsiders. The brand may be linked to a corporate Purpose, a set of values, a lifestyle or even a product. The link will vary from company to company.

Only great brands have a moral content; in great companies, both the brand and Purpose stem from the same moral roots. In truly great companies, as we shall see, the brand, the ethics and the Purpose all align together. This can happen in a self-conscious manner (as with The Body Shop, whose Purpose involves building a brand that displays its altruism) or in a seemingly effortless manner (as with Berkshire Hathaway, where no one doubts the fit between the firm's ethics, its reputation and its brand).

PURPOSE VERSUS VISION, MISSION AND VALUES

As executives often try to manage their reputation externally to motivate consumers and citizens, they often view their "vision," their "mission" and their corporate "values" as the internal counterpart: a way to drive employees' behavior.

Consider these two visions: "To dominate the global food service industry" (McDonalds). "We will become number one or number two in every market we serve, and revolutionize this company to have the speed and agility of a small enterprise" (General Electric).[8] These are exciting, motivating targets, and as such important management tools, but there is nothing particularly moral about them. They have force because they draw on and strengthen the sense of belonging and commitment employees feel to an ambitious enterprise, not because they feel "right."

There are plenty of companies with a strong Purpose—for example Wal-Mart under Sam Walton and Berkshire Hathaway under Warren Buffett—in which it's difficult to detect an explicitly stated vision. Purpose creates a direction for the company, but not necessarily a snapshot of the destination. Indeed, Sam Walton's story is an excellent refutation of the argument sometimes advanced that leaders need a "mental image of a possible and desirable future state of the organization . . . an all-important bridge from the present to the future."[9] Walton had a very clear image of a possible and desirable *current* state of the organization, a much hazier one of the future. What mattered was serving the customer today, not building the organization for tomorrow.

Purpose is not a *corporate mission*. First, missions are often identified with mission statements, and, as everyone knows, these are often utterly trivial: a description of the current product attached to some not quite sincere aspiration. More serious is the relation between mission and vision that some companies posit. Goldman Sachs's mission is "to provide excellent investment and development advice to major companies"—nothing wrong with that—and its vision is "to be the world's premier investment bank in every sector." In these statements, and there are many other similar ones throughout the corporate world, the mission is about the output and impact of the company, and is given a moral twist ("excellent"), while the vision is about the success of the company in the future and is amoral ("premier").

At some of our clients (not Goldman Sachs), an implicit deal has been offered to the workforce: "If we follow our mission (which, by the way, is a good thing to do anyway), we will achieve the vision." Curiously, the amoral vision becomes a justification for the quasi-moral mission, rather than the other way around. This breeds cynicism, with the result that the mission is seen as just another management tool, a way of getting from here to there. This is not a viable role for Purpose.

Finally, Purpose is not *a set of corporate values*. Corporate values differ from Purpose in two respects. They are often not moral and they are often not concerned with the destination of the organization.

Corporate values often involve no moral commitments by employees. Instead they are simply ways of regulating behavior. They are designed to ensure the smooth running of the company—reducing transaction costs, as economists might put it. Peter Jenson, a divisional president at what was then Smith Kline Beecham, put it thus: "The key is to have a team of people with fully aligned attitudes and values. Then you spend your time getting things done and don't waste your time explaining why you are doing it."[10] To the extent that they go beyond the most minimal standards, these values are intended to ensure conformity ("the way we do things around here") and a sense of belonging. The implicit deal is: Adopt these values and you will fit in. If you do not conform, you will be more easily identified, and then ostracized, asked to leave or reduced to impotence. "If you remain outside our value system you have to go, however talented," is a typical management comment.[11]

When a company is driven by a Purpose, the vision, mission and values flow naturally from that Purpose. People don't need to be "aligned"—they already have been attracted to the organization, as employees or customers, by its Purpose. Corporate leaders get distracted by their vision, mission and values, in the same way that they get distracted by concerns about reputation, compliance, ethics and public identity. Those seem like the most direct ways to address their concerns about their standing in the world at large, or with their own employees. But in fact those are inadequate ways to address those concerns. The only effective route is the fundamental route: developing and deploying a clear and consistent organizational Purpose.

RECLAIMING ETHICS FOR PURPOSE

Most people associate Purpose with ethics. So, how about ethics and Purpose? What role can ethics play in a Purposeful company? They are extremely important as the articulation of the high ground that makes the Purpose viable. Companies with different Purposes will find different kinds of ethics important.

The point is well illustrated by contrasting BP's solar energy program and its Third World development activities. BP has invested in solar energy and is aiming to reduce its dependence on greenhouse gas–producing petroleum; hence the slogan it introduced with its new corporate identity, "Beyond Petroleum." This is part of a wider set of initiatives designed to address global warming. Chief Executive Lord Browne and his colleagues want to make money, but they do not want to lock themselves into resisting moves to save the planet. In this instance their moral ideas support their strategy—solar energy is a potentially serious business for BP. Crucially it is also a sensible long-term investment, given the problems we all face with oil. There is a mutually reinforcing fit between Purpose and commercial objectives. BP has been criticized for the slogan, and for overselling what it's doing, but not seriously criticized for the program itself. BP has the high ground.

Browne himself has described this kind of activity in terms of Purpose: "Our purpose . . . is to be one of the world's great companies. That means delivering results and doing our business exceptionally well day to day. But it also means aligning our activity with the world's needs, leading change and being a force for progress in everything we do."[12]

This is the language of discovery: To lead change and be a force for progress in an era of climate change means venturing into the unknown. BP will continue to occupy the high ground so long as it maintains the spirit of invention and exploration—so long, for example, as it credibly demonstrates its goal of being the industry leader in solar power. This also means that BP cannot simply follow standards set by others—or even settle for being one step ahead of the game. It has to stay in front of other companies, like DuPont, which are simply seeking to embed "sustainable growth" in their business models. This is not to criticize DuPont—it is doing far more than many of its rivals. But it has not made environmentally driven discovery part of its Purpose, as BP has; and it will not enjoy the same benefits or face the same risks.

The situation is different when BP is attacked for joining a consortium that is building a pipeline across Turkey and has negotiated certain extra-territorial rights from the Turkish government. Oil companies have a patchy record in their relations with the Third World, partly because they have delegated moral responsibility to corrupt national governments (such as those in Angola and Nigeria). BP, however, leads the industry in its development and human rights programs and policies—it feels it has been "unfairly treated" by the Non-Governmental Organizations (NGOs) that monitor multinational activity. These NGOs, on the other hand, remain skeptical of policies that they suspect are no more than reputation-driven restraints on what BP would really like to do.

The trouble is there is no mutually reinforcing fit between BP's Third World policies and its strategy for developing and producing from new fields. It is not that the two are inconsistent, just that the policies appear to have nothing in them for BP, except the maintenance of its reputation and perhaps its executives' consciences.

BP's leaders may well have as sincere moral ideas about human rights as they do about the environment. I applaud this, but whereas the latter is now supporting a strategy, and creating long-term returns, the former appears to be merely a restraint on its strategy and a defense of its reputation.

DuPont is another interesting example. Its leaders have set themselves the goal of turning DuPont into what they call a "sustainable growth company." That is, they intend to increase its rate of financial growth while reducing its negative impact on the environment. CEO Chad Holliday has explained that "sustainable growth will be the common denominator of successful global companies in the 21st century," although it clearly is not at the moment. This *may* be no more than pragmatism of the kind any company looking after its stakeholders must engage in—in this case pre-empting government regulation and ensuring that the company is well positioned to respond to regulation. A test of whether it is just this or is instead part of a Purpose is how the plans play out inside the company. Are the plans seen as a burden by the top team and other managers, as another constraint on strategy? Or do they animate and inspire the top team and their colleagues, and form one of the drivers of the strategy?

PART II

GREAT STORIES OF PURPOSE

INTRODUCTION

Ideas are like trees falling silently in the forest—if they're not put into action, they might as well disappear. What is potent about the idea of Purpose is that history is rich with examples of men and women who took the idea and boldly forged ahead, carving out great success for their enterprises and immortality for themselves.

In the next few chapters, I will return to examine more closely the life stories and business careers of leaders who, each in a different way, shaped the nature of the industrial society we live in. Each created great organizations—profitable, influential and long-lasting. Each of them accomplished this by choosing a different form of Purpose on which to base their enterprise: Discovery (the love of the new), Excellence (the pursuit of the intrinsically beautiful and elegant), Altruism (the urge to increase happiness) and Heroism (the drive to achieve).

Their stories are well-known—you have no doubt studied some of these men in school. That familiarity is a great advantage. It saves me the trouble of taking you through their biographies and allows me to tell their stories through a very narrow window: through the role of Purpose in their decisions and commitments.

The great example of Discovery is Thomas Watson, the creator of IBM. The classic representative of Excellence is the investor, Warren Buffett. The Altruist I will profile is Sam Walton, founder of Wal-Mart. Finally, I will look at two heroes, Henry Ford and Siegmund Warburg, who could not be more different from each other—but who each, in his own way, epitomizes the nature of heroic achievement in business.

CHAPTER FOUR

TOM WATSON'S PASSION FOR DISCOVERY

Tom Watson, a man of immense creativity, designed a process of training and thinking and built a great team with it. Because corporations are large entities, requiring the executive talents and leadership of more than one man, this approach gave Watson the wherewithal to become the predominant leader of innovation in the Information Age. Innovation is, of course, not invention per se, but the realization of results from invention. Watson sailed into the future on an unfamiliar, abstruse conceptual machine called a computer, and it took him to a new world.

Tom Watson's entire life was a journey of discovery. When he took a troubled company and started it on its new course, he spoke of its future in gloriously abstract terms—"a vision of something way beyond our present conception."[1] Later he saw the potential for "progressive" men (like himself and Franklin D. Roosevelt) to counter the effects of the Depression and continue the technological revolution started in the twenties. He took the risks needed to do this, and his resulting success encouraged him to think of his company, IBM, as an institution, still engaged on a quest, but now instead a bigger one, on the international stage. Finally, he passed the baton to his sons in the fifties, recognizing that electronics would lead to places that were still "beyond our present conception."

In 1939, IBM had a turnover of just $34 million—about $450 million in today's terms. That was a reasonably big business—though tiny compared with Ford or General Motors.[2] In the previous four years the company had achieved excellent sales growth, an average of 16 percent a year, largely because of the new Social Security measures that required companies to operate complex payroll procedures, for which IBM's machines were used. But even from 1918 to 1935, when sales had grown just 4.5 percent a year in real terms, Watson still enjoyed capitalism's great honor—he was the highest-paid executive in America.

IBM dominated the still quite small data processing industry. Watson believed very strongly that IBM had to retain this position in the industry and he would always take the risks needed to maintain this leadership. During the early years of the Depression, he invested over $1 million in a research and development facility—an amount that could have brought the company down had not the Social Security legislation increased demand for payroll processing. Later, during World War II, he expanded production facilities for war-related work while maintaining his domestic data processing capacity and paying ex-IBM employees in the services 25 percent of their salaries, promising them a job when peace returned. After the war he had 2.5 times the factory capacity he had before, but he insisted on maintaining this capacity; in a couple of years, demand caught up.

He inculcated the view that the company should be dominant among his colleagues, including his sons, Tom and Dick. Thomas Watson Jr. makes clear in his autobiography that he could not have lived with himself had he let IBM lose this position, and he took it out hard on his colleagues in the 1950s when competitors appeared to be leapfrogging the company. As the data processing industry expanded with the advent of electronics in the late forties and fifties, Tom Watson Jr. pushed IBM to expand at a breathtaking rate.[3]

Watson Sr. turned a temporary competitive advantage into a sustainable one. It is possible to explain this achievement in terms of a personality—his hold over his colleagues and in particular over his son Tom—that created an organization constantly striving to lead. I believe his personality was only as effective as it was because of the Purpose he subscribed to and communicated to his colleagues.

Success, Watson said, was based on enthusiasm, and enthusiasm was based on knowledge. Salesmen needed to *discover* their customers' problems and *discover* solutions to them. "THINK" became the company slogan, appearing on placards in all the offices. Managers and salesmen were encouraged to think creatively to come up with ideas about how to make service improvements. Then, once they had come up with the ideas—getting information onto punch cards faster, for example—Watson would focus efforts on making the improvements.

Watson understood how a technical lead can create a near monopoly, which generates high profits, and which in turn pays for the research and development needed to maintain the technical lead. So he started hiring research engineers, including James Bryce in 1917, who 19 years later would be honored by the U.S. Patent Office as one of the ten greatest living inventors. During the twenties and thirties Bryce and his team produced a steady stream of patents for the company. Almost all of these were for the tabulating division—not because of any strategic decision by Watson but because that was where the commercial, and therefore the technical, opportunities lay.

Executives and managers were quite emotional about Watson, telling him such things as "how deeply grateful we are to you," and "you are the best friend I have" and "no one could be happier serving with and for you than I am." This was due in part to the way Watson combined charm, generosity and harshness. He was always willing to credit the good work of others, and, from the mid-twenties at least, he made a point of treating the shop floor workers with respect, visiting factories and entering into conversation with individuals about their work. He was a leader on pay and working conditions and later he set up a country club for all employees on equal terms.

But as well as presenting this benevolent face, he could be stern and harsh, haranguing managers and demoting those who disagreed with him or dared to complain, and on one occasion sacking an entire year of male graduate recruits because the females in the year were not being allocated jobs within the company. He did not tolerate dissent. As Watson put it to a class of trainees, "Sometimes young men disagree with our ideas or our policies because they know better ways. Such young men never make a success with us." His combination of warmth and coldness could be particularly cruel and manipulative and the result was that his subordinates craved his blessing, like the children of a capricious father. It was a classic case of leadership based on dependency.

WATSON'S JOURNEY
OF DISCOVERY

Thomas Watson Sr. was hired in 1914 as the president of the Computing-Tabulating-Recording Company, the original "data processing" company, whose founder Herman Hollerith had invented the punch card tabulating machine. Watson himself had a past as an ace salesman for National Cash Register, and a conviction (later overturned) in Dayton, Ohio for illegal sales practices. (He was accused of engineering sales of faulty cash registers and then selling NCR replacements when the originals failed.) Watson always claimed he was innocent and blamed local Republicans; this experience made him a lifelong Democrat and ultimately paved the way for a close friendship with U.S. President Franklin D. Roosevelt. Perhaps the experience may have helped him keep a relentless focus on the Purpose closest to his heart—the journey of discovery which he took on full-bore when he joined CTR (symbolized most strongly by his choice of a new name for the company, "International Business Machines," bestowed ten years later). Almost from the start, he felt he was on to something, even if he did not quite know what it was. The sentiment was expressed in Watson's favorite IBM company song, "Ever Onward":

> There's a feeling everywhere of bigger things in store
> Of new things coming into view.
> Our aim is clear: to make each year exceed the one before
> Staying in the lead in everything we do.

IBM was not just a community; it was a community with a Purpose.

Watson had the restless curiosity that was well-suited for this kind of journey. He described himself in the early 1920s as having a "keen mentality that is always alert and searching." At a meeting in the late 1920s he said to his subordinates, "The reason I feel so good and want to talk so much today is that I have just been out in the field a couple of weeks calling on offices and learning about the business." Until the end of his life he would spend months each year traveling around the United States and the world, doing just that.

As well as understanding the strategic importance of research and development (R & D), he was fascinated by new products and ideas. He was not himself an inventor or an engineer, but he would have ideas—for example, for a railway ticket printing system, or for special tabulators for bank branches. These were often impractical because he was always driven by customer needs rather than by the technology—the opposite of Henry Ford, who saw the implications of the technology but was uninterested in what customers wanted. When Watson pressed his ideas on his engineers, he helped them focus on the customers. Twenty years later he was slow at first to see the implications of electronics, since he simply could not see why customers would want to speed up calculations that fast. But once he realized they did, he relentlessly pushed the company forward.[4]

As the 1920s progressed, opportunities became ever clearer to Watson. IBM may have had 80–90 percent of the tabulating machine market, but Watson reckoned the existing market was only about 5 percent of its potential size. His quest for the new made him sensitive to the potential, and to the immensity of the challenges.

After the Wall Street crash in 1929, Watson was all the more ebullient. He called together his top team and announced that "the main issue" facing management was not how to retrench, as might have been expected, but "building the IBM and making it a bigger and better business." In 1930 there was a 50 percent decline in the market for office equipment, so IBM had to find new markets for its machines, both in the United States and abroad—and it did, with sales holding up in 1930 and 1931, and even growing in real terms. The journey had become more perilous, but for a man with a Purpose it was essential to continue advancing. Between 1929 and 1932 Watson effectively bet the firm and increased his manufacturing capacity by 33 percent.

In January 1932 Watson announced that he was spending $1 million on a new research and development facility. He had always looked after his engineers well; now he built them a beautiful building, with wood paneling, marble stairs and air conditioning. They could have any machinery they needed.

But by 1934 Watson was overextended. Sales had just about held up, but the number of employees had increased by 20 percent since 1930, to over 7,500. The new R & D facility seemed an extravagance and it looked like Watson's bet might not pay off. Some directors even talked of replacing him. But the crisis passed and in 1935 Roosevelt's Social Security measures were voted into law by Congress. Demand for IBM's machines started to increase sharply, with sales up 7 percent in 1935 and 16 percent in 1936. Watson's investment in capacity and R & D *had* paid off. He had been rescued by his friend Franklin Roosevelt's New Deal.

The war created yet more opportunity for Watson. Because he had geared up for war contracts, he knew that once the war ended he would have capacity and manpower for a major expansion in data processing, and by 1943 he was planning for it. By deciding to maintain capacity at war levels he in effect bet the firm again.

WATSON'S PURPOSE

Watson *inherited* market dominance in data processing. He *created* an organization that both needed to and was able to retain this dominance. But loyal staff, subservient managers and a celebrity CEO were certainly not enough to achieve this. The famous eccentricities of the company—the dark suits, the company songs, the ban on alcohol—were only the outward signs of an organization with a strong leader. What mattered wasn't the quirks of his character but his Purpose, which bound people together and inspired them to action.

It was in the nature of the Purpose that Watson was constantly seeking out and creating the new: He pursued this consistently. He was not interested in convention—salesmen wearing dark suits were *unconventional* in those days, and he made them do it for a reason—as a symbol of allegiance. Similarly he was not so concerned with what time he or his colleagues arrived at the office—what mattered was that they thought about what had to be done. Salesmen should think about their customers' requirements and managers should think about the implications of their salesmen's reports. Just as the engineers had to discover new ways of tabulating, so salesmen and their managers had to discover how to improve their customers' businesses and IBM's service. Because they were on a journey into fresh territory, they had to shake off convention and follow the (existentialist) prescription: "Think of each situation afresh and try and see what ought to be done for the best."[5]

The existentialist philosophers tell us we are all on such a journey of discovery during our lives; for Watson, IBM was his life and its journey was his journey. He made choices freely and accepted the consequences of those choices—most strikingly when he felt free to bet the company on several occasions (in the Depression and after World War II) and face the possibility of bankruptcy.

Watson's Purpose animated his company. His subordinates were clearly *not* existentialists; for the most part they abandoned their personal, individual freedom (including the freedom to choose, to make up their own minds) in favor of the collective will of the company. In effect, they delegated that freedom to Watson himself. They had to if they wanted to stay. But that did not just mean flattering the leader. It meant acting as he would do. It did not mean thinking his thoughts, it meant thinking in his unconventional style—within of course the limits set by the company's technology and objectives. It meant never assuming that the status quo—the comfortable, monopolistic status quo—would last. It meant striving to improve IBM's products and constantly inquiring about customers' needs and how to improve IBM's service.

As the company matured, so this Purpose became ever more deeply entrenched and institutionalized. IBM was different from other businesses—for example, apart from factory hands, it almost only recruited graduates straight from college. No one with experience of other organizations was allowed in to dilute the atmosphere.

This created a magnetic environment for the young men who joined IBM between the thirties and fifties, in some ways similar to the encompassing atmosphere among new ordinands in the Catholic Church. These young men were entering an institution that was to take over their lives.

Upon retirement, Watson turned over power with an ease and grace uncommon in such autocratic leaders. Here again, the Purpose provided an explanation. He knew his son would do things differently than he would (and that turned out to be true), but he also knew that the changing technology called for another individual to lead. IBM's power diminished only after several generations of leadership, when in the 1980s and early 1990s it tried to become a conventional company. By then, the dark blue suits *were* a symbol of conformity; even IBM's customers preferred conventional clothes. But the leadership of IBM had come to feel that the machine and the suit gave them their power, not the ethic of discovery. And IBM began to slide.

Even in the 1980s, some of the original Watson ethic remained—for example, in the team that created the IBM Personal Computer. And in the 1990s, in part by drawing upon its original legacy of discovery, Tom Watson's company was once again able to reinvent itself as an innovator in services by going beyond mainframe and advising clients on integrated solutions. In the end, it was neither the machine nor the suits that had mattered. It was, and could only be, unconventional thinking—the thinking that had, once, guided its leader to an all-animating Purpose.

CHAPTER FIVE

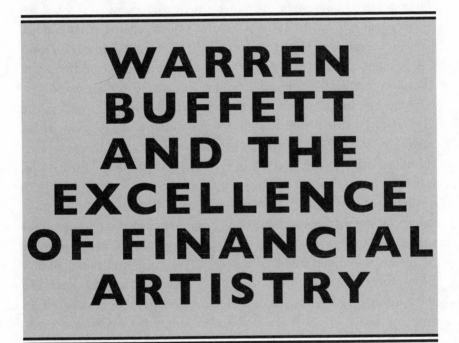

WARREN BUFFETT AND THE EXCELLENCE OF FINANCIAL ARTISTRY

Purpose has flourished for half a century in the career of the best-known and wealthiest investor in America—Warren Buffett, who entered the investment business in 1951 with $10,000 savings and is now worth $30 billion. For those who wonder how he did it—and why—he has written a series of disarmingly straightforward "letters" to his shareholders, which set out his investment principles.

Buffett was born in 1930, the son of a Midwestern stockbroker. The Depression had just begun and his father's business was in difficulty. At the age of 5, Warren decided that he was going to be rich. At 14 he had accumulated enough from his newspaper route to invest $1,200 in land, which he rented out to a local farmer. At 19, he went to Columbia University to study with one of the founders of the investment analysis industry, Ben Graham. After Columbia, he spent a few years working for his father and for Graham's fund management business, meanwhile converting his $10,000 savings into $140,000. Then in 1956 he set up his own investment partnership.

Between 1956 and 1970 (when he wound up the partnership), he achieved an annualized return of 29.5 percent, against the Dow's 7.4 percent. Between 1965 (when he took control of Berkshire Hathaway) and 2002, he achieved an annualized return of 22 percent, against the 10 percent of the Standard & Poor 500.[1] Berkshire Hathaway is now primarily a holding company rather than an investment trust, but Buffett continues to beat the market. This should be impossible, according to many professors of finance. So how did he do it?

His strategy was to identify secure long-term cash flows undervalued by the market, and then buy large stakes in the relevant companies. That strategy would be a blueprint for success for any number of investors—and it's hardly a secret. What differentiates Buffett from others who agree with his strategy is that Buffett also has had a Purpose driving his activities, a Purpose around which he fitted his strategy. The two neatly dovetailed. "Wanting to be rich" had nothing to do with it.

BUFFETT'S
INVESTMENT STRATEGY

In the Berkshire Hathaway annual report for 1977, Buffett described the four tests he applied to potential investments: "We select our marketable equity securities in much the way we would evaluate a business for acquisition in its entirety. We want the business to be one: (a) that we can understand; (b) with favorable long-term prospects; (c) operated by honest and competent people; and (d) available at a very attractive price."[2]

These tests may seem so simple as to be unhelpful. Fortunately Buffett has been quite willing to explain them. He has defined an "attractive price" as one comfortably less than the company's "intrinsic value," that is, the discounted value of future free cash flow. Then he acknowledged the difficulty of assessing these prospects, hence his first test: He was only interested in businesses he could "understand," or at any rate learn about quickly. This really meant sticking to industries that were predictable. Technology businesses were out, not because he and his partner, Charlie Munger, lacked the mental equipment to grasp the current state of technology, but because neither they, nor probably anyone else, could predict its future state. "If we have a strength, it is recognizing when we are operating well within our circle of competence, and when we are approaching the perimeter," he wrote.

Buffett and Munger had the *prudence* to recognize their own limitations. They needed to be cautious because the "favorable prospects" that formed his second test had to be rock solid. As he put it, "We favor businesses and industries unlikely to face major change . . . we are searching for operations that we believe are virtually certain to possess enormous competitive strength ten or twenty years from now."

Buffet once said that his ideal investment was a toll booth on the only bridge in town. In other words, he wanted potential for a monopoly or near monopoly franchise that could generate growing revenues. Such opportunities are rare. Buffett had the *patience* to wait for opportunities, and the *courage* to commit a significant proportion of his funds when they arose.

Buffett was interested in fundamentals, not the short-term impact of events. This gave him a great advantage when the underlying strength of a business was obscured by superficial problems. In 1964, for example, American Express had a world-leading brand name and two products, travelers' checks and charge cards, that looked set to grow hugely as travel itself expanded with the advent of jet engines. However, the company was mired in a short-term cash problem at one of its smaller subsidiaries, and the stock was cheap. Buffett invested 40 percent of his partnership's worth in this one stock; within two years, it had tripled in price. Similarly, in 1988 Coca-Cola had enormous potential for continued overseas expansion, together with a

management team that had started to show that it could reap this potential; although the stock price had improved over the course of the
eighties, in Buffett's view it still did not reflect the long-term and relatively risk-free nature of that potential. Buffett invested 35 percent
of Berkshire Hathaway's tradable portfolio in Coca-Cola. Ten years
later the price had increased almost six times.

Buffett's third test, "honest and competent people," might sound
as if it should be shared by any rational investor. In practice he has
applied the test in a quite distinctive way. First of all he has looked for
managers who "work because they love what they do and relish the
thrill of outstanding performance. They unfailingly think like owners
(the highest compliment we can pay a manager)." Secondly, when
buying a private company, he has made clear that "We like to do business with someone who loves his company, not just the money that a
sale will bring him. . . . When this emotional attachment exists, it signals that important qualities will likely be found within the business:
honest accounting, pride of product, respect for customers and a
loyal group of associates having a strong sense of direction."

The "like to do business" criteria goes beyond calculation. It is
also a matter of *aesthetics:* "We intend to continue our practice of
working only with people whom we like and admire. This policy not
only maximizes our chances for good results but also ensures us an
extraordinarily good time."

He has made the point in even more striking terms: "We would
rather achieve a return of X while associating with people whom we
strongly like and admire than realize 110 percent of X by exchanging
these relationships for uninteresting or unpleasant ones."

Aristotle might have said the same. He wrote that this kind of ad-
miration was a strong basis for *friendship;* this was not purely a private
affair but the "bond that holds the community together"—and, as
such, one of the greatest goods.[3]

BUFFETT'S PURPOSE AND HIS INVESTMENT STRATEGY

Buffet's strategy only worked because he had the prudence to recognize the limits of his competence, the patience to wait for genuine

opportunities and the courage to back his judgment to the full. He also had the sensitivity to recognize admirable traits in others.

But these are not the only exceptional qualities that turned the principles into success. As well as these virtues, he has fantastic skills. He reads at least 2,000 annual reports a year and is famous for his photographic memory. When asked why he did not have a computer in his office, he said, "I am a computer." When he allocates capital—putting ⅓ of the company's resources into a single stock, for example—it is on the basis of a comprehensive knowledge of the market and the companies traded in the market. Because of his genius for remembering and for mental arithmetic, this knowledge does not have to be filtered through other people's brains. His confidence in an investment is confidence in his own judgment, not in that of a subordinate.

This self-confidence makes it easier for him to remain unswayed by emotion or intellectual excitement, whether his own or others'. Similarly he has rejected Wall Street–style "fashion" investment partly because it does not work, and partly because it "does not completely satisfy my intellect."

As is well known, he does not deploy these virtues and skills because he wants the trappings of wealth—he lives on a relatively modest salary. Rather, it seems, he just enjoys the process of investing well and making money. As he put it, investment is his "canvas"; as with an artist, the creative process and the output are indistinguishable. It makes no sense to ask why he wants to go on making money, it is just what he does. He pursues investment excellence for its own sake. The wealth is not even a score to prove that he is successful—he has gotten beyond that.

For Buffett, his role in life is primarily to allocate capital so as to maximize return on equity, and fulfillment to him is excellent performance of that role. This is a textbook case of Aristotelian Purpose, which involves the search for *eudaimonia* or well-being, understood as a kind of fulfillment or flourishing achieved by performing one's role in the community. Buffett's investment is not "ethical" in the sense that he searches out especially ethical companies, and from time to time he has even engaged in short-term risk arbitrage. But he draws a sharp distinction between the activities of arbitrageurs like T. Boone

Pickens and James Goldsmith, who "are not creating value . . . they are transferring it from society to shareholders" and the profitable businesses he backs that are adding value (making "the steak taste better," as he put it). His role is useful to the community.

His Purpose makes investing a joy. There is something almost primitive about him, allowing Buffett a kind of eternal youth. A New York investor visiting him at his home in Omaha noticed about him a "ring of innocence reclaimed." A woman friend said that when she was with him they were like "kids shooting marbles." And as Buffett put it to a friend, "some days I get up and I just want to tap dance."

This joy has in turn helped sustain for decades the excellence of his activities. Indeed it is worth quoting Aristotle on courage: "Rash people are impetuous, eager before danger arrives, but shifty when it is actually present; whereas courageous ones are keen at the time of action but calm beforehand." Buffett's ability to stand apart from the emotion of the stock market displays precisely the *measure* of the virtuous man that Aristotle praised.

BUFFETT AND THE MANAGEMENT OF ACQUIRED BUSINESSES

Buffett has also managed businesses effectively once acquired. This might seem surprising—he is after all by no means the archetypal conglomerate chief executive. Again, he has set out the route to success in his letters. It turns out the principles guiding his management of businesses are entirely consistent with those guiding their selection:

> At Berkshire we feel that telling outstanding CEOs . . . how to run their companies would be the height of foolishness. Most of our managers wouldn't work for us if they got a lot of back seat driving . . . nevertheless, Berkshire's ownership may make even the best of managers more effective. First we eliminate all of the ritualistic and nonproductive activities that normally go with the job of the CEO [i.e., no meetings with Wall St., the press, board etc]. . . . Sec-

ond we give each a simple mission: just run your business as if (1)
you owned 100% of it (2) it is the only asset in the world that you
and your family have or will ever have and (3) you can't sell or
merge it for at least a century.

This loose approach to management works because it is founded on
the set of good personal relationships that Buffett has cultivated. This
does not mean he spends much time with individual managers: Ken
Chase, who managed the Berkshire Hathaway textile business, recalled that the telephone calls were short and infrequent. The relationship is perhaps best described as that between comrades in arms,
a variety of friendship Aristotle described, built on a respect for good
qualities rather than warmth of sentiment. The result is that his managers feel a personal responsibility to him.

Buffett has always expressed his respect for his managers publicly
in his shareholder letters, and has made plain that he would not jeop-
ardize these relationships for the sake of short-term profit.

Buffett has at times even foregone the best possible deal in order
to build relationships. For example, he paid more than he needed for
shares in Wesco, a California savings and loan, in order to avoid any
bad feelings with its management. There was an SEC investigation,
and the investigator expressed his puzzlement at Buffett's overpaying.
Buffett pointed out that "it's important how the Wesco management
feels about us. . . . Lou Vincenti [chairman of Wesco] doesn't really
need to work for us. He likes working for us."

And indeed Wesco management performance improved significantly under Buffett, as has that of many subsidiaries. Buffett would
not normally pay more than he needs—he is not an over-generous
man (if anything he can be stingy)—but in the words of his biogra-
pher Roger Lowenstein, he is "uncanny as a motivator."

Good performance is also encouraged by Buffett's straightness on
executive pay. His policy is to "pursue rationality" (again, echoes of
Aristotle, for whom man's defining task is "rational activity"). Buffett
means that he relates pay to individual performance; in the case of his
chief executives, he relates it to percentage return on equity. Share
price movement based on market mood, or higher profits resulting

from retained earnings, or good performance elsewhere in the group, are not relevant because they are not strictly rational measures of performance.

Buffett is also good with people running the businesses he has had minority stakes in. He had an excellent relationship with Katherine Graham, for example, chairwoman and major shareholder in the *Washington Post*. After buying a stake in her company and joining the board, he became something of a mentor to her. To the frustration of some of the *Post* executives, he used this relationship to stop profits from the newspaper being dissipated in less profitable ventures, with the result that between 1974 and 1985 it retired 40 percent of its shares, and earnings per share went up ten times.

In some ways Buffett has maintained a similar set of relationships with his investors. In the early nineties he claimed, perhaps implausibly, that he knew, by sight if not by name, 90 percent of his 7,500 shareholders. More important, he has consistently said that he does not want just any old shareholders. He wants "high quality shareholders," that is to say, "rational shareholders" who ensure a "rational share price" (rational again!), reflecting the underlying value of the company. Accordingly, he has discouraged institutional investors, who are the most likely to be influenced by market mood, and for years he did not split his stock, making the price of entry high—in the year 2000 shares traded at over $70,000.

His attitude is well reflected in this letter to shareholders:

> Charlie and I hope that you do not think of yourself as merely owning a piece of paper whose price wiggles around daily and that is a candidate for sale when some economic or political event makes you nervous. We hope you instead visualize yourself as a part owner of a business that you expect to stay with indefinitely, much as you might if you owned a farm or apartment house in partnership with members of your family.

And indeed he has been successful in creating a sense of community among shareholders. This is not a commonplace trait among corporate leaders these days. A recent Halliburton annual meeting was held in a small Oklahoma town (near where it has its headquarters), making it difficult for dissident stockholders to communicate their distress at the company's substandard performance of its government contracts in Iraq. At the annual meeting of Home Depot—a company noted for declining revenues, an extravagantly paid CEO and an over-generous board of directors—the directors didn't bother to show up and the CEO moved the get-together to a quick and uneventful conclusion.

But a Berkshire Hathaway annual general meeting is a little like the agora of ancient Athens. Citizens can listen to and question their leaders—or buy insurance, jewelry or other goods and services provided by Berkshire companies. Buffet's annual reports display the Aristotelian virtues of *truthfulness* and *wittiness* that are so lacking in most public documents, but that are powerful tools for building community.

BUFFETT: AFTER HIM, WHAT?

The extraordinary thing about Buffett is that he is such a pure example of Aristotelian Purpose. He has demonstrated no interest in discovery or the new—he simply lacks intellectual curiosity about matters which do not impinge on investment performance. He is not particularly compassionate—at one point he wouldn't even *lend* his daughter some money for a new kitchen—and he has shown absolutely no desire to build an organization (as opposed to a community). The company has a tiny head office, and no one but the two partners has ever made any decisions. (Buffett did once take on an apprentice investment manager but that did not work out.)

Shareholders have frequently asked what will happen when Buffett dies. From the outside, it does not look as if he has created an enduring organization—his company is just too small to be a community of comrades. Has Buffett been so concerned with excellence that he has had no time to care about such things?

On the contrary. Buffett is too shrewd to be so psychologically imbalanced. It is not like him to believe, "Après moi, le deluge."[4] He and his partner may not have a bench filled with young talent. But surely, they know where those junior executives can be found—and, more, they know that young executives who appreciate their style of investing and management will find Berkshire Hathaway. Buffett's codes may not survive intact. But it is reasonable to conclude that talented, Purposeful men and women will surface who will do the best they know how for Berkshire Hathaway and its shareholders. If one is looking to create an intrinsically excellent and elegant enterprise, one can't ask for more than that.

For his philanthropic interests, Buffett has already found the right man for the job: In June 2006 he announced that he would give the bulk of his $40 billion fortune to the Bill and Melinda Gates Foundation. Buffett is such an example of Aristotelian virtue that he is able to recognize the excellence in others, in this case Bill Gates, someone who is even richer and more successful than him, and who also happens to be younger!

CHAPTER SIX

SAM WALTON'S ALTRUISTIC COMMITMENT TO THE CUSTOMER

Business stories about Wal-Mart in recent years could make you conclude that it is run by Satanists. In these accounts, managers lock employees in stores overnight. They find clever ways to deny overtime pay to workers. And they pay so badly that many, many employees get health care at the government's expense.

It is hard to believe that Sam Walton, who created the culture of Wal-Mart, would have endorsed some of its recent policies. His Wal-Mart was fueled by altruism. His passion for customer service and customer value was not, I believe, undertaken at the expense of the

Wal-Mart employee. Because Sam Walton, though hard-nosed and hard-driving, was nonetheless very aware of the power of consensus.

Walton's leadership skills were first noticed at the University of Missouri, where he became president of the student body. His political style was to greet people in the street before they greeted him, whether he knew them or not. That way, classmates came to think they knew him and liked him, and that he liked them right back. Walton found similar techniques useful throughout his life.

Walton was naturally friendly, but he was also intensely competitive. In the words of an early colleague, "What motivates [Sam Walton] is the desire to absolutely be on top of the heap"—or what he called, in his own words, "a true passion—some would say obsession—to win."[1]

His charm, his gift for merchandising, his willingness to experiment and imitate others, and above all his "bias towards action," as he put it, helped him become the largest retailer in the United States. But whether as a means to winning, or because he wanted it for its own sake, there was something else driving him and his company. That was the desire to create the greatest amount of happiness for the largest number of people. For Walton, growing up in the relatively impoverished region of rural Arkansas, that meant helping as many people as possible raise their standard of living: giving them material goods in a homogenized but comforting atmosphere.

In the process, he became known for displacing local retailers and uprooting downtowns—and much of that may be indefensible. But it does not change the altruistic nature of his enterprise: Wherever a Wal-Mart opened, people moved up into the middle class. In that sense, he was a forerunner of one of the most intriguing ideas propagated by business strategists today: the idea, as put forth by CK Prahalad, that there is a "fortune at the bottom of the pyramid." In other words, the socioeconomic pyramid—and those who will serve the humble, particularly the humble of India, China and other emerging nations—will enrich themselves by doing good.[2]

Walton used everything and everyone to accomplish this goal. He drove himself and his employees ruthlessly, and he was even more ruthless in squeezing pennies out of his suppliers. He also tirelessly exploited his natural friendliness and charm. But if the frugality was natural, so was the friendliness. He had the kind of tendency to empathize with others that, as Hume said, lies at the heart of morality: "Sympathy is the chief source of moral distinctions."[3] Over time—not from the start—this empathy turned what would otherwise have been simply a strongly competitive strategy into a Purpose.

In short, Sam Walton was no saint. He created a very tough company. But Purpose was at its core. He could have become a successful Southern discounter without a Purpose. But he could not have gone on to build what is now the world's largest company without that Purpose and without knowing how to make money out of it.

COMPETING WITH CORNER STORES

In 1945, Walton opened his first variety store, a franchise of the Ben Franklin chain, in Newport, Arkansas. Over the next five years he built its turnover from $72,000 to $250,000. His success was based on four things: finding cheap suppliers; employing effective display and promotion; discounting; and engaging in a constant stream of merchandising experiments—which often meant copying the competition. Effective promotion involved popcorn and ice cream machines at the entrance to the store, a carnival atmosphere and the force of his own personality. "Mr. Walton had a personality that drew people in. . . . It was like he brought in business by his being so friendly," reported a clerk.

In 1950 he was kicked out of the store by his landlord and he had to start again in another town. This time he picked Bentonville, further to the north, and he repeated the strategy that had worked before. After two years he was ready to open a second store, and by 1960 his chain of 15 variety stores was turning over $1.4 million.

But Walton recognized that variety stores were threatened by larger "discounters." This form of retailing had grown rapidly through the fifties, reaching an industry turnover of $6 billion by 1962. Discounting meant selling a wide range of nonfood merchandise at rock-bottom prices in low-rent, out-of-town outlets. He proposed to Butler Brothers, owners of the Ben Franklin brand, that he start a chain of discount stores for them. They refused—and he was forced to start his own chain.

Walton opened the first Wal-Mart in 1962, and over the next eight years he opened another 17 stores in Arkansas, Oklahoma and Missouri. He employed the techniques he had used in his variety stores—except now he was riding the wave of discounting, which during the same period expanded threefold. He offered rock-bottom prices, big promotions on the pile-it-high, sell-it-cheap model and money back guarantees. Price was more important than quality—he got product where he could—and his premises were scruffy—an old bottling plant and a converted cattle yard. Most important, he targeted small towns where there was no discounting competition.

This expansion could not be financed from cash flow, and by 1970 Walton was heavily in debt. This was both irksome personally and an obvious constraint on growth, so he decided to go public. An initial offering on the Over-the-Counter market was comfortably oversubscribed and the rate of expansion stepped up.

After the mid-seventies, however, the growth rate slowed, consolidation started, and K-Mart and a handful of other leaders began to set higher standards. In this more competitive environment, many of those who had milked their territories went out of business—of the top 100 discounters in 1976, only 24 remained in 1992.[4]

COMPETING WITH LEADERS

In 1976 Walton was not yet an industry leader. He had about 5 percent of K-Mart's turnover, and, as he put it, "so much about their stores was superior to ours back then." But suddenly he found himself competing head to head with K-Mart in a number of locations.

The clash prompted him to focus on competitive strategy; he improved the physical fabric of the stores, the merchandise mix and presentation, while continuing to drive down costs. At the same time he recruited a team of managers that went on to create the distribution and information systems responsible for much of Wal-Mart's future success and growth. He and his managers built an organization that was better at managing discount stores than anybody else in the United States.

The speed and breadth of the turnaround against K-Mart was striking. By 1990, K-Mart's sales per square foot were $150 to Wal-Mart's $250. In 2002 K-Mart was bankrupt and Wal-Mart was the largest company in the world.

Walton won this war because he created four advantages—price, merchandising management, logistics and service.

First, as he grew, he maintained the drive for low prices. His buyers bargained harder than anyone else's, and his organization remained slimmer than anyone else's. One vendor called Wal-Mart "the rudest account in America." How did the company get its buyers to remain tough? The answer lay in what the head of buying would tell them: "You're not negotiating for Wal-Mart, you are negotiating for the customer. And your customer deserves the best price you can get. Don't ever feel sorry for a vendor. He knows what he can sell for, and we want his bottom price."

Similarly the organization was kept lean because Walton would persistently ask how such and such a position or department was going to help get a better deal for the customer. There were minimal personnel and public relations departments, and no regional offices (other than distribution centers). On buying trips, expenses were so tight executives often had to share hotel rooms and walk rather than take taxis.

Second, Walton created an organization that kept top managers close to the individual stores—and thus the customers—even while the company grew dramatically. He himself had always been a superb merchandiser. Now, as the company grew, he continued to spend two or three days a week in the stores. In doing so he set an example for all managers.

Walton's approach to merchandising was simplicity itself: Imitate the competition. As a manager put it: "I remember him saying over and over again: Go in and check the competition." It also involved a constant stream of experimentation. David Glass, his successor, said: "He gets up every day bound and determined to improve something . . . he is less afraid of being wrong than anyone I've ever

known, and once he sees he's wrong, he just shakes it off and heads in
another direction."

This experimentation was by no means random: It was guided by
information, and Walton was a master at gathering and using information. He went everywhere with a famous yellow pad and later a
tape recorder, asking questions and recording information, about his
own and his competitors' stores. Throughout his career he went
through the figures for every store each week. Information, he felt,
kept him close to the stores and the customers.

From the start, managers met once a week, compared notes and
acted on decisions straight away. Later, when the company was much
bigger, regional managers based at headquarters would fly out to
their territories for four days, tour their stores, and then convene for
meetings on Friday and Saturday. Decisions about changes to merchandise or other issues would be made at the meetings and be given
to store managers by the end of the day; they would be acted on over
the weekend. Walton's "bias towards action" prevented the system
from clogging up, and at the same time kept managers close to the
stores.

Regional and district managers were essentially part of a communications system; there was no time, and certainly no money, for
them to build the kind of layered decision-making bureaucracy that
afflicts most large companies. This focus on detail and efficient communications helped headquarters delegate decisions to the stores
more effectively than the competition. Store managers had discretion
in allocating space, designing displays and ordering merchandise, and
had access to the information they needed to do this efficiently. In addition, they and their hourly paid workers could feed their experience
upward and see it acted on fast.

The investment in information systems, together with an indus-
try-leading distribution network, constituted Wal-Mart's third advantage. The company had built its first distribution center and
established its own fleet of vehicles in 1970, because it was cheaper
than relying on suppliers or third parties. Despite Walton's skepti-
cism about the costs of information technology, Wal-Mart was the
first discounter to install computerized inventory control, in 1971,

when it was still an insignificant player. In the late eighties Wal-Mart was a leader in creating direct links between its computers and those of its suppliers. It had some of the lowest levels of stock outs and its distribution costs were half the industry average.

Walton and his colleagues have always placed most emphasis, however, on their fourth advantage. In his own words: "Satisfied, loyal repeat customers are at the heart of Wal-Mart's spectacular profit margins and those customers are loyal to us because our associates treat them better than salespeople in other stores do." Ask any small businessman why his business is successful; he will say something similar. However, Walton's ability to stick to this formula even as the company was growing was remarkable. Indeed Walton put *more* emphasis on this as the company expanded.

Discounters have to keep their margins low, which means keeping payroll low. Originally in his efforts to minimize costs he had always paid the least he could, even below the minimum wage on occasion. While he had always been a great personal motivator, he had not seen the link between how he rewarded staff and how they treated the customer—and perhaps, in the early days, price had been more important anyway. In the early seventies he came around to the view that "if you want the people in the stores to take care of the customers, you have to take care of the people in the stores."

Basic wages remained low, but in 1971 Walton set up a bonus-and-share plan for staff, which, because of the subsequent success of the company, has made some quite junior employees several hundred thousand dollars. He did not claim that this plan was exceptional, but by the time he wrote his autobiography in 1992 he could say, "the more you share your profits with your associates—whether it's in salaries or incentives or bonuses or stock discounts—the more profit will accrue to the company."

Walton was strongly anti-union, and engaged in aggressive tactics to keep unions out. The only reason employees might want a union, he said, is when "management has done a lousy job of working and managing with their people." To him, this meant more than just rewarding people fairly; managers also had to be "servant leaders"—

sharing information widely, encouraging junior staff to act on their own initiative and encouraging promotion from within.

Walton could do this himself superbly. "After a visit, everyone in the store has no doubt that he genuinely appreciates our contributions, however insignificant" a store manager recorded. He adopted an open-door policy, asking people to speak to him if they had any concerns. He insisted that he and other managers give intelligent answers to associates' questions, and everyone was kept informed of their stores' sales, profits and inventory turns.

Walton glamorized what were otherwise humdrum jobs. He self-consciously married "the traditions of small town America, especially parades with marching bands, cheerleaders, drill teams and floats" with some of the ideas he picked up from a trip to Korea and Japan in the early 1970s. He would also push people to be as outgoing as he himself had been at college. In the 1980s he once used the satellite system to ask store staff to pledge that "whenever you come within ten feet of a customer, you will look him in the eye, greet him and ask him if you can help him." His ideal was associates who genuinely cared about customers and felt a moral obligation to help them. In Hume's words, they should be "useful or agreeable" to others.

WALTON'S PURPOSE

Until the mid-seventies, Wal-Mart was more profitable than its peers because of Walton's merchandising and motivational skills and his natural competitiveness. These, rather than Purpose, were the major source of his advantages. The company was small enough, and the competition weak enough, for his personal strengths to carry the day.

From the mid-seventies he had to compete against larger, more successful companies, but Wal-Mart grew at an even faster rate, while maintaining the highest margins in the industry. And this is where his Purpose assumed its rightful place in his company.

Everything revolved around the customer. If, for example, his buyers got an especially good deal, Walton would pass the gain on to

the customer rather than increase his margins. This was good commercial customer relationship-building—but it also allowed him to
tell buyers that they were *negotiating for the customer*. It was the resulting sense of obligation and Purpose that kept buyers tough. Similarly,
management information systems were designed to help managers be
more sensitive to *what the customer wanted* and then act on this knowledge, while the distribution systems were designed to get the merchandise they wanted into the right stores as quickly as possible. It
was the Purpose that kept the systems focused, simple and responsive.
This in turn helped everyone remain true to the Purpose—for example, having senior managers on the road, helping the in-store mer-
chandisers, became a constant reminder of the importance of the
local customer to headquarters. And store staffers were encouraged
to feel a personal duty—even to make a pledge—to *help the customer*.
It was this Purpose that maintained the high morale and standards of
service.

Such a Purpose—to serve the customer—is easy enough to declare. In the late eighties K-Mart's Chairman and CEO, Joseph An-
tonini, imitated Walton and exhorted staff over the company's
telecom system to put the customer first; it did not work. The difference? Wal-Mart was distinguished not by the content of its Purpose
but by the employees' commitment to it.

Walton wrote his autobiography while suffering from terminal
cancer, so he was perhaps inclined to write in moral terms. What is
interesting is the nature of the morality he described. He argued that
driving down prices was a way of giving back to the community,
rather defiantly adding, "Whether you buy into the argument or not,
we believe it." He summed up his impact on customers and associates
by saying, "I believe that millions of people are better off than they
would have been had Wal-Mart never existed."

Most entrepreneurs value teamwork as a necessity—Walton valued it for its own sake. He said it was "more the goal of the whole
thing, rather than some way to get there." He got pleasure from the
fact that many hourly paid employees, "learn to stand up tall, look
people in the eye and speak to them, and they feel better about

themselves, and once they start gaining confidence there's no reason they can't keep on improving themselves."

However, he was also very demanding of his colleagues and could be quite gruff. Managers had to come to meetings every Saturday and seven o'clock starts were the norm. A colleague on a buying trip recalled how they would finish work at half past midnight and Walton, retiring while the others went for a drink, would demand they meet for breakfast at six. The others might protest, but Walton insisted they would find something useful to do at that hour.

For all his competitiveness and toughness, Walton had a great capacity for empathy. This is the root of Humean ethics, which prescribes that we should make others happier—our ability to empathize means we are ourselves happier when others are happy. Fortunately for Walton, his empathy fitted perfectly with the commercial requirements of discounting and the need to create happy customers. His Purpose and strategy were as one.

Was Sam Walton concerned that the company's size and its growth dynamic might weaken its Purpose? Yes. He even speculated in his autobiography that the customer might be better served by five $20 billion companies than one $100 billion company. He went on to write, "What's really worried me over the years is . . . that we might someday fail to take care of our customers, or that our managers might fail to take care of and motivate our associates. I also was worried that we might lose the team concept or fail to keep the family concept viable . . . as we grow."

The Wal-Mart in recent headlines—the giant box that swallows everything in its postal code—would be beyond Walton's imagining. He was not a visionary. He had a single gift, and it worked for him to the end of his life. There was, as a result, no need for him to doubt himself. What he did for the customer—that was God's work.

The scores of altruistic companies starting out today will face similar challenges to those Wal-Mart faced in the 1970s. They will need to be ruthless on behalf of their altruistic Purposes. (Sam Walton succeeded brilliantly at that.) And then, when the shadow side, the inevitable unintended consequences of their Purpose, becomes clear—for every altruistic endeavor wreaks some toll on someone, whether intentionally or not—they will need to reframe their action to keep their altruism intact. That's the far more difficult challenge, and it's not clear yet whether even Wal-Mart, in the absence of their founder's presence, will be able to rise to the occasion.

CHAPTER SEVEN

THE HEROIC PURPOSE OF HENRY FORD AND SIEGMUND WARBURG

HENRY FORD

Henry Ford was rich, one of the richest men in the world. But money was a by-product for him. He looked at the early automobile and knew he could build one better and cheaper. Once he figured out the "how," his career was a long open road, with very little real competition in the crucial early years. Only later would he discover that life is not a straight open highway—and that he had no talent for sudden turns and sharp curves.

Ford's great strength was the purity of his heroic Purpose—he wanted to change the world through his automobile, and dominate the resulting industry. He let nothing, not even the realities of finance, stand in his way. In 1906, he had a furious argument with his original backer. Alexander Malcomson wanted to develop an expensive car, responding to current market demand. Ford wanted to develop a cheap car, using standardized parts. Ford won, threw his partner off the board and bought his shares. With the share transfer complete, he said to one of his mechanics who was driving him home, "This is a great day. We're going to expand this company, and you will see that it grows by leaps and bounds. The proper system, as I have it in mind, is to get the car to the people."[1]

The Ford Motor Company, founded in 1903 with just $28,000 in cash, did indeed grow. It grew with all the speed of a software company or a dot com—but with one huge difference. It resulted in vast factories spread across the United States and the world, and a complex vertically integrated supply chain extending from iron ore factories and a rubber plantation to a railroad, a shipping fleet and a small airline. The story of Ford's rise—and subsequent decline—has often been told in terms of strategic brilliance and failure. I think it is better understood in terms of Purpose. That is, as a single-minded effort to change the world.

FORD'S SUCCESS

Henry Ford was born in 1863, the son of a Michigan farmer. As a child, he was fascinated by all things mechanical and at the age of 16 he took a job at a machine shop. Over the next 20 years, he established himself as a highly competent mechanical engineer, rising to the position of Chief Engineer at the Edison Illuminating Company (later to become Detroit Edison, this was an electric power and light company aligned with Thomas Edison's original electric power company in New York).

While Ford was building his career in Detroit, Daimler and Benz in Germany were separately developing the first motor vehicles powered by the internal combustion engine. News trickled into America in the late 1880s and early 1890s, and Ford turned his mind to developing an engine and later a vehicle. Working in the evenings in a shed at the back of his home, and funded only by his salary, he made slow progress, but by 1896 he had completed his first model. By 1899 he felt sufficiently confident to resign from Edison and, with a small group of backers, set up the Detroit Automobile Company. One of the causes of his confidence was praise for his vehicle from Thomas Edison himself, who had met the young inventor at an electric power company. No doubt the discovery-driven Edison recognized someone of similar focus; but Ford's drive and concentration was oriented differently. Unlike Edison, he seems to have been less interested in invention for its own sake, and more interested in seeing how far he could take it in shaping the world.

But that would mean putting aside short-term rewards in favor of long-term possibility. The automobile industry was then four years old in the United States, producing a total of around 900 vehicles a year. It wasn't growing fast; after little more than a year, Ford's company closed. Ford complained later that the other shareholders saw the company as a mere "money making concern" rather than as "a vehicle for realizing my ideas."

For entrepreneurs like Ford, who are following a Purpose from the beginning, control is always an issue. In the next 18 months, Ford joined and left a second venture, The Henry Ford Company—he had learned from his first experience that "thinking first of the money instead of the work brings on fear of failure and this fear blocks every avenue of business." As a result "the way is clear for any one who thinks first of service, of doing the work in the best possible way." He soon started development on the car he wanted to make, a simple, light and efficient car—a "family horse," as Ford called it—and attracted the backing of Malcomson, a wealthy coal merchant. A new Ford Motor Company was formed.

From the beginning, Ford's clarity was exceptional and unwavering. In 1903, he said: "The way to make automobiles is to make one automobile like another automobile, to make them all alike, to make them come through the factory all alike, just as one pin is like another pin when it comes from a pin factory." This simplicity would lead to low prices, and low prices would ensure that "competition is eliminated before it starts." At the same time it would greatly increase demand, which would allow Ford to lower prices still further and so create a virtuous circle. Profit per car might fall but scale advantages were such that overall profits would rise. What is more, this happy scenario would not just benefit Ford; it would also benefit "the average American citizen" who would now be able to "own and enjoy his own automobile." As he said to men in his plant, he wanted to produce a car that working men could buy. He was going to "democratize the automobile."

And, not incidentally, fulfill a heroic mission. In its first full year the company assembled and sold approximately 1,700 cars. Then in October 1906, Ford launched the Model N at only $600—40 percent cheaper than his previous basic model. Sales for 1907 shot up to 8,000 units; profits topped $1 million. Suddenly Ford was one of the major players in the industry. This level of success confirmed that he was right: A vehicle that met the real needs of ordinary people would quickly gain dominance.

Ford began almost at once to start work on a successor, the Model T. Launched in 1908, by 1910 sales climbed to more than 18,000 units and company profits to more than $4 million. This was a good performance but despite more than doubling sales between 1907 and 1910, Ford had not increased his market share significantly.

In 1910, he was ready to implement his ideas in full. The company moved to a new factory, enormously increasing capacity. That fall Ford cut the price of the cheapest Model T from $900 to $680. Sales exploded and, stimulated by repeated price cuts, continued to explode until America's entry into World War I nearly seven years later. By 1914 the T was selling almost 250,000 units at prices from $500; by volume, Ford had 48 percent of the U.S. market and a virtual monopoly of cars under $600. By 1917, Ford was selling 730,000 Model Ts, starting at $345. None of these price cuts were needed to match the competition or ensure that demand was maintained—Ford instead seemed to be acting consistently with Nietzsche's principle that "under peaceful conditions, the militant man attacks himself."[2]

FORD'S ADVANTAGE

Ford dominated the bottom of the market because he was better equipped to fight a price war than his competitors—and as a result he did not have to fight a price war at all. The full range of cars was made from a single chassis; this same basic model was produced for 19 years. This simplicity and the strength of the basic design underpinned Ford's success.

Simplicity of design opened the way to mass production. Ford was not the first person to understand economies of scale or the virtues of system in the factory, but he applied these principles with a single-mindedness that none of his competitors matched. He was the one who could, in Nietzsche's words, "grasp at the future with a creative hand."

Retooling was constant—Ford would throw away equipment only a few months old if this was needed to make improvements to the car or efficiency gains in production. And improvements were not limited to the factory. Ford and his colleagues looked at the entire flow, from the mining of iron ore to the sale of cars by the dealers, and made changes where necessary.

The biggest change took place between 1912 and 1914, when Ford, inspired by meat-packing factories, installed the first moving assembly line in car manufacturing. This increased productivity sensationally: Making a chassis, which had taken over 12 man-hours, now took less than 3, dynamos now took 7 minutes to make instead of 27, and so on.

Ford did not create this edifice on his own. Even before he set up his first venture, he had attracted men willing to work with him for nothing. By 1912 he had built a powerful team; the energy they brought to bear made the phenomenal changes and growth possible. And they all recognized that Ford was the driving force. As one of them put it, he had the necessary foresight, originality, shrewdness, clarity of thought and temerity. "Most of all he was resolute in applying the foundation principles of mass production: simplicity of design, speed and continuity of quantity production, huge sales at ever-dropping prices and small unit profits."

It was this resolve that inspired his team. It was this inspiration that created a system that, for a time at least, no one else could rival. To state the obvious: He was their hero.

How did Ford, an ill-educated mechanic, come to understand the dynamics of the industry so much better than anyone else? How did he maintain his sense of direction between 1900, when he first formulated his ideas, and 1910, when he started to implement them in full? How did he manage to build such a successful team, to turn his plans into reality? The answers are not found in Ford's strategy, but in his Purpose.

FORD'S PURPOSE

Like many entrepreneurs, Ford did not really want to make, let alone enjoy, more and more money. Indeed he did not watch the cash in the company very closely; in the early days his colleague Couzens, who looked after the money, was probably vital to his survival. Ford was happy to throw away comparatively new machinery, and he never assessed the return on his investment. In 1917 he fought (and lost) a law suit against the Dodge Brothers, two minority shareholders (and founders of the Dodge auto brand) who wanted him to distribute dividends rather than invest in lower prices and expansion.

As one of the wealthiest men in the country, asked the plaintiff's lawyer, what was Ford trying to do? Ford replied that he was trying to employ as many workers as he could, give them high wages, provide the public the benefit of a low-priced car, and "incidentally make money. . . . If you give all that, the money will fall into your hands; you can't get out of it." This remark lost him the case; the judge ruled that money for shareholders should not be incidental, and ordered the dividends paid. Ford subsequently bought out the Dodge Brothers as quickly as he could.

If money was incidental, what drove Henry Ford? He wanted to reshape society with the automobile, but he was no champion of modernity as such. His plants may have been the perfect examples of vast centralized production, but privately he invested in several small village factories, a form of industrial organization he hoped (in vain) would revive and *improve* rural life. A similar motivation initially inspired his manufacture of tractors, and he was especially pleased that the T sold so well to farmers. Even though rural factories never took off, the car did make an enormous difference in the countryside, for example relieving the isolation of farmers' wives like his mother.

During the early years of the company, he had expressed the rather naïve hope that the car would be an engine of political change: "If you get people together so that they get acquainted with one another, and get an idea of neighborliness, the car will have a universal effect. We won't have any more strikes or wars." The same idealism was apparent in the time and money he spent trying to put an end to World War I. In general Ford was more concerned with improving things than meeting market demand, about which he could be quite contemptuous.

A similar desire to improve seems to have prompted his agreement to Couzens's proposal in 1915 to double the minimum wage of his adult male workforce to $5 a day. This has been analyzed exhaustively as a shrewd business calculation; productivity did increase in the years following and Ford became a national figure as a result. Five dollars a day was only the most visible part of a whole program of good employee relations introduced at this time—more systematic wage rates and increments for good performance, sick leave, an eight hour day, protection from arbitrary dismissal by foremen and so on.

Like the Model T, these better conditions and the extra pay were meant to improve things, in this case the lives of the workers. To ensure that they did, and that the extra cash was not simply dissipated, a team of investigators, part of a new "Sociological Department," was set up to visit employees in their homes to detect drunkenness, bad housekeeping or rack-renting landlords. Help was available for those who wished to move to new homes, and immigrants were coached in the American way of life, including English language lessons. To a far greater extent than its rivals, the company trained unskilled workers—in 1916 Ford set up the highly successful and enduring Ford Trade School for youths. Ford treated his workforce harshly and despised those who needed "an atmosphere of good feeling" but he seems to have wanted to create opportunities for disadvantaged groups. He had a good record of hiring African Americans and in 1919 was employing 1,700 severely handicapped and 9,000 partially handicapped employees in a workforce of 45,000. Particularly striking was the program to hire ex-convicts and Ford's proud remark that "Only 3 out of 600 convicts in my factory have failed to make good."

Ford was not first and foremost a social innovator, and he was not committed to any of these projects in the way he was committed to the cheap car. Famously, inflation quite soon eroded the value of the $5 day and by the mid-1920s real wages were scarcely above their original level. The arbitrary power of the foremen to sack workers was reasserted and, with little in the way of surplus wages to monitor, the Sociological Department was wound down. In the twenties the regime at Ford's was much like that in other factories; by the thirties it was worse, and Ford's labor relations involved hiring thugs from the Detroit underworld and physical violence. Good relations were strictly for the good times.

What explains these inconsistencies? Perhaps it was Ford's fascination with the mechanical. He was a mechanic, not a psychologist or philosopher, even if the public at the time wanted to attribute to him an improbable wisdom. The one consistent element in his activities and ambitions was the way he used machines as a force for change—and, because organizations were also a kind of machine, he believed they too could improve things and people. What mattered was the machine, or the company, not precisely what was done with it.

In this Ford was very much the Nietzschean. Despite Ford's claims about democratizing the automobile, he was less interested in what people wanted than in exercising his will to improve the world. Despite the variety of social projects he pursued, he seems to have been less concerned with human welfare than with effectiveness and the exercise of strength. What the casual observer might think were Ford's ends—working men enjoying their own cars, for example— were merely means to this overarching end. Again Nietzsche's words are relevant here: "One loves ultimately one's desires, not the thing desired." No doubt Ford would have scoffed at this remark, but the German philosopher who preached "vast hazardous enterprises" that would educate the world and end the "frightful rule of folly and chance" was setting out the Purpose that the American industrialist pursued.

It was a Purpose he pursued consistently. It underlay all his ideas: democratizing the automobile, engineering peace, improving rural life, educating a new workforce. And it underlay the constant drive to improve both product and process, and made the risks involved in massive expansion seem worthwhile. This Purpose gave him a strong direction, and circumstances—or what writers on strategy call "the business environment"—made it possible for him to pursue this successfully.

And the Purpose made him pursue the direction resolutely. Ford worked diligently on a car that could be reduced in price, even though it was years before this would happen and he had no idea how it would be achieved. The same Purpose gave him the strength to set up in business for the third time in 1903; to eject Malcomson in 1906; to start looking for a larger factory site in 1906, little more than a year after moving to a new site; to cut prices when the factory was operating at capacity in the prewar years; to fight a legal battle with shareholders in 1917; and then to buy out these shareholders in 1920, effectively borrowing the money against the company's future profits.[3] As Nietzsche puts it, "It is not the strength but the duration of great sentiments that makes great men."

And this resolution attracted others. Ford built a team of young men who sensed the Purpose could work and thus came to share it. Ford may have been an autocrat from the start, but for a long time he did not have to intervene very much, spending most of his efforts on product development. The effective work of this team was central to his success.

DECLINE IN THE 1920S

After a wartime lull, unit sales built up quickly, rising to 2.2 million units worldwide and a 57 percent U.S. market share in 1923. But that was the peak. The company did not achieve the same volumes again until the 1950s and never the same share. Worldwide sales fell to 2.1

million units in 1924 and 1925 and to 1.8 million in 1926, when Ford's U.S. share was only 34 percent.

By then, competitors were finding it easy to copy Ford's production techniques and erode the cost advantage he already had. Ford had never attempted to keep what he did secret; indeed, competitors were free to come and inspect the plant or read one of the books containing detailed illustrations of his machinery and methods.

The situation was made worse by a migration of managers to General Motors and other competitors. Ford had always been quite explicit that he would not share power with anybody else, in stark contrast with the collegiate style being developed by Alfred Sloan at GM. As Ford put it to a visitor: "That's the only way to get anywhere, one man rule"—as good an example of the Nietzschean *Ubermensch* speaking as any. This became more marked after World War I. The team morale that had driven the company in the prewar years faded; the more independent-minded managers were fired or left. The subordinates who survived and progressed were men who did what they were told.

With the scale dynamics more widespread and the competition imitating his techniques, Ford lost his price advantage. By 1924 the Chevrolet was the better car. The T still sold far more units—it was cheaper and had a huge reputation—but Ford was coasting. After 1919, Ford refused to allow significant improvements to the T, and the engineering department was poorly organized and unmotivated. Feedback from dealers was ignored. Positive initiatives from subordinates tended to be disrupted by Ford's idiosyncratic personal interventions. Even the attempts at improvement by Edsel, Ford's son and by this time nominally president of the company, were brushed aside.

The nature of demand was changing too. Now that so many people had a car, and now that technical performance had improved so much, buyers were looking for improved design. Possession of a modern-looking car became a status symbol; the T, which once had been the status symbol of its generation, now looked old-fashioned. Henry Ford refused to respond to this change in consumer taste and to allow any changes to the body styling of the T: As far as he was concerned a car was a machine for "getting you there." His exasperated subordinates would have recognized the "will to stupidity" that Nietzsche described as a feature of strong men.

A PURPOSE OUT OF
TUNE WITH THE TIMES

Ford Motor Company's relative decline in the twenties has often been explained in terms of strategic choice, a failure to respond to changing market conditions and an ossification of decision making brought about by the willfulness of an old man. But Henry Ford was only 60 in 1923, the peak year of company sales, and in 1927 he threw himself into the successful development of the Model T replacement. Perhaps some of the company's problems in the 1930s and 1940s are best explained by the aging process, but the failure to adapt the strategy in the 1920s can be more fully understood in terms of Purpose.

Ford was disparaging about the rising importance in the industry of fashion and cosmetic design:

> It is considered good manufacturing, and not bad ethics, occasionally to change designs so that old models will become obsolete and new ones will have to be bought either because repair parts for the old cannot be had, or because the new model offers a new sales argument which can be used to persuade a customer to scrap what he has and buy something new. . . . Our principle of business is precisely to the contrary. . . . We want the man who buys one of our products never to have to buy another.[4]

Ford's heroic Purpose had devolved into a non-competitive strategy. The whole management team could share Ford's Purpose, but once the competitive situation started to change, that lockstep commitment didn't matter. Ford was not interested in innovation, or making customers happy, or even excellence for its own sake. Ford's Purpose made it hard for him to adapt.

At bottom, it was simply Ford's good fortune that his Nietzschean Purpose fit the prewar situation well. As the strategy derived from Purpose became less successful, it lost its binding force in the company. It was no longer clear where the Purpose was taking the company, making it almost impossible for others to share it. It no longer underpinned the company's morale. Ford became more and more isolated, while the organization was held together by its own momentum, or even fear, rather than by Purpose.

Ford became a hero once he stopped trying to discover and started concentrating on effectiveness. But effectiveness was only one arrow in a manufacturer's quiver. Ford refused to change or grow. And so the hero outlived his Purpose.

SIEGMUND WARBURG

In a sense, the iconoclastic European banker Siegmund Warburg was Henry Ford's opposite—an unapologetic elitist with no interest in the common man or mass-market products. During his early years, in pre-Nazi Germany, he was privileged to see how business elites operated, and he imitated what he saw. Later, in England, he took his heritage and his vision and dressed them in the financial equivalent of the bespoke suits and custom shoes that he wore (and that he insisted his staff wear). The result was a business that took fastidiousness to a new level—a business that made a virtue out of superiority. What could be taken for arrogance was, in his case, Purpose.

His story effectively starts in 1931, when the 29-year-old Warburg went with his cousin Jimmy and his uncle Max to see the chancellor of pre-Nazi Germany. They had a plan for the rescue of a leading German bank, and with it the German banking system. The proposal was turned down; the bank collapsed. Max was familiar with such frustrating encounters with national leaders, having been an occasional advisor to the Kaiser before World War I.

Thirty-three years later Warburg, too, would become an unofficial adviser to a national leader, in his case English Prime Minister Harold Wilson. Sneered at by some of his competitors for associating with the socialists, he was being true to his—and his family's—idea of a banker, involving himself with national and international issues. By this stage, in 1965, Warburg had moved to England, and his company, S. G. Warburg, was one of the top two merchant banks in London.

After WWII, it employed just 15 people but it grew rapidly in the late forties and fifties. In 1959 it achieved worldwide fame by securing control of British Aluminum for Reynolds Metals and Tube Investments in a hostile takeover that went against the unwritten "club rules" of the City of London. Indeed, the firm faced extreme pressure from the financial community (the Bank of England, the other major banks, even the Prime Minister) to abandon the deal, but refused to back down. Three years later S. G. Warburg organized the first dollar denominated bond issue outside the United States for Autostrade Italiane, an innovative response to the imminent Interest Equalization Tax in the United States, which allowed the firm to dominate a completely new market.

Warburg was enterprising and opportunistic, and he and his firm were highly disciplined, placing far greater emphasis on coordinated teamwork than was common in the City at the time. But what drove the team? What kept them together through the regime of discipline, fear, long hours and sometimes abuse that Warburg imposed? And what drove Warburg himself—universally described as a "magnetic" or "mercurial" character with infinite charm, barely controlled emotions and no talent for small talk?

The answer, I think, lay in Warburg's almost nostalgic idea, formed in Hamburg in the 1920s, of what a banker should be, and powered by his strong sense of heroic Purpose.

STARTING IN LONDON

In 1921, Warburg came to work for M. M. Warburg and Co. In 1930, he was made a partner. He then asked to head up a Berlin branch. He stayed in Berlin until 1934, when he correctly read Hitler's intentions toward the Jews and emigrated to England.

Warburg arrived in London with approximately £5,000 in cash (perhaps £300,000 in today's money). His naturalization petition was sponsored by the Rothschilds, the Hambros and the Barings. He would work for a new firm, the New Trading Company, which was already in the process of being set up in London by a group of Dutch and German banks, including Warburg's Amsterdam firm. Warburg had a small personal stake, 10 percent, but he was not the boss. The first managing director was a well-connected old Etonian, Harry Lucas.

There were initially just three employees. Like any small company of this kind, it took such work as was available—its main business seems to have been acting as an intermediary for those seeking finance—and it achieved modest success. After four years there were nine employees.

After the war, all the top executives were German or Austrian refugees. These men brought a distinctive, "German" style of doing business, and Warburg imported some of the practices he had known at M. M. Warburg and Co. in the twenties and thirties. For example, all directors read all correspondence prior to the morning meeting and all outgoing mail was read and countersigned by a second executive. There was always more than one person familiar with a client's affairs, and the smallest client got the same level of service as the largest—one of Max's rules.

Warburg himself kept on top of everything that was going on. He traveled extensively, but, wherever he was, each day he received a summary of all incoming mail, a log of all telephone calls, minutes of meetings, a list of lunch guests, the schedules of directors, a review of the financial press, a list of shares bought and sold, and reports on the state of current client accounts and proposals. When in London he worked the firm's network himself. He prepared carefully for the two daily client lunches—he would shake hands and chat with invitees to the first and sit for the second, which was for the most senior clients. He was reputed to stock his conversation with aphorisms he had either read and memorized or carefully made up in advance. He wrote regularly to his large range of contacts and was even criticized by his rivals for wasting time on people who would never generate business—but of course some of them did. Unlike those rivals, he and his colleagues thought about the business they would be doing two or even five years into the future, and how they would achieve it.

Above all, he insisted on meticulous standards from his subordinates. As he used to put it, "we must do things with style. We must achieve the results."[5] Letters, he advised, should always be written with the desired reply in mind and constructed to achieve this. In any case, any letter with spelling mistakes or poor grammar had to be re-typed. Strategy for a deal should include carefully worked-out fall-back positions, and in the event of failure post mortems had to be carried out. Someone even had the job of recording all the mistakes made and what was done about them. Such diligence required long hours—the company became known as "The Night Club" and employees made a point of being visible in the evenings.

The firm was thus a highly disciplined machine, which did things more thoroughly than its rivals. It also benefited from Warburg's outstanding network of contacts. A third advantage was the perspective he and his fellow directors brought from a different time and place—paradoxically, this helped them be less hidebound by convention than their competitors, and thus more likely to respond to the underlying logic of a situation. A final advantage, much commented on, was Warburg's fantastic charm—he was the supreme salesman, both in winning clients and placing securities.

This unique combination of strengths helped the company grow significantly during the late forties and fifties—from profits of £40,000 in 1948 to £1,000,000 in 1957.

WARBURG'S PURPOSE

Warburg engineered legendary deals. He referred to his kind of banking by its traditional name, *haute banque*. Even in the early days, he would make remarks such as, "Either a firm is in *haute banque* or it does not exist." The idea was explicitly elitist, and suited Warburg's hankering for a world in which an intellectual and moral elite could thrive. As he put it in his private notebook,[6] "I still hope for a new aristocracy, a new elite, whose qualities will be a suspicion of luxury and the accumulation of goods, a respect for substance rather than appearance, for quality in preference to quantity, and a fierce nobility and independence of judgment." Prominent among such an aristocracy would be the banker, whose strict independence would allow him to give his clients advice that the City crowd either had not thought of or would not dare follow.

Warburg's Purpose was to belong to—and create—such an elite. Why? Because, as he said, "The real object of the vital impulse is to bring the diverse potentialities of the human being to their highest possible level." That is, he valued the achievements of the elite for their own sake.

In this he was directly inspired by Nietzsche, who had longed for the dominance of the *Übermensch:* "It is the business of the very few to be independent. It is a privilege of the strong." With independence and strength went solitude: "He shall be the greatest who can be the most solitary . . . the man beyond good and evil." Warburg had echoed these words in a funeral oration for an uncle in the 1930s: "Lightning and thunder could flash from his eyes—the lightning of vision and the thunder of indignation, an unholy thunderstorm that, far beyond good and evil, tried to crush everything petty and ugly." His uncle had had "the most difficult courage that exists, the courage of loneliness and independence."

He aspired to the same courage himself.

This was easier for Warburg than for other men because he had a profound belief in his own superiority. His doctor, to whom he made long confessional statements during the last decade of his life, reported that Warburg was "completely egocentric and fundamentally conceited. He thought most other people were fools." Or as Nietzsche had put it, "The noble soul has reverence for itself." So it is not surprising that he retained such tight control over his firm, insisting on a discipline that he believed came naturally to the elite, and that was essential to controlling those who might otherwise fail. His conviction in others' inferiority also explains why he was so little concerned by the complaints of the Governor of the Bank of England during his first great transaction, the hostile takeover of British Aluminum. It also explains why he had such a taste for financial engineering, which, after all, depends on spotting market imperfections—that is, other people's stupidity.

On this he could be eloquent. "Most of the important people in the City," he remarked, "will knowingly make blunders, with the sole aim of sparing themselves any conflict." He had a visceral hatred for the resulting "tolerance towards mediocrity." He was anticipating, 20 years in advance, the research of behavioral economists who build human foibles and misperceptions into their models of market activity. As the years went by, the financial markets did not seem to improve. In the sixties he said, "Promotion there [in banks] is based, today more than yesterday, on the co-opting of mediocrity by mediocrity."

As Warren Buffett also observed, being the same as everyone else, fitting in to the prevailing mood, is the most popular way of making money in financial markets. The more alert will make more money than the less so, but overall such activity adds little value and is parasitical; investors and companies pay a high price for the market liquidity that is its only product. Siegmund Warburg—like Buffett—disliked the mediocrity and blind following of fashion involved, and also like Buffett he made money by being smarter. But he was driven by different forces than Buffett. The American investor delighted in the power of reason; Warburg delighted in victory, in being better for its own sake, being truly *haute banque* when others were mere pretense.

Although he hoped for a "*new* aristocracy," his aspiration was tinged with nostalgia for a world that he had glimpsed as a young man. He also valued and wanted to preserve the traditional disciplines of a private bank and the international friendships of a private banker, as close to the spare comradeship of the elite as could be hoped for in real life. His elitism implied style, and Warburg valued style for its own sake. As well as writing immaculate prose, everyone in his office had to be immaculately dressed, but with old-fashioned restraint. "If you notice the tie a man is wearing, it is too loud," he once remarked, and he is said to have turned down a client because he was wearing monogrammed shirt cuffs. Style also extended to what one talked about: He preferred to recruit trainees who were lucid about Plato and Thomas Mann rather than those who only knew economics, and he flattered his clients by sending them gifts of books.

Style was the outward form of the discipline needed to make his firm truly elite. It was also part of Warburg's display, the charm that flattered and won over clients. As he put it, "You have to become someone's friend to be their banker." For all that, his doctor believed he was a deeply lonely and unhappy man, and like many such men he had strong emotions, both positive and negative. He was constantly giving people generous presents, but, if the occasion dictated, would display a fierce temper, throwing telephones out of the window and tossing crockery around the office. His charm was like that of an actor: controlling these emotions, holding them in check when he was called on to play the part of the banker. In one moment, he would recite laboriously learned aphorisms; at another, he would consciously put on a tantrum to achieve an effect. He really was, as Nietzsche would put it, "the play actor of his own ideal." It was this balance between emotion and his idea of the banker that fueled the web of relationships that in turn helped bring him such success.

That same balance created an unusually intense atmosphere within the firm. He would latch onto new recruits and build them up, along with his expectations of them, and, when, as almost always happened, they failed to live up to his ideals, or they asserted their independence (a quality he was cruelly ambivalent about), he would be disappointed, sometimes it is said to the point of tears. Employees would be flattered when he put his arm around their shoulders and gave them his close attention. But, as one employee put it, "one lapse and one immediately saw his face close." In this, Warburg was strikingly like that other Nietzschean, Henry Ford, who developed a series of intense relationships with key members of his team. Almost all of these soured and the individuals left, leaving Ford isolated.

We can see the great contrast in Warburg's mind between two kinds of people. On the one hand are the elect, the elite, Nietzsche's "higher class of men," the "free spirits" who understand what is fundamental in life, who exercise independent judgment, and thus whose advice is of enormous value. Such people have no time for the trivial and are immersed in the great dramas of the human condition. Hovering above such people, but also part of this "higher class of men," aloft on their superiority, are the bankers, who treat their clients too as part of this elite. Then there is everybody else, irretrievably mediocre, conventional and lusting after pleasure and money, Nietzsche's "lower order of human beings."

✑

Ford and Warburg could not have been more different as individuals, but they were driven at root by the same Purpose. Their firms were propelled by the principal characteristic of heroism: To dominate their rivals and build an enduring advantage by establishing the standards of their industries. For Ford this was the mechanistic standard of the integrated supply chain, for Warburg the elitist standard of *haute banque.*

PART III

HOW PURPOSE BUILDS GREATNESS

INTRODUCTION

A ll of these stories suggest that Purpose is the starting point of greatness in companies.

But what is a great company? We know it when we see it. But what are the signs of greatness? What transforms a good company into a great one?

Some would say that the greatness of a company is evident in its climate—in other words, in the morale of its employees. When there is high morale, people feel that they do great things simply by working for their company. The company does great things itself, and they are a part of it.

But morale is a tricky indicator. During the Internet boom of the late nineties, any number of companies had morale that would make the cheerleaders of the Dallas Cowboys jealous. And why not? The stock prices were rising. Recently arrived secretaries, freshly rewarded with stock options, were worth millions of dollars—on paper. Executives gave speeches in which they claimed "Trees can grow to the sky." And, daily, the stock prices rose.

Those who worked at a dot com company during those years will remember the strange sense of unreality that accompanied this false prosperity. How reassuring it felt—and yet oddly dissonant—to watch the executives claim credit for rampant growth, and to assert that they knew why it was happening, and that it would last forever. How odd it was to see the envy on the faces of friends and family who worked at "old-line" companies, and who had been left out of the gravy train. A friend at AOL recalls the cheering in the office at the end of a week when the stock had gained five points a day and his net worth topped $20 million.

The crash—the puncturing of the "Internet bubble"—brought the end of "theoretical wealth" and corporate valuations that had no connection to reality. And with that came a dramatic drop in morale. The brilliant executives were revealed to have no greater knowledge than the kid who delivered the mail. The formerly rich were found to have no intrinsic superiority to the rest of us. And as for morale, who could be more depressed than an employee who had been a paper millionaire, and who has just discovered that his meager base salary is all he has left?

Another definition of greatness holds that it can be judged by a company's ability to innovate. This is true—but exaggerated. At many companies during the dot com boom, "change" and "technology" were intellectual currency—buzzwords for any new initiative. "Reorgs" were common, as if cleaner reporting relationships constituted genuine achievement. But novel action in itself has no meaning—if anything, it may disguise an inability to figure out what really needs to be done. The fact of the matter is that, in most organizations, there is more wealth created by continuity of a smart strategy than by constant change. That is why long-term investors tend to make more money, over the course of a year, than day traders.

Others would suggest that greatness is the mark of a winner. A firm is on its way to becoming great if it has a competitive position; otherwise, it will languish among the mediocre. To put it in the words of the great race car driver Sir Jackie Stewart, "What counts is whether you are in pole position or not." Unfortunately, the winner of any given contest is not necessarily the one with the greatest capability. Circumstance always plays a part, and so does the way the contest is set up. Indeed, history records many people with notable failures early in their lives who went on to remarkable achievement—Abraham Lincoln, Mahatma Gandhi, Winston Churchill—and lifelong winners who ultimately contributed very little in the way of greatness. Companies, too, may hold a highly competitive position for reasons that have little to do with their own intrinsic greatness—except for their great luck.

Still others would equate greatness with performance: The firm that consistently achieves the highest measures and metrics is the greatest firm. In his book *Good to Great* Jim Collins implicitly takes this view; his criteria for "great" companies are those with stock price performance that outperformed the market and their own industries for at least 11 straight years.

I see two problems with any quantitative indicator of corporate greatness, even one as well-reasoned as Mr. Collins'. First of all, performance is inherently qualitative—there is no reliable way to translate the many facets of a company's quality into the narrow bandwidth of a numerical metric or ranking. At best, a performance metric will isolate some aspects of a company's greatness while providing the illusion of a comprehensive view. And because numbers are easy to manipulate, greatness can be overlooked or hidden all too easily, while mediocrity (or willful manipulation of the numbers) can be elevated.

How then do you know a great company? By the quality of its action: The capacity to accomplish sustained, powerful and valuable results. When you consider the greatness of a company, you understand why the "stakeholder" idea of a company's purpose—the idea that a company exists to serve its shareholders, customers, employees, suppliers, regulators and neighbors, balancing its obligations and duties to each—is precisely wrong. A great company is one that embodies a Purpose in such a way that its quality of action is high. Such a company will naturally produce results that exalt the lives of shareholders, customers, employees, suppliers, regulators and neighbors. It won't need to take on their demands as an obligation.

A great company, in short, not only sustains itself, but it provides continuing evidence of the value of its existence. It not only makes a product or provides a service that people want, but it does so in a way that makes people glad that this particular company has come into existence, if only because of the great way that it plays its role.

What kind of results do great companies produce? That depends on the company and the situation. The great companies at this moment in time—one might include such obvious examples as Toyota, GE, Microsoft and IBM, and no doubt each reader of this book would have his or her own list—have each been great in their own way. But they all manifest that greatness in some common ways.

- They are great places to work; the collective morale of their employees is high.
- They are great innovators; they introduce new ideas and execute them powerfully well.
- They are great competitors; they never give up fighting for position.
- They are great leaders; they set an agenda that is worthwhile to follow.

In the chapters that follow, I want to explore the connection between Purpose and each of these attributes of greatness. I will argue that Purpose increases morale, strengthens the ability of the firm to innovate, solidifies position and guides leadership. In all these ways, explicit attention to Purpose can lead companies closer to their potential for greatness.

CHAPTER EIGHT

PURPOSE AND MORALE

MORALE AND ACTION

How do you raise morale? That's a big challenge in an age of relative transparency, when employees can learn much more about their employer than that employer might ever want them to know. And it's even harder when good people are relentlessly head-hunted and there is always a would-be employer with an offer you can't match—stock options, bonuses, perks, to say nothing of a bigger paycheck week after week.

Still, we count talented employees with strong morale as our greatest assets. And the reasons are obvious. They embrace action, bring energy and resourcefulness to their tasks and make the most of the tools at hand. They are engaged by the nature of the work itself, and less driven by the rewards and punishments of incentives. Therefore, they make decisions more purely related to the strategic goals, and to the Purpose, of the enterprise.

Employees who lack morale are a drain. They work by rote and seem listless, curiously detached from their surroundings. No wonder the Prussian general von Clausewitz believed that in war the physical factors are "little more than the wooden hilt, while the moral factors are the precious metal, the real weapon, the finely-honed blade."[1]

A Towers Perrin study published in January 2003 found statistically significant correlations between employee morale and returns to shareholders over a five-year period. A 2002 survey by PricewaterhouseCoopers found strong correlations between absenteeism (a surrogate for low morale) and low profit levels. A survey of 592 of the largest U.S. companies published in 1986 established a significant relationship between the existence of management policies designed to improve motivation and strong financial performance. A survey of 968 companies published in 1994 showed similar results.[2] A 1998 McKinsey study of 77 large U.S. companies found that the top 20 percent in terms of financial performance also outperformed on 13 of 19 McKinsey measures of intangible "employee value."[3] A survey of leading corporate executives, conducted in 2004 by the Aspen Institute and Booz Allen Hamilton, confirmed a link between financial performance and values, showing that financial leaders were more likely to make "values" explicit by codifying or articulating them.[4]

Those who put more trust in market performance than in surveys should note that anyone investing each year from 1998 to 2002 in companies appearing in *Fortune*'s "Best 100 Companies to Work For" list would have achieved almost double the average stock market returns.[5] If the market as a whole had performed as well, at least $500 billion would have been added to the value of the U.S. stock market.[6]

Such statistics don't necessarily indicate that high morale leads to higher profits, but they do suggest a virtuous circle. Good morale and good financial performance tend to be infectious—they breed more of the same, and they also seem to breed more of each other.

But good morale cannot be constructed directly. One does not go up to an employee and either shout at them or plead with them to raise their morale. Only when conditions are right does morale go up. It's thus helpful to think of good morale as being supported by four building blocks—rewards, tasks, community and Purpose.

You can hear the importance of these four blocks in the four kinds of questions people commonly ask about someone's work. They ask whether the individual is being treated well (rewards). They ask whether he enjoys his work (tasks). They ask if he fits in and is loyal to his employer (community). And they ask if he is committed to the results, is driven, or, in terms currently favored among U.S. executives, whether he or she "has religion" (Purpose).

Rewards is the first block. They are the extrinsic incentives loved by the economists. While they are necessary in any commercial organization, they are rarely a source of advantage since they are so easy to imitate. Instead, they are a hygiene factor: If you get them wrong, they cause you all sorts of problems.

Tasks is the second block. When a task is sufficiently enjoyable, it can be the primary source of morale, the most important of the four blocks. Few tasks are like this, however, and the less enjoyable the task, the more important are the other blocks, each of which can provide rational or emotional justification for the task.

Community is the third block. Members of a community tend to feel loyal to it and will "go the extra mile"; a company that is also a community has an advantage over one that is not. Unfortunately, strong communities that lack Purpose tend to be rather static places, and their members will remain passive until attacked.

Purpose is the fourth block. Members of a community that also share a Purpose will not wait to be attacked before fighting. They are ready for action and will go out to improve their fate even when things are going well.

Each of these building blocks can be managed through the range of human asset management tools listed in table 8.1. Those followed by an asterisk are tools primarily used by the company's leaders.

It is my view that Purpose, along with a sense of community, generates commitment—and that a *combination* of Purpose and community will work better than either on their own. The mix of the two elements needs to be right. Too little conscious Purpose and the company will be inward looking and lose its creativity and its ability to move forward. Too little community and the company can fragment, or even become paralyzed. To generate the right kind of morale—to

MORALE

PURPOSE

COMMUNITY

TASK

REWARDS

maximize effective action—the general manager has to get this mix right. Then he will be developing morale that can create enduring advantage.

REWARDS

As Napoleon said, an army marches on its stomach. In business that means money. Community and Purpose can be important in business, but they do not operate in the same way as they do in politics or religion. We might share a Purpose with colleagues and believe strongly in what we and they are doing, but at the end of the month or week, we get paid. Rhetoric aside, for the vast majority of people that is, and always will be, a very important part of why they are working. However meaningful work in a corporation may be, not many billionaires choose to be middle managers.

If you reward a certain kind of action, you "reinforce" that action, which means that is the action you will get.[7] Bonuses can send optimistic or pessimistic signals about the future. Relative differences in pay send signals about status. And pay raises and promotions (or lack of them) can be seen as positive (or negative) feedback on performance. After Henry Ford introduced the $5 day, workforce productivity and rates of absenteeism and turnover improved markedly, not because of any direct incentive effect of the new pay deal, but because of improved attitudes toward the job. On the other hand, survey evidence suggests that the generally low levels of pay raises between 2000 and 2002 depressed morale, particularly in fields like IT, where employees had got used to constant increases.[8]

One of the most important of these emotional effects is the impact of the perceived equity or inequity of the rewards.[9] At the Italian firm ST Microelectronics, one of the world's leading microchip manufacturers, executives took a pay cut during a downturn in the early nineties. Morale—and the company's long-term growth and profitability—were maintained.[10] Process is also key to perceived equity

Table 8.1 Human asset management tools

1. Rewards
Remuneration
Pay – absolute amounts
Pay – relativities and perceived equity
Pay – processes and perceived equity
Performance based pay – cash
Performance based pay – shares
Personal perks

Other tangible benefits
Training
Career development
Promotion
Termination

Intangible benefits
Praise
Constructive negative feedback
Decision rights
Consult rights
Victory messages
Teleconferences and video conferences
Creation of heroes
Internal status (titles, clubs etc)
External status (the business card)
Other symbolic awards (prizes etc)

2. Task
Operational stimuli
Goals
Deadlines
Crises
Internal competition

Task negotiation
Task design
Participation in task design/suggestion
  schemes
Communication and discussion of
  strategy
Delegation of control
Increasing responsibility
Encouragement of experiments
Creation of challenges and use of skills
On the job development of skills

Fitting people and task
Recruitment
Training
Professional development
Transfers
Team development

3. Community
Events and rituals
Office parties
Off-sites and conferences
Company songs
Rituals (e.g., Monday morning meetings)

Other communication
Symbolic communication (names, logos
  etc)
Use of status symbols
Stories about the history of the
  organization and individuals within it
Stories about current staff
Stories about the competition
Communication about company /unit
  performance and plans
Public relations – external perceptions
Induction
Peer to peer communication

Relationships and structure
Work unit design
Office design
Team building exercises
Informal interpersonal relationships
Involvement in recruitment,
  terminations and career development
  plans
Participation in decision making
Job rotation and movement across the
  company
Encouragement of personal networks

*Training, rewards and facilities
used to build community*
Training
Professional and Career Development

(continues)

Table 8.1 *(continued)*

Pay policy – relativities (perceived equity)	**4. Purpose**
	Internal and external communication of the purpose*
Equity participation	
Redundancy policy	Communication of unexpected victories and defeats (miracles)
Cafeteria	
Health services	Creation of the top team*
Uniforms	Dialogue*
	Moral identity stories*
Leadership	Stories about the history of the organization
Company leadership that encourages dependency*	
	Mottos, credos, visions and missions*
Team leadership	Prototypical actions and statements*

* = *a leadership activity.*

and thus morale; good process requires transparency—both about the bases for rewards and about the different options people have for how they take them. As the HR director of pharmaceutical company Astra Zeneca has put it, "Building transparency has at one stroke removed all unfairness . . . there are no side deals to be made. People see the processes as fair."[11]

TASKS

A task is a series of actions or activities coordinated by a goal. A manager can use the task to raise morale through the way he sets the goals and designs the task itself.

Research by psychologists in the mid-twentieth century demonstrated the power of these measures. Kurt Lewin, one of the founders of the field of organizational development, pointed out that people have a natural urge to complete a task, however mundane, and that most of us feel a tension until we achieve this. This is because the task occupies some part of our mind, which we naturally want to keep reasonably uncluttered. Thus goals have a natural energizing effect, even if we do not actually care about the end results.

In addition, the nature of the task itself can boost morale, up to a point. Some work is simply enjoyable, in exactly the same way that a game of tennis or chess is enjoyable. Typically the work is absorbing and demanding and satisfying at the same time, and sometimes, when things go really well, it creates what psychologist Mihaly Csikszentmihalyi has called "flow": very high levels of active concentration in which the worker loses all self-consciousness and is taken over by the activity itself, but remains in control.[12] This kind of flow often accompanies creative work, but research indicates that more humdrum tasks can also generate it. Probably the most universal principle about task design is the balance of "stretch": To be intrinsically enjoyable, a task should be easy enough that the person doing it feels proficient and competent, but enough of a "stretch" to keep the person from feeling bored.

COMMUNITY

Employees' need for community has been recognized ever since the 1930s, when it was identified as part of the early reactions to the mass production system and the assembly line. When workplaces are sufficiently open, warm and collegial, employees feel themselves to be part of a valued, ongoing set of relationships with colleagues, peers, and creative partners. This is experienced as a sense of community. Employees who feel that sense of community tend to be more motivated, make better decisions, suffer lower burnout, change employers less often, enjoy greater job satisfaction and feel more emotionally secure than those who feel relatively detached or isolated.[13] The evidence is quite clear: Community is not simply a nice thing to have. It is extremely valuable and productive to have employees driven by allegiance to the workplace, the company and the people with whom they work.

Enabling this sense of community—and the identification with the company and loyalty that go with it—is a "psychological contract" between employer and employee. This lays out what each side can expect of the other, over and above the minima stipulated in the legal contract. It is in turn rooted in the social norms and economic conditions that form the context for the employment relationship.

In Japan large companies have been the focus of loyalty for a significant proportion of their workers. In return for lifetime employment and emotional security, the traditional Japanese worker offered complete dedication to his employer. Behind this psychological contract lay a strong sense of mutual moral obligation, comparable to the obligations felt between parents and children in Japanese society. Indeed parents would attend the new recruits' initiation ceremonies at some companies, in effect handing over their parental responsibilities to their children's employer.[14]

In the United States, this kind of commitment has been less prevalent. There has long been a tension between ideals of team spirit and conformity on one hand (known as the "organization man" syndrome, after William H. Whyte's phrase describing managers of the 1950s), and autonomy and entrepreneurship on the other (known best, perhaps, by Tom Peters' phrase "the brand called 'me'"). But by the end of the 1970s the conflict between these two models seemed to be over. The organization man had lost; by the nineties he was virtually dead. The traditional psychological contract—loyalty in exchange for stable employment and career prospects—had been torn up in the vast majority of commercial organizations. The social norms underpinning this contract, the expectations of loyalty each party had of the other, no longer had any force. A survey conducted in the early nineties revealed that only 2 percent of managers believed loyalty to the company was the route to success.[15]

Paradoxically, however, the end of the organization man made the value of community more apparent than ever. Managers everywhere now recognize that the frontline employee has to be empowered in a way that only a few pioneers preached or practiced a generation ago. Everyone recognizes that the Toyota production system, in which the sense of belonging is a critical element (because Toyota uses it to help develop employees' collective awareness of quality and effectiveness), is superior to traditional American methods. Nobody wants to deal with a call center clerk who can only follow rules and cannot handle problems.

Whatever the size of the organization, most people will feel a greater sense of identification with their employer if they are actively engaged in decisions affecting their work and kept briefed on broader decisions. Communications must be full and honest—a hint of condescension or dishonesty is counterproductive—and comments and suggestions must be listened to and genuinely valued. Sam Walton provides an outstanding example of the benefit of good communication. It would have been easy for him to hide behind the need for commercial confidentiality and not give employees real information about the business, or to stop listening to suggestions on the basis that he had heard it all before; Walton resisted these temptations, and it paid off.

It is tempting to propose a glib approach to the morale problem—training and communication. But it is not the training and communication itself that is important in earning loyalty, rather it is the subtext of mutual respect. What is insulting—deeply insulting—is to suggest, as some business writers come close to doing, that with a little clever management or training, anyone can achieve intrinsic fulfillment or a sense of belonging from their work. We do not live in Aldous Huxley's "brave new world," in which humans are programmed into alphas, betas and so on, with the epsilons wholly fulfilled by the most menial tasks.

Instead, there are two clearly viable ways to build community in the workplace. The first is to foster, encourage and further develop the natural communities that form within companies, in the offices and factories, among people at every level. The second is to recognize that in our world the causes of stress, motivation and morale are complex and diverse, and each individual's attitude toward work will be different. A leader who approaches employees with clear, honest self-awareness and an explicitly communicated respect for each employee's uniqueness will, over time, earn back mutual respect.

And that, at last, is where Purpose comes into play in building morale.

PURPOSE

In any given organization, there are too many people to treat them as individuals; and yet they each must be regarded as unique. Each demands a distinct relationship with the organization and recognition tailored to his or her personal contribution; and yet each must join together with a sense of common solidarity.

Purpose is the solution to this dilemma. It is the only vehicle available to leaders for approaching large numbers of employees at once—and still maintaining the kind of mutual respect needed to build community.

The psychologists Abraham Maslow and Carl Jung suggested that an individual could and should progress from mundane to higher concerns during the course of his life. Jung characterized this progression as first meeting one's obligations (career, family and so on) and then in the second half of life gradually developing a fully integrated self. Maslow characterized it as first meeting lower-level psychological needs (for security, love and self-esteem) and then finally striving to reach one's "full potential" and to be "true" to one's nature. Ultimately for Maslow that involved other people: "Self-actualizing people are, without one single exception, involved in a cause outside their own skin, in something outside themselves . . . some calling or vocation in the old sense."[16]

Jung and Maslow believed that only an elite aristocracy were ever likely to achieve this. But experience and observation show us that many, many people, from all levels of society and all walks of life, can make this kind of progression. Some people will end up doing it on their own, but for many individuals, a relationship with an organization or group can provide a platform for self-transcendence and power. The group provides a ready-made "larger scheme of things" when the individual is hard-pressed to know what his or her personal vocation really is. One of the best corporate examples of this is IBM: In its heyday, it turned otherwise ordinary individuals into *members* of a corps.

✺

An organization with a strong sense of Purpose does not just make people feel better. It also creates a strong sense of direction and obligation. Indeed it raises morale at least partly *because* it creates this sense of direction. This combination of energy and direction makes it effective at stimulating action.

One result of this is that making small day-to-day decisions becomes easier. Managers cannot determine the best course of action, on the basis of first principles, every time they have to decide on something. Even if they had the mental capacity to do so, this would cause chaos, since different decisions made around the firm by different managers would as often as not be inconsistent with each other. A number of shared understandings are vital if there is to be coherence—particularly in a world where more and more decisions are delegated to the front line.

The point has been well made by a GM manager: "There are some fundamental beliefs you have to share with a group of people. And if you don't have those fundamental beliefs, then the rest of the stuff—the little things—have nothing to hang on to, so they don't become as meaningful to implement on an individual basis."[17]

A lab manager at Hewlett-Packard demonstrated this kind of shared understanding when he said: "We simply should not be in markets that don't value technical contribution. That is just not what Hewlett-Packard Company is all about."[18] Bill Hewlett and Dave Packard have repeatedly stated that the company exists to use technology to make a contribution to society. As a result managers know what the company is "about"—they do not need to consciously conceptualize technical contribution as HP's competitive strength, though they are always on the lookout for ways of making that contribution. They are focused on opportunities for innovation.

Purpose makes these fundamental beliefs about the company salient. Purpose adds color and therefore strength to what might otherwise be dry prescriptions from the top. In a well-known story, 3M's Purpose to "solve problems" made one engineer so responsive to a customer's dilemma that he invented a new form of masking tape, which he later developed into Scotch Tape. Another famously responded to the difficulties he himself had finding his page in his hymnbook by inventing the Post-it Note. The point about these familiar stories is not how wonderful it is that individuals can invent products; the point is that the Purpose heightened those individuals' sense of their own role and hence their responsiveness to the problems they encountered. It generated action. Other firms could hire excellent engineers, but it was excellent engineering and this sense of role that produced 3M's flow of winning products.

Company leaders may be more flexible if they are confident that employees share the Purpose. 3M's famous 15 percent rule—which allows engineers to spend 15 percent of their time on private projects—is productive and possible because both the engineers and their leaders agree that 3M is about solving problems. After Danish hearing aid manufacturer Oticon was reorganized from a conventional hierarchy to a collection of projects, anyone could propose a project. The chief executive even accepted that it was fine to embark upon a project without top management approval—the real test of a project's validity was whether you could persuade anyone else to collaborate on it.[19] He only granted this freedom because he recognized that the employees shared a strong Purpose: to improve the lives of the hard of hearing.

In short, Purpose—and the community that it infuses—makes action easier because it creates a shared understanding about what is important. This stimulates initiative and cooperation, helps employees stick to the point and makes many irritating bureaucratic controls redundant.

Morale is crucial to fuel the engine of action. Purpose gives morale traction. Together, they can lead to greatness.

FROM MORALE TO ACTION

For all the importance companies place on extrinsic rewards (money and recognition), the research shows that such rewards are more effective when combined with the "intrinsic" motivators—task, community and purpose. This is not just because intrinsic motivators are cheaper (good job design, for example is cheaper than bonuses) and available during good and bad times (a lower bonus than the year before can easily demoralize workers) but because they are linked to a worker's sense of self-determination. Any employee who is motivated intrinsically has, in some way, chosen that position—or at least has chosen to apply a degree of creativity, persistence and grace on the job. Genuinely intrinsic rewards provide a reason for people to genuinely invest themselves in a job or a company, without being manipulated or bought.

However, while extrinsic rewards, tasks, community and purpose are all important over time, the evidence does not show that all means of motivating morale are an important part of the mix in *every situation*. If my employer wants to motivate me, the relevance of any reward, extrinsic or intrinsic, will depend on how strongly I want a particular outcome, along with my expectations about how much effort it will take to obtain it and how effective I will be. If what I want most strongly is cash for my son's college fees, or a promotion that will provide security, or health insurance, then that may drive me to work hard, while the intrinsic purpose may have little meaning. On the other hand, if I came to the company to realize my creative ambition, then the intrinsic purpose may matter more than the level of pay. What motivates one person may have little effect on another, and the motivation for an individual may vary dramatically at different times of life. For all these reasons, the more tools the manager has in his armory—the more forms of motivation available—the better.

In the long run, morale tends to be maximized when there is a mixture of both Purpose and community, in a balance where neither is much stronger than the other. Too great an identification with the company for its own sake will result in a fall off in creativity, a lack of flexibility, risk aversion and even unethical behavior. Organizations showing some of these symptoms include the Roman Catholic Church today, torn by scandal in the United States, where traditional loyalty to the institution has protected the hierarchy; IBM in the 1980s, where corporate pride weakened the capacity to innovate; and the UK Conservative Party, during much of the past decade, where tribal loyalty replaced a sense of purpose as the unifying principle. For those in strongly competitive markets, these faults can be catastrophic, as IBM found. Loyalty to the organization needs to be tempered by commitment to the cause.

In all cases, the "right" balance will depend on the situation—and on how the situation is changing. An organization that has been on the attack, but which is tired and in danger of fragmentation, may need more community as it comes to defend itself. An organization that has been on the defensive, but is now moving into attack and is in need of creativity, may need more Purpose.

Finally, the net effect of conscious attention to morale is a climate more conducive to greatness. As an executive of the company, you will not be the judge of this climate. It will be judged by your employees, customers, shareholders and neighbors—your stakeholders, in other words. But you can set the criteria by which you will be judged. All four of the Purposes highlighted in this book—altruism, discovery, excellence and heroism—have their own form of high morale. The employee of an altruistic company is ennobled by belonging there. The employee of a discovery-oriented company is charged with the spirit of a freely chosen new enterprise. The employee of an excellent company has the gratification of participating in work of great obvious value. And the employee of a heroic company feels the spirit of the winner. These motivations will last as long as the Purpose holds true; an effective executive ensures that all of the other morale-building tools, including rewards, community, and tasks, have been designed and set up to reinforce the Purpose that will make the company great.

CHAPTER NINE

PURPOSE AND INNOVATION

An Innovation is any development that creates change. It could be as big as a jet engine or as small as a tiny improvement to production line processes. Or, as the economist of innovation Joseph Schumpeter put it, it can be a new kind of food: "It should be stressed at once that the 'new thing' need not be spectacular or of historic importance. It need not be Bessemer steel or the explosion motor. It can be the Deerfoot sausage."[1] I'm interested in innovation—in innovative strategy, technology, products and services. I'm especially interested in the two million suggestions made in a year at Toyota through the employee suggestion scheme—because 85 percent of them were adopted.[2] That could not happen without a strong, consistent Purpose. Was it a Purpose of excellence, discovery, heroism or altruism? To answer that, one would have to know the nature of most of the suggestions.

Standard strategic analysis "explains" advantage, for both countries and companies, principally in terms of innovation. As Michael

Porter puts it: "Innovation has become perhaps the most important source of competitive advantage in advanced economies."[3]

Some companies can defend their existing strengths for a while without innovation, but as everyone knows, patents expire, consumer tastes change and competitors come up with new ideas. Innovation is not at the top of the agenda for all industries—many packaged grocery products, for example, are fantastically stable—but it is somewhere on the agenda for all industries. At the same time, this reliance on innovation has often led companies away from their Purpose, into a series of expensive blind allies. In 2005, Booz Allen Hamilton conducted a study of the one thousand biggest spenders on innovation—the companies with the largest research and development budgets around the world. They found no significant correlation with any measures of corporate success. None. Not profits, not revenues, not growth or shareholder returns.[4] In other words, the simple decision to invest in innovation is not enough. How you invest, and especially how innovation serves a larger Purpose, determines the value of your investment.

It's my view that Purpose helps innovators see beyond current convention—it improves the quality of innovation. And Purpose counters the natural risk aversion that large companies have to innovation. It thus increases the *quantity* of effective innovation, often without raising the price tag.

Purpose makes an innovator more aware, or sensitive, because it is *itself* a response to the environment, and one that engages the innovator strongly. We might even say that a Purposeful response, if genuinely felt, is an innately innovative response because it provides a context for paying attention to the needs in the world outside.

Think of innovation as taking place within a mental space. In a company without Purpose, this space has three dimensions—understanding of the technology, understanding of the customers, and understanding of the competition. In a company with Purpose, this three-dimensional space becomes four-dimensional, the additional dimension being understanding of the Purpose—discovery, excellence, altruism or heroism. The extra dimension makes it easier for the innovator to think outside existing conventions. In the absence of

Purpose, "what the customer wants" can be interpreted in a very conservative way—extrapolating past purchasing patterns, listening to focus-groups and consulting qualitative research data.

The innovator has every reason to identify the essence of practices in other industries and repackage them for his own use—like Ford, who adapted meatpacking techniques, or like Aristotle Onassis, who pioneered cruise ships by borrowing from the hotel industry. The innovator may reconfigure components into new products, like the engineers at Sony who developed the Walkman. The innovator may glimpse potential benefits in new technologies, like the engineers at Seiko who developed the quartz watch or those at Apple who worked on the graphic user interface. He or she may simply see economic logic in a situation masked by current convention, like Siegmund Warburg helping Reynolds Metals take over British Aluminum. Or he or she may realize how the peculiarities of his or her organization can generate new customer benefits, like Nathan Rothschild in the 1820s, who used his international network to make local payments to international bond holders.

Purpose itself is not, strictly speaking, *necessary* for this kind of innovation. I do not think that Michael O'Leary, for example, who has changed the rules in the European airline market, would insist that Purpose drove his decisions at Ryanair. What is necessary is an ability to see beyond the existing market dynamics. Entrepreneurs have no problem with this, but large successful organizations often find it more difficult—this is why companies dominated by brand marketing departments often fail to innovate effectively. Purpose's contribution is to help avoid this kind of constraint, to help innovators see beyond existing dynamics and industry conventions.

Purpose also provides a degree of emotional certainty that makes the prolonged openness of mind required for innovation easier. Sometimes innovating means *not* doing something and instead waiting for the right opportunity. Warren Buffett is a good example; his commitment to excellence gave him the patience to refrain from investing when there were no real opportunities, even though the rest of the investment industry thought there were. Masaru Ibuka, the

founder of Sony, had clear ideas about the reasons for its incorporation—"to establish a place of work where engineers can feel the joy of
technological innovation, be aware of their mission to society and
work to their heart's content." Such clear ideas, driven by the Purpose of discovery, made it tolerable that he and his colleagues "sat in
conference . . . and for weeks [after the company was founded] tried
to figure out what kind of business this company could enter, in order
to make money to operate."[5]

A clear Purpose helps *anchor* this kind of open-mindedness as
well. Buffett's investment decisions were highly calculated. Companies like Motorola and Microsoft have a very clear idea of what they
are trying to achieve. The goals driving particular research and development programs are not necessarily moral, but where there is a Purpose underpinning the business of the firm, then there is an
unavoidable moral discipline that engages individuals.

Having a Purpose does not guarantee greater sensitivity to market signals. It can make people more bigoted and isolated, as we saw
with Henry Ford. The "right" Purpose—one in tune with the
times—is more likely when developed collectively, reflecting more
than one person's response to the environment. It is also more likely
when it is aligned with the company's commercial strategy. An innovator's Purpose also strengthens his or her will, an important factor
because the outcome of innovation is always highly uncertain. Even
to embark upon the process of innovation requires an act of will, including the will to persevere no matter what may lie ahead. When
Henry Ford first started tinkering with the prototype that turned into
the Model T, he may have thought he knew what would happen, but
it was hardly the same kind of knowledge as that produced by a cost
accountant who prices all the inputs for a given output. Similarly, any
successful result from a research and development lab depends on a
decision to pursue a line of enquiry, the end product of which is un-
predictable, to some discernable result.

Daniel Vasella, CEO of Novartis, has been explicit about using
Purpose in this way: "One way we try to foster innovation . . . is to
align our business objectives with our ideals. . . . I believe that people
do a better job when they believe in what they do."[6]

PURPOSE AND
RADICAL DECISIONS

It has long been observed that most fields of activity have ingrained ways of doing things that all involved take for granted. Because each player takes into account the expected behavior of the other players, these habits often become unconsciously established as limits in the minds of participants. In a market of competing innovators, such habits tend to limit the scope for competition. Players tend to mistrust any innovation from outside; they become like boxers in a ring, anxiously watching each other, landing punches and going round in circles. One company may win a battle, but no company ever wins the war—and, with it, the peace.

Some companies avoid this stalemate. They innovate radically, and instead of just winning battles they achieve peace, either by so changing the rules that they come to dominate the industry, or by carving out their own niche, which they alone occupy, at least for a while. This is the achievement of enduring advantage; once this state is reached, radical achievement breeds further radical achievement. Competitors no longer feel constrained to innovate "just enough" to beat the competition. They are free to discover new forms of competition.

Each of our entrepreneurs refused to play by the rules—they were driven by Purpose to innovate in a radical way. Tom Watson was driven to search out the potential of the data processing industry, the scope of which he thought he alone recognized. But he did not want to just lead the industry, which he did anyway; he wanted to bring it to its potential. Accordingly, he took huge risks and invested heavily in research in the 1930s, helping to make IBM impregnable. In doing so he created a tradition of innovation that helped keep the firm dominant and at the edge of development, even when technological competition became tougher in the 1950s.

Sam Walton's management system was driven by his single-minded commitment to offer the best possible prices to his customers. Built up over many years, it was nonetheless a radical innovation for his industry, and other companies, such as K-Mart, were forced to imitate him. But they lacked his Purpose, and it was he and his successors who made the system work and came to dominate the industry.

Henry Ford wanted to use machinery to improve things, and that meant democratizing the automobile. Accordingly, he invested hugely in capacity, installed the moving assembly line, slashed prices and attempted to control the entire value chain from raw materials to showrooms.[7] He created new forms of advantage—scale, automation—that for a time, at least, allowed him to dominate the industry.

Siegmund Warburg knew that he had to be one of the elite. He did not mind running a small bank, but he could not tolerate simply doing routine work for routine clients. Accordingly he innovated and pushed his clients to innovate, inventing the hostile takeover industry and the Eurobond industry, both of which he came to dominate.

Warren Buffett wanted to be an excellent investor—which meant being a rational investor. He knew that the best way to achieve this was by staying as far away as possible from Wall Street. Unlike our other entrepreneurs, he has not dominated or changed his industry, but he has achieved a kind of peace. Instead of winning an empire he has established autarchy, his own island where he is supreme and left alone. He is spared the endless battles for relative position faced by other investment managers. He does not choose to be like Napoleon, to set out to conquer the world. He is content to stay in his hometown of Omaha.

In their book *Built to Last*, Jim Collins and Jerry Porras have presented some other examples of entrepreneurs and corporations that have been driven by Purpose to innovate in a radical way, and that ended up changing their industries. These include Walt Disney, who, they tell us, wanted to make people happy. When he made *Snow White*, the first full-length animated feature film, people thought he was mad; he came to dominate this part of the industry. In the fifties he set up Disneyland—without any market data to indicate there was demand for this new product. Again, he was driven by Purpose to take a risk, he innovated and he changed the industry.

Masaru Ibuka set up Sony in the aftermath of World War II, and he set out the "purposes of incorporation," which included feeling "the joy of technological innovation." In the fifties he decided to work on a transistor radio. "People are saying that transistors won't be commercially viable," he said. "This will make the business all the more interesting."[8]

Bill Allen, chief executive of Boeing from 1945 to 1968, said that the company he led was "always reaching out to tomorrow" and that it employed people who "eat, breathe and sleep the world of aeronautics." A stream of radical decisions led to the development of new airliners—the 707 in the 1950s (the first commercial jet), the 727 in the early 1960s and then in 1965 the 747 (the first wide-bodied jet). Discounted cash flow just did not come into it. "We will build it even if it takes the resources of the entire company," Allen told a doubtful nonexecutive in 1965. It nearly did require all of those resources—but of course Boeing retained its enormous lead over its rivals, such as McDonnell-Douglas. Allen was driven by Purpose to take a risk; he innovated and Boeing changed—and continued to dominate the industry.[9]

And then there is Bill Gates. His Purpose—to get Windows onto every desktop in the world—was a modern version of Henry Ford's plan to democratize the automobile, and Gates' company grew at the same heady speed, making him, like Ford, the richest man in the world. But like Ford, now that Gates has come close to achieving his Purpose, there is a dilemma. He continues to win his battles, but he has not established a peace. His software near-monopoly is eroded daily by new developments on the Internet, in open-source software, and in the nature of computer-based devices, to say nothing of challenges from regulators. Should Microsoft keep its old Purpose, honed across three decades? Or should it adapt and change the industry rules again? Perhaps consideration of this question prompted Bill Gates' announcement, in June 2006, that he would retire as chief executive of Microsoft.

These examples do not mean to imply that changing the rules is only for big businesses. It is worth remembering that Walton's approach brought him success as a small businessman before he became a big businessman. He changed retailing in Bentonville before he changed it in the Midwest or in the United States as a whole.

The key to changing the rules and winning dominance is to make decisions. This applies as much in a village market as in a global market. Henry Ford's competitors reckoned they could make a surer stream of profits from the mid-size and luxury markets. Walton's competitors allowed him to grow to critical mass in the semirural Midwest while they were milking more lucrative urban markets. Buffett's fund management rivals all preferred to estimate how other fund managers would respond to new information rather than to judge purely on fundamentals.

If you doubt Purpose can generate enduring advantage through innovation, I invite you to compare the performance of the companies in the following table with those of their rivals.

Table 9.1 Seven companies that have enjoyed enduring advantage

	Purpose	Type of Purpose	How Company Rewrote the Rules	Financial Results[a]
Ford	Use machines to improve the world	Heroism	Made money from cheap cars and mass production	c. 100 percent p.a. real return 1903–1919
IBM	Seek out the new "beyond our present conception"	Discovery	Aimed to solve customers' problems	9 percent p.a. real earnings growth 1915–1956
S.G. Warburg	Maximize the achievements of the elite	Heroism	Encouraged hostile takeovers and Eurobonds	23 percent p.a real earnings growth 1948–1969
Wal-Mart	Give the customers a good deal	Altruism	Introduced very low prices to small towns	27 percent p.a. real earnings growth 1971–1992
Berkshire Hathaway	Invest excellently and encourage excellent managers	Excellence	Invested large stakes on fundamentals	22 percent p.a. real returns 1965–2003
Disney	Make people happy	Altruism	Created new product types	18 percent p.a. real returns 1923–1998
Sony	Innovate in a useful way	Discovery	Invented portable, convenient products	10 percent p.a. real earnings growth 1967–1999

[a]*All figures are adjusted for inflation. Figures for Ford are based on the initial investment of $100,000, cash dividends paid and the price at which Ford bought out other shareholders in 1919—$255m (Nevins 1954, 1957). Figures for IBM are based on earnings, which grew from under $1million when Watson took over in 1915 to $87 million when he died in 1956 (Maney 2003 and Company reports). Wal-Mart earnings grew from $3 million to $1,608 million between flotation in 1971 and Walton's death in 1992 (Vance and Scott 1994). S. G. Warburg figures are based on figures from the Mercury Securities 1969 annual report (the last year Warburg was a director) and Chernow (1993). The figures for Berkshire Hathaway are based on the 2002 annual report. Sony figures are based on annual reports. Disney figures are based on figures in Bill Capodagli and Lynn Jackson, The Disney Way (1998).*

CHAPTER TEN

PURPOSE AND COMPETITIVE ADVANTAGE

To enjoy a competitive advantage is to be able to generate more wealth than other companies in the same industry year after year. Not all companies want or need to achieve this. Most public companies do.

Michael Porter is one of the most influential writers on the subject, and I agree with much of what he says. So let's start from his analysis. His most important point is that companies can only achieve *sustainable* advantage through what he calls "strategic positioning," that is, by occupying a distinctive and profitable market position—a combination of product, price and distribution method—that competitors either cannot or choose not to imitate: "Competitive strategy is about being different. It means deliberately choosing a different set of activities to deliver a unique mix of value. . . . If there were only one ideal position [in an industry], there would be no need for strategy. Companies would face a simple imperative—win the race to discover and pre-empt it."[1]

Porter says, "The essence of strategy is choosing what not to do." To choose one position, is, inevitably, to reject others: "The more Ikea has configured its activities to lower costs by having its customers do their own assembly and delivery, the less able it is to satisfy customers who require higher levels of service." Those who try to get the best of both worlds and "straddle" different positions all too often fall between two stools—as an example Porter cites Continental's failed attempt to imitate Southwest with its Continental Lite brand while still maintaining certain traditional features of its service.

A successful strategic position will depend, says Porter, on a distinctive and complex array of "activities," and the design of this array should permeate every aspect of the company. In Porter's words: "Different positions (with their tailored activities) require different product configurations, different equipment, different employee behavior, different skills, and different management systems." Without such an array, he says, a strategic position is little more than a marketing slogan. With it, it may be possible to dominate a segment. But establishing such an array is difficult and expensive. For some companies, the marginal costs will be greater than the marginal benefits.

Domination of a segment may not be the only way of achieving superior profits, but it is probably the most reliable way. And basing that dominance on an array of activities that fit together and support each other will clearly make it more difficult for someone else to appropriate, imitate . . . or steal.

Anyone reading Porter—and certainly anyone wanting to implement Porter—is bound to ask just how this fit between a position and all the activities supporting it is to be achieved, and, more importantly, just how it can be achieved so that others are reluctant to try to imitate it. It was not simply that Ford decided to build the Model T and Highland Park. We want to know how the choices on the blackboard became reality. After all, these decisions could have been made by anyone—and yet it was significant that the Ford Motor Company, and not, say, Pontiac or Dodge, was the company that made them.

In most cases, the companies making such decisions could take action because they enjoyed distinctive strengths or a position in the industry well-suited to that decision. Firms do not all start from the same place, and the additional costs and difficulties of moving to the strategic position will vary from firm to firm. The disincentive effect of strategic positioning—and of course the differential probability of success with any strategic positioning—depends on several key distinctive factors. And as we shall see, an articulated Purpose is the crucial missing link in developing all of them.

STRENGTHS:
ROUTINES AND RELATIONSHIPS

Thucydides analyzed the battles between Athens and Sparta in terms of the city states' respective strengths and weaknesses. Modern investment bankers tend to use this approach, seeing firms as collections of assets rather than as holders of strategic positions. Strengths and assets are always complemented by coordination, the action that allows their effective deployment. According to Prahalad and Hamel, "The real sources of advantage are to be found in management's ability to consolidate corporate-wide technologies and production skills into competencies that empower individual businesses to adapt quickly to changing opportunities."[2] The key to success, they go on, is the ability to "co-ordinate diverse production skills and integrate multiple streams of technologies."

"Consolidate." "Coordinate." "Integrate." Please notice that while these are all parts or functions of corporate activity (technologies, production skills, individual businesses), the activity itself is focused on the corporation as a whole. These terms all imply the fact that underlying the corporate strategy as a whole will be a web of routines (things people do) and relationships (connections among people). Coordination, which is the distinctive activity of the firm, depends on effective routines and working relationships.

Writers on strategy during the past 20 years generally agree that the most important and obvious part of this web of routines and relationships exists within the firm, connecting colleagues. But they also tend to state that it extends beyond the firm, to customers, suppliers, experts, joint venture partners and regulators and so on—to anyone whose input is important to the firm's output. Some of these routines and relationships are formal—like the budgeting procedures, or the innovation management procedures that some firms adopt, or the allocation of decision rights. Some are informal—the personal networks that allow individuals to access knowledge across and beyond the firm, or to assemble teams on an ad hoc basis, or to influence the way decisions are taken and so move events forward. But whether formal or informal, these routines and relationships represent the reason why a firm can be more than the sum of its parts, and they all contribute to making coordination (and thus "fit") possible.

Those routines and relationships, in turn, are shaped by the organization's Purpose (and the conception that employees have of it). They rest on a set of understandings shared among everyone involved. If the organization's purpose is mere expedience, people will tend to do things and have contact with people to gain only short-term advantage. If the organization's Purpose is altruism, discovery, excellence or heroism, then people will tend to be guided, consciously or not, by those values when doing regular tasks and building relationships at work.

It was shared understanding that made the codes of behavior developed at S. G. Warburg more than bureaucratic rules. It was shared understanding that made the group of young men around Henry Ford work effectively together, even though there were few formal roles and reporting lines. It is shared understanding that allows Warren Buffett to manage his conglomerate with such a light touch.

These shared understandings underpin all kinds of *organizational strengths*—motivated employees, effective teamwork, knowledge sharing and coordination, efficient factories, creative product development teams, good brand management, a spirit of cooperation, flexibility and so on. Particularly important is the way these understandings facilitate learning from experience—the learning that ensures that strategy and operations remain closely connected. And it is this kind of learning that ensures that the positioning and the fit is more than a boardroom presentation and a fantasy of top management.[3]

These kinds of understandings do not just happen. In my experience such understandings have to be built, slowly. They require a degree of openness to the other party—to their concerns and agenda—and a willingness to adapt to that agenda. This willingness to adapt, to give as well as take, flourishes only when there are long-term relationships between the parties. In other words the short-term coordination, systems and patterns of behavior that make for an effective firm are only the visible part of long-established, carefully built relationships of trust. As John Kay puts it in his excellent study of what makes for corporate success:

> If there is a single central lesson from the success of the Japanese manufacturing industry, or from Benetton . . . it is that the stability of relationships and the capacity to respond to change are mutually supportive not mutually exclusive requirements. It is within the context of long term relationships, and often only within that context, that the development of organizational knowledge, the free exchange of information and a readiness to respond quickly and flexibly can be sustained.[4]

In a similar way, communities of expertise are highly significant for modern business, whether they are in Silicon Valley, the fashion industry, the advertising industry, pharmaceuticals or some other market. The Purposes uniting at least some of the professionals in these industries are moral insofar as they go beyond money and create a sense of obligation. Companies benefit from these Purposes because they make it easier for community members to remain abreast of the latest industry developments, as well as to exploit contacts with experts, potential partners, potential recruits and so on.

For most businesses the most important relationships beyond the firm are with customers: Why do supermarkets invest so much energy in helping local schools? Why do art galleries and dress shops invite customers to "private views"? Why do the call centers of sophisticated companies encourage staff to engage with callers in a personal rather than mechanical or subservient way? Why does American Express call its cardholders "members"?

Even businesses that have no human contact with their customers do this. For them branding is at least partly about making the consumer feel he has an exclusive "relationship" with the brand. Sometimes, for example in the high fashion industry, consumers even feel part of a "community" of fellow customers, a community that contributes to their identity. Once such relationships are established it is relatively easy for the companies behind the brands to sell their products, and by the same token difficult for rivals to break in.

Some companies—a small minority—encourage their customers to join a Community of Purpose. The Body Shop tries to make its customers feel that by buying its products they are sharing the company's Purpose (to protect animals, the environment and local ways of life). Some commercial art galleries try to make their customers feel they are sharing in a mission to uphold cultural values. Some newspapers try to make their customers feel that they are part of a political or social mission. It is arguable that some consulting firms do something similar with senior managers in client companies.

Some of our entrepreneurs demonstrated the power of Purpose to strengthen relationships in this way. Siegmund Warburg's Purpose added to the legendary charm with which he built his web of connections. Warren Buffett's Purpose infused his relationships with his customers—that is, his shareholders—some of whom were inspired by it. Tom Watson and his salesmen built relationships with their customers on the strength of his Purpose. And countless professional relationships are strengthened by a service ethic or commitment to excellence.

PURPOSE AND ADVANTAGE

So far, in effect, we have said that Purpose provides the raw materials from which competitive advantage is created—the underpinning for more effective routines and relationships. But Purpose also shapes the patterns of behavior that make the raw materials fit together effectively. Michael Porter would be quite right to complain that social complexity, or good landing slots, or even scale advantages, on their own and in the absence of a strategic position, only contribute to operational effectiveness. What matters is that these things are harnessed to a particular position—that they are tailored in a way that supports that position. Purpose helps achieve this, in three ways.

First of all Purpose is a consistent guide for those making the countless small decisions that add up to a strategic position: How much should we spend on customer service? What kind of training do we need to give customer-facing staff? Is this product enhancement worth investigating? There are never definitive rules for answering such questions, and there are limits to the rational calculations managers can do. Accordingly, they often have to guess the answers, guided consciously or unconsciously by their perceptions of what the organization expects of them. An active Purpose helps ensure that perceptions of organizational expectations do not sink into habit. When there is an active Purpose, it is the Purpose that guides the answers, rather than just mindless company convention.

Second, the Purpose, if it has any bite, will have influenced the choice of the strategic position itself and helped the strategists identify those features of the firm that can contribute to achieving that position. It represents a kind of lens through which the firm's strengths can be seen, and thus acts as a guide as to how best they can be used. Henry Ford's heroic Purpose—to use his "machine" to improve the world—made the size and efficiency of his plant loom large; thus it became important to engineer a car that could exploit these features and that could be produced in vast numbers. With a different Purpose, that engineering strength could have been put to a very different use—perhaps to produce "the best car in the world," the stated ambition of Charles Rolls and Henry Royce at about the same time. Had Ford adopted the Purpose of "excellence," as Rolls Royce did, he probably could never have executed his idea of the democratically priced and engineered car, because the Purpose gave him a way to inspire the others in his company. Purpose guided Ford's strategic positioning as well as the day-to-day actions of his team; it related the two, and helped provide consistency to the firm.

Third, Purpose provides this consistency over time as well as at any given time. The past action that *created* the strengths and the future action that *exploits* them are linked: What we did yesterday influences what we can do tomorrow. Specifically, the skills, inclinations and patterns of interaction of employees and suppliers that have been established by the Purpose of the past will determine strategic positions that are feasible in the future. The nature of the Purpose thus influences tomorrow's strategic position.

Companies without Purpose are always in danger of losing direction—of constantly changing their strategy and so losing the necessary continuity. This means that they have no chance of achieving a hard-to-imitate strategic position—there is simply not enough time. Such companies are often said to have "lost their way." Another danger, in reaction to this, is that of deifying a strategy, and continuing to follow it when it is no longer viable. A&P, Sears and many other retailers fell into this trap during Wal-Mart's first great wave of national expansion: Confronting a new competitive business model, they assumed they could best survive by keeping their old strategy intact.

Purpose makes both of these forms of failure less likely. For where there is a Purpose lasting through time, a common set of principles guides opportunistic purchase of assets, development of new products and brands, formation of relationships inside and outside the firm—*and* the choice of strategic position. The same Purpose stimulates and guides the formation of assets, and guides how those assets can be used to achieve a strategic position and thus advantage. Assured of this underlying continuity, the company can have the confidence to develop its strategic position creatively.

PURPOSE AND
ENDURING ADVANTAGE

Michael Porter believes that well-chosen specialization, supported by a system of activities designed to deliver on that specialization, will be both more profitable and more difficult to imitate than doing what everyone else does, however good one may be at that. Sustainable advantage—defensible advantage—depends on strategic positioning.

But even strategic positions can lose their value, either because they are eventually imitated, or because changing tastes and technologies make them irrelevant. Companies that become fixed on a particular position can be wrong-footed when the market changes. If the company is to maintain its advantage over the longer term, something else is required.

A strong Purpose, built on moral ideas that have stood the test of time, helps to provide this "something else." This is because it stimulates successful innovation and the successful formation of new relationships; and it is these that create the strengths and assets that in turn underpin a successful position. The awareness and willpower that Purpose strengthens make it easier to advance the company into successful new positions, even before the value in the old has worn out.

A Purpose is never fully achieved, so it remains a constant, relatively unchanging stimulus. It helps prevent complacency even after successful positioning reduces the immediate economic incentives to create something new. Watson, Walton and Warburg were all driven to continue innovating even when they had established themselves as leaders and had relatively little to fear from rivals.

Look at any company that has been successful over a very long period. It will tend either to own strong brands in relatively stable markets—where a strategic position is sustainable over the long term—or to be guided by a strong Purpose that has allowed it to constantly reinvent its position. Examples of the former are Unilever and Procter & Gamble, with their timeless solidity and timeless brands. An example of the latter is IBM, which, after losing its Purpose in the 1980s and failing disastrously to adapt its strategic position, rediscovered its Purpose in the 1990s.

Operational effectiveness can create competitive advantage in the short term, but it will quickly be eroded. Strategic positioning extends the life of a competitive advantage, making it sustainable at least into the medium term. Purpose creates even longer lasting advantage than strategic positioning; it is thus a kind of third frontier of advantage—enduring advantage. Whether you are defending a hill or developing the right weapon to take it over, having a Purpose—beyond the obvious one of survival—will enable you to bring your advantage to bear.

The first two columns of the following chart, Table 10.1, are adapted from Porter's *Harvard Business Review* article "What Is Strategy?"[5] and summarize the key differences between the strategic view he characterizes as dominating the 1990s and his own view of strategy, based on specialization and strategic positioning. The underlying disagreement is over whether specialization allows you to defend your position. If it does, then you should specialize (Porter's view). If it does not, you should think of yourself as in a permanent race with your competitors to be best at what you do. To be sure, specialization is likely to prolong your advantage—but perhaps not for as long as Porter assumes. Another source of sustainability is needed, and this is where the third column of the table comes in, based on my view of strategy and advantage. The most likely source of this sustainability is Purpose, which helps the company discover and align itself around new strategic positions while remaining faithful to certain central traditions.

Table 10.1 Three views of strategy and competitive advantage (columns one and two by permission of *Harvard Business Review*)

The Implicit Strategy Model of the 1990s	*Sustainable Competitive Advantage (Porter)*	*Enduring Competitive Advantage*
One ideal competitive position in the industry	Unique competitive position for the company	Sequence of competitive positions for the company, stemming from Purpose
Benchmarking of all activities and achieving best practice	Activities tailored to strategy	Action, routine activities, assets and strategy that all reflect Purpose
Aggressive outsourcing and partnering to gain efficiencies	Clear trade-offs and choices vis-à-vis competitors	Trade-offs and choices driven by competitors and Purpose
Advantages dependent on a few key success factors, critical resources, core competences	Competitive advantages that arise from "fit" across activities	Competitive advantage that arises from "fit" *and* assets/strengths *and* action
Flexibility and rapid responses to all competitive and market changes	Sustainability that comes from the activity system, not the parts	Mid-term sustainability that comes from activity system. Long-term sustainability that comes from Purpose

CHAPTER ELEVEN

PURPOSE AND LEADERSHIP

L eadership is the ultimate advantage. When it's present, it makes all other advantages possible. And poor leadership can turn even the best advantage into a disaster. Leadership is the prism through which I see all of ancient Greek history—my country's origins are a study on the value of effective leadership.

If leadership is genius, then it is only effective because it is tightly linked with management. Leadership does not float in and out of an enterprise like an inspiring butterfly coming in the window; it's not charismatic words and great deeds served up without a context. Like everything else, leadership has to work on a daily basis. That is why, if we were picturing it, we might say that great leadership is a roof that sits atop a framework of sound management.

Management is nothing more—or less—than the art of getting things done. As anyone who has ever managed anything can attest, there's a huge gap between that statement and its application. "Things refuse to be mismanaged long," Ralph Waldo Emerson says. Not so. If you have ever worked at a firm that's lost its way, things can be mismanaged for a long time, right until the business spins into a death spiral.

And yet we are told—in the classic management texts, anyway—that the elements of successful corporate leadership are obvious and eternal: persuasion, clear headedness and discipline.

In my experience, discipline is sometimes as much as 90 percent of what is needed to maintain and nourish a company. In stable conditions, the discipline of rewards and rules may sustain the habits necessary for steady profits. At the other extreme, in a crisis, discipline allows management power and willpower to be maximized, and most employees will cooperate when the alternative is bankruptcy or being fired. A reasonably resolute leader can quickly recast the tasks that individuals have to perform, and crisis creates its own energy and group cohesion in the short term.[1]

But in many situations in between—those which are neither routine nor crisis driven—discipline is not enough. As a company starts to emerge from the crisis, who will energetically support the turn-around manager? Fear will bring people into line; what will keep them there? And what will stimulate the creativity and initiative that creates advantage?

If discipline is not enough, then people will tend to look next to the personal qualities of the leader. And it is certainly true that some individuals have the power to motivate followers and persuade them to do things that they would otherwise not do. The quality can seem almost magical, and employees fall under the spell of such leaders.

It is true that in any group a leader will emerge—indeed even leaders chosen at random tend to increase the group's efficiency.[2] Those who possess a good grasp of the task at hand and a degree of "emotional intelligence,"[3] essentially a sensitivity to others' feelings, will have even more of an impact. This is often the role of the top team of the enterprise, who will carry the company's Purpose to their direct reports, from which it will typically cascade through the enterprise in conversation after conversation. But I'm more interested in aspects of leadership that go beyond the reach of face to face relationships to generate effective action across the entire company.

One answer, according to some leadership ideologues, is to be the super-energetic boss, on top of everything. The plan he adopts, it seems, is less important than the characteristics of the man himself. This role has been described lucidly by Larry Bossidy, chairman of Honeywell International, and Ram Charan.[4] The leader grabs the organization, and by sheer strength of character forces it to wake up, to change, to respond to opportunity. He follows every decision through, he works relentlessly to have the right people in the right place. Because he really understands the business and the key issues that underpin success, he is able to focus on these and so avoid the twin evils of micromanagement and over-delegation.

It is ironic that the shortcomings of this approach were so vividly illustrated by the problems Honeywell itself suffered after Bossidy resigned in 2000; he had to be called back as chairman 15 months later to deal with them. If an organization is lucky enough to secure the services of a Bossidy—and that is quite a tall order—the downside is that it can grow dependent on his input; when he departs, the firm does not know what to do. Of course, Bossidy might argue that, in Honeywell's case, the problems can be put down to a failure of succession planning. But this is an important part of his model: If such an able character as Bossidy is unable to follow his own prescription, in this case succession planning, what does this say for the prescription?

The leader as superhero is too difficult a job for most candidates. As one writer reviewing the literature put it, it seems the business leader has to be "a cross between Napoleon and the Pied Piper"[5]—a great decider and a great persuader. With such high demands, it is hardly surprising that another commentator has concluded, "most organizations today lack the leadership they need. And the shortfall is large. I am not talking about a deficit of 10% but of 200%, 400% or more."[6] In many circles, leadership has become a kind of black box, a magic formula along the lines of: "Problem + Leadership = Solution." This is evident in both the widely popular literature on the subject and the combination of inflated salaries and short tenures that public company boards are granting their CEOs. Perhaps most unrealistic of all, leaders are expected to change company culture in short order, when, in reality, cultures—the habits and shared beliefs of employees—take years to form.

Because most men and women know they can never be superheroes, a second approach is to follow one of the many management fads. Since the late 1980s, a wide array of such techniques has become available: Total quality. Benchmarking. Best practices. Flexible manufacturing. Value creation. Strategic intent. Continuous improvement. Cross-functional teams. Revitalization. Restructuring. Reengineering. Organizational transformation. Business process redesign. Organizations as orchestras. The new organization. The knowledge-intensive organization. The learning organization. The self-designing organization. The hybrid organization. The post-entrepreneurial organization. The post-industrial organization. Knowledge workers. Empowerment. Diversity. Entrepreneurs. Intrapreneurs.[7]

Devotees of each of these fads insist that they should not be designed as a mere "program," but as a fundamental approach to rethinking and redeveloping the management systems of the enterprise. However, they always come in as a program, and rarely last longer than two or three years. In fact, that is arguably their purpose. They are brought in, whether consciously or not, to divert attention from the painful, universally acknowledged fact that systems are not enough and action is difficult.

A third approach is the elegant non-solution—to give up. There are plenty of CEOs who "delegate" and as a result "preside" over their companies rather than manage them. These CEOs are, literally, useless. They set targets, and then wait and see whether the targets are met. If they are, these executives collect their bonuses; if they are not, the executives get fired.[8] For example, the CEO of one of the world's largest corporations once complained that he had no power—all he could do was "approve or disapprove someone's capital budget and . . . approve or disapprove someone's headcount—that's it." Here was a man with more levers at his disposal than almost anyone else in the world, and he had lost the will to pull them.[9]

The problem for executives like this is that they know that the old model of command and control is outdated, and that it will not work in an environment in which strategy formulation is delegated to business unit managers, or even lower. These executives have quite sensibly abandoned this model, but they have not found a replacement. They also know they cannot run a very large business by sheer force of personality—at least not their own personality.

As it happens, with the right level of discipline and a clear sense of Purpose, leadership can make a real difference. It can create a stream of profits over and above those expected from the firm's assets. This requires great skill. However, it does not require superhuman capabilities. The so-called shortage of leaders only exists because the job of the CEO has been mis-specified—*diverse components of leadership have been rolled into one job*, and this has resulted in an expectation that is often impossible for one person to fill. The "crisis of leadership" can be dealt with by breaking leadership down into these components, and then hiring a team who among them have the skills needed, and who will work together sufficiently closely to ensure those skills are integrated.[10]

This does not mean that there is no role for the CEO: He has to manage the leadership team. Nonetheless, if I am correct, then a firm's success will depend less on the board choosing the right hero and more on its achieving the right balance in the top team as a whole.

I have written about five entrepreneurs who dominated their companies. All large companies need this kind of entrepreneurial drive—but in the absence of a Walton or a Ford, a Watson or a Warburg, the responsibility can be shared within a team.

What, then, are the different components of leadership? They are the *four preparations that always have to be made for any collective action*, and they are as follows:

- Think: Devise a direction or outline plan.
- Inspire: Generate collective support for this direction and the kind of action that will be required.
- Mobilize: Make sure that all the relevant individuals agree to cooperate and to accept specific roles.
- Empower: Set up the systems needed to maintain momentum.

These stages, appropriately, spell "TIME." The stages are iterative rather than purely sequential: Deciding what to do may depend on knowing what tasks various people will cooperate on; and working out how to do something may depend on the systems likely to be available. But the underlying logic of the stages is very simple and probably universal. The same basic pattern applies to a family outing, a charity appeal, a military action or the launch of a new business. The methods can be hierarchical or team based, systematic or chaotic, but the same basic logic applies. The processes may be democratic or authoritarian, but in any case the leadership team has the responsibility of ensuring that they happen and that action results.

There are three reasons for which, if I may say so myself, I like the TIME framework and why I recommend it to anybody who wants to understand leadership.

First, as my colleague Gary Neilson, Booz Allen Hamilton Senior Vice President and co-author of *Results* (2006), has observed, it is written at such a level of abstraction that it cannot be wrong!

Second, it proposes an analytical approach to leadership, which allows for action. One can use it to assess individuals and to assemble leadership teams. There is nothing that can be done to improve leadership without effective assessment. That is why our firm, Panthea, has focused on developing leadership assessment methodologies that are designed to be at least as reliable as the most reliable methods that financiers use to assess tangible assets.

Third, I like this framework because it connects leadership, at least linguistically, to the notion of time. Time, and integration in time and over time, is vitally important for leadership. Integration in time happens during what I call Campaigns, which will be the subject of my next book.

Having said all that, I will now use this framework, and in particular the first three components, to describe how leadership teams develop and use Purpose.

THINKING

Give a leader a Blackberry, a dozen direct reports, some commitments to charity and a seat on a few corporate boards—and then ask him to think? There isn't time. He can't possibly do it.

But thinking is the starting point of change. Without it, you cannot possibly discover your Purpose, choose your strategic position and align the two. And by "thinking," I don't just mean analysis—I mean a creative leap. And, not, please, one of those "out of the box" insights. As the acid-tongued business writer Michael Lewis has pointed out, as soon as someone says, "Let's think outside the box," you can be guaranteed he never will. A creative leap, in contrast, requires time; ideas have to ripen, associations have to be revealed, you may even need to read a book (and not necessarily one about business). That rumination might well be followed by a high-level dialogue with a trusted adviser.

Most of the entrepreneurs in my case started with a clean slate, but this is not the situation facing the leaders of most existing companies. They have a heap of existing resources at their disposal, and inherit a whole range of practices designed to coordinate those resources and ensure cooperation. Perhaps they will conclude that these practices—and the knowledge, skills and habits associated with them—are valueless, and they will strip the assets and start again. But that is unusual; normally they inherit something of value that their stakeholders want them to make the most of.

First, the Purpose itself has to be decided on—or rather discovered—by the leadership team. There are two basic constraints: It must fit the moral ideas of those the team hopes will join the Community of Purpose, and it must support an achievable strategic position that will generate wealth.

The Community of Purpose will always include the top team, of course, but how widely it extends beyond the top team will vary. Henry Ford established a small, informal community of key managers whom he enthused with his vision. Sam Walton, by contrast, tried to create a mass movement of Wal-Mart employees, all keen to present the customer with a good deal.

Sometimes the community may extend beyond the firm—or at least there may be constituencies whose moral preferences should at least be considered when developing the Purpose, even if they are never the driving force. Purpose is never simply a public relations or branding tool, but if it helps to strengthen a brand in the eyes of customers who approve of it, then that's all the better. Food companies such as Duchy Originals (owned by the Prince of Wales and committed to organic farming) or cosmetics companies such as The Body Shop (which does not allow testing on animals) have benefited significantly from the Purpose of their founders in this way.

Intelligent decisions about Purpose are based on analysis of the environment, as well as on the firm's strengths and weaknesses. This type of analysis may not be sufficient for effective action, but it represents a necessary first step. The goal is to align Purpose with strategy. Then the same actions that create the firm's wealth will also lead it toward its Purpose.

Private companies, the "Tom's of Maine" of this world, can afford a trade-off between morals and wealth; if advancing toward the Purpose means a reduction in profits, the owner-manager can make that choice. A public company does not have this luxury. Its managers have to make quarterly or half yearly earnings reports to analysts and fund managers, who for the most part will have little interest in Purpose unless it can be shown to advance profits. These external pressures mean that Purpose will degenerate into empty verbiage unless it is well-aligned with strategy.

Watson, Buffett, Walton, Ford and Warburg were entrepreneurs for whom material success and Purpose were entwined. What was more significant about these entrepreneurs' careers was the way *the same actions* that created wealth also drove them toward their Purpose. For Watson, thinking about customer needs was both the route to success and a moral obligation. For Buffett, investing in businesses with managers committed to excellence—a very good investment strategy—was simply what he wanted to do. Walton believed that boosting associates' self-esteem was worthwhile in itself and good for business. Ford cut the price of the Model T and thereby both democratized the automobile and achieved huge profits. For Warburg, victory in a takeover battle confirmed his elite status and brought financial success. For none of these businessmen was there a moral dilemma between Purpose and profit. There was no question of "Today we will look for profits and tomorrow we will do what we really want to do." They were, as one might say, not just Sunday Christians, but Christians every day of the week.

Having said that, there was nothing automatic about this fit between morality and strategy. It is quite definitely not the case that there is a morality for every source of profit and a source of profit for every morality. The experience of the Ford Motor Company in the 1920s is clear evidence of that. The Purpose did not change, but the world did—and the profits fell. Watson's Purpose did not match the existing products of CTR (as IBM was originally called) when he took control: His vision had nothing to do with computing scales or time clocks, and these businesses were sold. Company leaders have to *manage* Purpose and strategy so that they are aligned. If they drift apart, then the organization starts to follow two masters—and is unlikely to satisfy either fully.

A firm's failure to integrate strategy and Purpose creates a dangerous divorce between its economic power and its legitimacy. Without legitimacy, more and more raw power is required and a company can never achieve stability; without power, legitimacy gradually oozes away.

Note that in this model Purpose is not simply a motivational tool—a beneficial organizational feature like a good cafeteria or an efficient suggestion scheme, ultimately designed to increase wealth. Instead, it is an objective in itself, with at least equal status to that wealth. Companies maximize wealth when they pursue Purpose, and vice versa. The most successful companies have a single strategy and strategic position that helps them advance toward both objectives at once. That is what aligning strategy and Purpose means.

Let us look at a few examples. It would be reasonable for Unilever to make increasing prosperity and reducing poverty in its Third World markets part of its Purpose, or the Purpose of part of its operations. Its former chairman Niall Fitzgerald has spoken eloquently on the subject of poverty,[11] and the company has a long history of involvement and improvement in the Third World, ever since William Lever received a one-million acre concession in the Congo from the Belgian government. Its businesses have a significant impact in the Southern Hemisphere, its global reach is one of its advantages, and its managers have long recognized that widely dispersed prosperity in these markets will significantly improve profits. Like any business it has to control costs, but its distribution networks, brands and quality systems are much more important to its competitive advantage than minimizing labor costs. It is already setting standards in less-developed countries, through its own operations and through its influence on suppliers. In doing so it is supporting its strategic positioning around quality product brands. If the company pulls such initiatives together, it can also gain all the benefits of Purpose.

Unilever's great rival, Procter & Gamble, is perhaps also discovering a Purpose in this direction. It has declared that it can deliver shareholder value by addressing the "frustrations and aspirations of consumers at all economic levels"—in other words by serving the poor as well as the prosperous. Proctor & Gamble's leaders are aware that the poor constitute a huge potential market—80 percent of the world's population. Part of this strategy involves working with partners to develop products such as a low-cost water purifier, antibacterial soap and nutrient-fortified food.[12] This kind of initiative could be part of a sophisticated PR campaign, or it could reflect part of a developing Purpose.

Note that P&G has a different Purpose from Unilever. Unilever is acting altruistically to reduce poverty; P&G is moving heroically to claim a market. When they compete, as they inevitably will, they will each attract different networks of customers, suppliers, distributors, and partners. The winner will probably be the company whose Purpose and strategy are most attuned to the needs of the global business environment over the next ten years.

Table 11.1 Seven Questions to Discover Purpose

1. What strategic positions fit our assets and other strengths?
2. What community of Purpose does this imply?
3. What can we learn from the heritage and heroes of the firm?
4. What other constituents do we need to satisfy?
5. What are the ethical ideas of these groups (including us)?
6. What are the implications for the Purpose of possible strategic positions?
7. What changes to assets or people are needed to create a fit?

The same kind of considerations make clear that it would be absurd for Microsoft to adopt a similar objective: Africans living in remote villages are not going to be writing software or benefiting from the arrival of PCs anytime soon, and Bill Gates had to admit rather ruefully after a trip to one impoverished settlement that "these guys aren't, like, buying things on E-bay." Gates has been generous personally, but software is not a driving issue in rural Africa, and a heroic company like Microsoft has little opportunity there right now.

ServiceMaster, the ancillary services company, depends for its economic success on being able to recruit and motivate low-wage employees. Its (Christian) Purpose requires that it treats its employees with respect, and this respect serves to reinforce employees' commitment. Purpose and strategy are perfectly aligned. The hotel chain Marriott is a rather similar organization, also dependent on recruiting and motivating large numbers of low-wage employees, and also animated by a Christian Purpose, as evidenced by its slogan "The Spirit to Serve." Since 1979 Marriott has targeted welfare recipients in its recruitment and training programs; it increased its efforts following the 1996 welfare reforms in the United States. This recruiting expressed its Purpose, in so far as it offered people the chance to improve themselves. It also met the requirements of its business, by accessing a large pool of low-cost labor.[13]

A possible plan of action based on this process is set out in table 11.2, and more details of some of the key stages are given in the epilogue.

INSPIRATION

To inspire means, literally, to breathe in—to intake. Inspiration is an act of transmission, generating ideas and passion and commitment from the community around us. Words matter, but eloquence has often come back to haunt the eloquent; we've all been "sold" (or sold others) on propositions that turned out to be less than brilliant. In an organization developing a Purpose, we want more—we seek an inspired leader who is a living example of his message. It's not

Table 11.2 How to Discover Purpose and Develop Strategy

Stages	Objectives	Processes
1. Review your strategy	Create a series of options that make use of existing strengths and draw out implications for assets and coordination	Strategy review
2. Draw out the implications	Identify implications for who is in the Community of Purpose and for the Purpose itself	Annex to strategy review
3. "Know thyself"	Understand your own moral ideas	Review the traditions in chapter two in terms of your own moral language
4. Understand company traditions	Understand what has seemed important to employees in the past—and what will be potentially important in the future	Research company history. Research current employee understanding of company traditions
5. Take a Purpose inventory of the top team	Understand the moral ideas of those you work with	Engage in ethical discussion. Listen to the moral language used
6. Take a moral inventory of the community	Understand the moral ideas of employees who are to be in the Community of Purpose and those of any relevant external groups whose moral ideas should be considered	Develop first take on Purpose and feed into employee survey. Create employee portrait for different segments, including employees' moral ideas. Research expectations of external stakeholders
7. Identify Purpose	Identify implications for Purpose of the outputs of stages 2, 3, 4, 5 and 6 and what has to be done to eliminate incompatibilities	Make a creative leap on basis of all data assembled. If the gap to be leaped is too wide—i.e. strong incompatibilities—hold structured dialogue, including advocacy for the Purpose and advocacy for the strategy

(continues)

Table 11.2 *(continued)*

Stages	Objectives	Processes
8. Create metrics and models	Create tools for predicting and measuring progress toward Purpose	Appoint Purpose champion to devise and test both metrics related to Purpose and models linking potential business decisions to those metrics
9. Test strategy and Purpose	Test if strategic position will deliver both Purpose and profit, and refine strategy or Purpose as necessary	Run likely scenarios through existing financial and new "moral" models. Accept minor problems— but do not ignore potentially serious tensions
10. Decide	Endorse Purpose and decide what—perhaps who—to drop	Buy/sell assets and/or replace key people

enough for the leader to tap into morality. He or she must be a moral leader.

This is a tall order. It calls upon all the gifts of a leader, from a deep connection to the organization's creation myth to a keen sense of the make-up of his or her listeners. At bottom, what we are seeking here is the moment when our community is created anew—and a fresh sense of Purpose energizes us to achieve a common goal.

John Kotter, one of the best-known writers on "leading change," recommends a step-by-step approach to building community: Create a sense of urgency. Build a top-level coalition. Develop and communicate a vision. Empower staff across the company as a whole.[14]

I have some questions here: Why should anyone care about "the vision" the CEO or the top team produces? Why should people commit to sacrifices in order to achieve that vision? How is it that people can come to believe in the aims of the company so strongly that it actually influences what they do day to day and gives them the energy to perform?

You have to do a great deal more than ensure that the vision is understood, a great deal more than communicate, communicate,

communicate. Jacques Nasser is a case in point. He was a charismatic individual who communicated incessantly during the years that he was chief executive at the Ford Motor Company (1999–2001). His message was the importance of the financial results of the company as a whole, and the virtues of a good p/e ratio. Perhaps for a while people were fired up by his personality—but in the end what did they care about p/e ratios? He failed.

Kotter and others seem to assume that people will be spontaneously motivated by the prospective success of the organization, that they will see its success as their own success, and that this will be sufficient to carry them through the pains of restructuring, or the drowsiness of a hot afternoon. But achieving this identification—this Community of Purpose—is precisely the task of leadership, precisely what needs explaining.

Company boards as well as company leaders need to take part in this task. The different effects of different styles of leadership will exercise a profound influence on the company's future character and indeed whether or not it develops a Community of Purpose.

One style of leadership in this realm has been described by, among others, Manfred Kets de Vries—a professor at INSEAD University who has applied the concepts of psychoanalysis to organizational issues. He points out that we are all to some extent emotionally dependent on other people, and a certain kind of leader plays on this dependency. This kind of leader awakens this dependency among subordinates, who then project their fantasies onto him or her. Leaders create emotional needs among followers, and then, when leaders choose, they satisfy this need. For example, the leader may assign a group of people a pivotal role in a change initiative, with enough ambiguity that only the leader's approval matters. Then he or she may inconsistently respond when asked, "How are we doing?" or "How do we judge success?" This can create an intense desire among subordinates to compete for approval and validation from the outside. Leaders may also use the same communications techniques to exercise similar power among people whom they do not often deal with directly. When a group shares such a dependence, a community rapidly clusters around a leader of this sort.

You are thinking what I am: This can lead to a dysfunctional, often narcissistic form of leadership. As follows: "Many top executives don't realize the extent to which people project their fantasies onto them; how much subordinates are inclined to tell them what they want to hear as a way of dealing with their own feelings of insecurity and helplessness; how willing subordinates are to attribute special qualities to someone simply because of the office he or she holds." [15]

This pattern of behavior, explains Kets de Vries, is rooted in transference—the tendency everyone has to turn new relationships (for example with the boss) into replicas of old ones, particularly those formed in childhood (for example with the father). Others have pointed out that this kind of deference to leaders is something we have inherited from our primate ancestors, and that it evolved through natural selection, since it prevented potentially lethal squabbles. Still others have argued that conformity and deference is the way we flee from the cognitive pain of making our own decisions, of being truly free.

The tendency to dependence in subordinates is often mirrored by the leader's need for praise—which psychoanalysts believe has its roots in the emotional wounds the leader suffered in childhood and that he or she is still trying to salve. (There is plenty of evidence that a disproportionate number of leaders have suffered childhood traumas—for example, 63 percent of all British prime ministers before Winston Churchill were orphans.)[16] Leaders of this kind also seek other emotional props—power, prestige and exorbitant levels of pay—to deal with similar problems.

Unattractive though it sounds when described in these terms, this kind of leadership can motivate. Shared dependency needs bind people together into a tight community larger than the immediate work group and can energize workers to fight for their leader. Tom Watson had a Purpose that inspired his followers, but he clearly also awakened dependency needs in his subordinates and this helped create an extremely powerful, motivated organization. Charles Forte, who in the 1970s and 1980s ran the UK's leading hotel chain, was another example, and he too presided over an efficient, profitable business. In both cases, however, their style was successful only because the companies they led did not have to fight powerful competitors or deal with the complexities of a constantly changing environment. Indeed the lack of competition meant that the organizations needed an internal energy source provided by the leader if they were not to become complacent and vulnerable—their monopolies could hardly be guaranteed to last forever.

The extreme case of a successful leader of this type is Joseph Stalin, who was much loved as well as feared and hated. He successfully defended the motherland during World War II, and inspired enormous efforts in monopoly industries from the 1930s to the 1950s. Henry Ford in his later years was another leader of this type—but when his company faced tough competition from the 1920s onward, it suffered accordingly. This type of leader is to be found most often in underdeveloped countries and underdeveloped companies.

It is not surprising that this leadership style can produce excessive identification with the firm—and that it can result in such damaging side-effects as low creativity, lack of flexibility, risk aversion and unethical behavior. It produces morale, but not all morale is good morale. In extreme cases, obedience and mutual praise become so satisfying to employees that real achievement—or the lack of it—is ignored.

But there is a style of leadership that does not rely primarily on dependency fantasies. A leader of this type achieves the most influence in a group when he embodies its values and characteristics and becomes its "prototype"—in contrast with the first kind of leader, who remains distant from the group, acting perhaps as its "father." This second kind of leader remains the focus for group members' fantasies—only now these are not just dependency fantasies but fantasies the group members have about themselves: They attribute to themselves the characteristics that the leader embodies and thus identify with both him and the group as a whole.[17]

Such leaders do not need to be charismatic. Indeed, often the leader's charisma is only the *effect* of the influence he has achieved, not its cause.[18] More important is that the leader appears to believe what he says, and appears to be very much part of the group—"one of us." This explains the popularity of leaders like Sam Walton and Warren Buffett, with their relatively modest lifestyles despite their great wealth. Madame Kiraç, managing director of Koç holdings in Turkey, explained that her father never traveled business- (or first-) class except toward the end of his life because he wanted to be a role model for his employees. Top management at many modern companies takes considerable efforts to ensure they are perceived like this. At sandwich shop chain Pret a Manger, the CEO had to spend two weeks making sandwiches when he first joined, and the whole top team spends one day a month working in the shops. They attend the weekly parties and are certainly not placed on a pedestal.

Excessive reward differentials, by contrast, tend to weaken this kind of leadership. The evidence is not conclusive, but laboratory experiments in 1998 indicated that people are less willing to follow leaders enjoying such differentials (other things being equal).[19] Research conducted by J. P. Morgan in the 1950s indicated that stock market success was positively correlated with narrow pay differentials within the top team.[20]

In addition to embodying characteristics of the group, prototypical leaders tell what social psychologist Howard Gardner describes as identity stories: "It is the leader who succeeds in conveying a new version of a given group's story who is likely to be effective."[21] This is because such stories or myths are "a way of making sense in a senseless world," to quote Rollo May, an earlier psychologist. He went on to say, "hunger for myth is a hunger for community."[22] In this, business leaders are like tribal leaders who establish themselves and create group identities by telling stories about the past. They are not simply repeating history or uncovering an identity that already exists, they are using a story to create an identity.[23]

Some of the most powerful such stories contain a Purpose and an aspiration,[24] as opposed to just a history. In these cases, it is the Purpose that defines the group—not just its past but its future. Howard Gardner gives some excellent examples of the messages that leaders in different walks of life have sent their followers.[25] Margaret Mead (1901–1978) was a leader within anthropology. Her message to her colleagues—the identity story she told—was, in Gardner's words,

"We anthropologists have the privilege of chronicling the cultures of the world, demonstrating that none is superior. We bring back the insights and convey them in plain language to our compatriots." Robert Oppenheimer (1904–1967) directed the Manhattan Project that resulted in the atomic bomb. His message to fellow scientists was: "We scientists have the skills to play a major role in the all important war effort. We must bury all differences and be able to work in secrecy." Alfred Sloan (1875–1966) was president of General Motors. His message was: "We in business are doing God's work. General Motors knows the best way to conduct business and has produced the most effective corporate family. We in the corporation are willing to help others."

The case stories in this book also involve prototypical leaders who told identity stories. Tom Watson told his colleagues, "We businessmen are going on a journey of discovery, and we have a duty to discover what we can." Warren Buffett told his senior managers, "We will be rational and maximize return on capital." Sam Walton's story to his associates was, "We discounters have a duty to serve our customers as well as we can." Henry Ford built around him a relatively small team who identified with him—mechanics, men who understood machines and their potential. He told the team, "We engineers are going to improve the world with the automobile." Siegmund Warburg told his partners and his employees, "We bankers are the elite; we will deliver results to the best customers, and do so with style."[26]

A related technique is to present the Purpose of the organization in ways that reach people emotionally. In the 1990s William Bratton was in charge of the New York Transit Police and, later, the city's police department. He slashed crime in both jobs—by some 39 percent in his first two years in the second post. A vital part of his success was getting his officers to support changed ways of policing. When he started at the transit police he insisted that all officials travel by subway—rather than the cars they had been provided with—so that they could see the problems for themselves. Later he insisted that all NYPD precinct commanders run community meetings, meet the local citizenry and find out their concerns. These were street-level rather than bureaucratic experiences and involved contact with people and their problems rather than just receiving data, statistics and quantitative goals. As a result they were moral experiences. They brought home the need for action to all involved.[27]

The opposite of this real-life focus is bureaucratic distance. There is always an emotional temptation, when the company's product is not that interesting, for managers to retreat into the realm of value-free abstractions—a comforting routine of moderate intellectual challenge, moderate interpersonal competition and the status that comes with working for a well-known and respected business.

The true leader can go beyond expressing the firm's Purpose. He can also awaken that Purpose—act as a kind of moral coach. In doing so he connects the follower to his own goals. The follower is then inclined to join the community emotionally. He feels loyal—and committed to action—not just because of personal relationships, or because of some "job for life" contract, or even out of emotional dependency. He feels loyal because he has found a community that furthers his Purpose.

Balancing Dependency and Purpose

Leaders can combine characteristics of both leadership types. Dependency—the need to belong—provides some emotional glue or comfort to what might otherwise be a rather demanding and rigorous regime of high standards and Purpose. Tom Watson was as effective as he was because he both awoke dependency needs *and* told a moral identity story. The dependency did not get out of hand because the salesmen saw him as the perfect salesman, as their prototype. Wal-Mart's highly charismatic leader enabled some employees to project dependency fantasies onto him; at the same time he encouraged them to be independent and to run their own stores.

Getting the balance right is particularly important when the environment is unstable. In that situation, the middle manager can no longer rely on standing orders or commands from above. He has to engage with the outside world and interpret it to the men and women he is responsible for. He has to convert its potentially confusing signals into a plan of action and motivate them to follow it. And he probably has to abandon old procedures and create new ones. In short he has to become what people think of as "a leader"—a presence that genuinely inspires by example and communication together.

When times are unstable a company needs both leadership from the top *and* delegated, face-to-face leadership. But delegated leadership is incompatible with top-level leadership based mainly on dependency. You cannot interpret the world to your colleagues if you only see it through *your boss's* eyes. You will not command the respect of your subordinates if you are a sycophant. You cannot create new ways of doing things if your main concern is obedience. Delegated leadership is designed to encourage flexibility, creativity and a reasonable degree of risk taking. But it is precisely these that are prevented by excessive identification with the company and dependency.

As a transition into a healthier style of leadership, I recommend the whole leadership team should act as prototypes and tell moral identity stories—sometimes exemplifying different styles of leadership that different employees will latch onto. This is an aspect of leadership that *cannot* be delegated. There will always be some dependency, some emotional glue. But when the leadership team gets this balance of emotion and reason right, it will have created an effec-

---

Table 11.3 Seven Steps to Creating a Community of Purpose

1. Create a top team, all of whose members are leaders.
2. Make efforts to be "one of us"—reduce excessive salary differentials, demonstrate respect, socialize widely.
3. Spend time on the "front line"—answering customer calls, working on the shop floor.
4. Tell identity stories that project the group's Purpose and aspirations.
5. Present the Purpose in ways that make it emotionally real for colleagues—for example by bringing them face to face with the consequences of their actions.
6. Engage in dialogue with individuals and groups, acting as a moral coach, awakening their Purpose.
7. If necessary deploy some of the techniques of dependency: Develop corporate rituals, bestow and withdraw favor to cement loyalty to the group.

tive and enduring Community of Purpose—and it will win employees' hearts *and* minds.

MOBILIZATION

It is tempting for a leader to play Patton. The creative thinking is behind him. He has inspired his subordinates. Now is the time to move: "L'avance, l'avance, toujours l'avance."

But by "mobilize," I mean something quite different. Mobilization is not a top-down, bureaucratic process—it's a negotiation. And a delicate one: Big picture ideas are being injected into day-to-day tasks. The leader's power is unquestioned here; now what he must demonstrate is his empathy.

Even when Purpose and strategy are well aligned, and employees throughout the company are committed to both and feel part of a Community of Purpose, they may not know what they should do on a day-to-day level. This is why the third component of leadership—ensuring individual cooperation—involves negotiating specific goals that are consistent with both strategic position and Purpose. It is these goals that translate the Purpose into something actionable.

In the typical large organization most operating goals are simply imposed on the team or individual: This works adequately provided that they are backed up with suitable rewards. But if the goals are to connect with the Purpose and have meaning to the individual or team, then they cannot simply be imposed. All the morale benefits of the Purpose will be dissipated if there is a perceived disconnect between what individuals give their hearts and minds to—their Purpose—and the goals and tasks they grapple with on a day-to-day basis. Not surprisingly there is plenty of evidence that when individuals and teams play a part in developing their own goals, performance improves.[28]

But this implies that the allocation of goals should be a negotiation, not an administrative task. The oldest joke in the management joke book is the one in which the noncommissioned officer says to the troops, "I want three volunteers, you, you and you." Unfortunately, many managers—who are happy to agree that the goals of a course of action should be genuinely shared by the team—are less happy to admit the consequences of this: They can no longer select volunteers this way.

Of course the boss can withdraw from the negotiation and impose an objective if he calculates that the resulting loss of morale will be less damaging than the change of direction the course of action would otherwise suffer. Both sides know that this is the bottom line, and this affects the dynamics of the negotiation. But the boss will not be able to achieve the best trade-off between morale and his desired direction if he does not negotiate in the first place. Indeed he may not even have identified the best trade-off—negotiations involve an exchange of information that can lead the parties to develop a solution better than either side had originally envisaged.

There will almost never be 100 percent support for the Purpose. When a community is built around Purpose, as opposed to dependency, there are bound to be disagreements (look at political parties and churches). Recruitment weeds out the most incompatible, but selection is never perfect, and, anyway, large, and especially international, companies will always have subcultures. More fundamentally, the whole process of awakening individual Purpose is inconsistent with imposing a single, monolithic view.

Fortunately, 100 percent agreement is not needed. What matters is that there is a center of gravity—sufficient consensus to move things forward despite the disagreements. This Purpose must be shared by the top team—since otherwise it will look like (and indeed be) a cheap attempt at manipulation or public relations. This is nonnegotiable.

Table 11.4 Five Steps for Turning Commitment into Action

1. Do a first take on the operating goals implied by strategy and Purpose.
2. Assemble teams suited to achieving these goals.
3. Negotiate and thus refine and develop the goals.
4. Continue to learn—draw out the implications of these negotiations for the strategy and Purpose.
5. Monitor support for the strategy and Purpose—do not expect unanimity, but ensure that there is a critical mass of support.

EMPOWERING THE ORGANIZATION

The exercise of power is not a zero-sum event. People need to know they will have the necessary tools to reach a new objective—and that, if the tools are lacking or more are needed, that they can ask for help. This is where leaders have a very undramatic but necessary role— they must make sure there are systems in place to maintain the company's momentum. And then they must take a deep breath . . . and delegate.

But contrary to how the "soft" literature on leadership would have it, empowering is not just about delegation. As the word suggests, it is about the application of power. Empowering is about structures—incentives, decision rights, information flows and work processes. All of these can be designed in ways that lead to inherently healthy organizations, with high-performance capacity, in ways that help a coherent Purpose be realized (and further developed).

I will not expand on all this, because the topic is excellently covered by Gary Neilson and Bruce Pasternack in *Results* (2006). One can apply the principle of "Purpose" and that book in tandem; indeed, they represent an integrated proposition developed in synch by Booz Allen Hamilton and Panthea.

I intend to describe the TIME framework in greater detail in future publications, including my next book on Campaigns. I only hope that the reader has been persuaded that leadership is not just about empowerment and mobilization, but that ideas are also important.

LEADERSHIP, PURPOSE AND ENDURING ADVANTAGE

Businesses are as much caught up in the war of ideas as politics, the arts and science. They are not part of some separate, value-free realm, and business leaders cannot pretend that what they do is value free, even if they want to. The business leader's role is to help his organization create sustainable competitive advantage, but I hope that if I have persuaded readers of anything, it is that this role and Purpose are closely entwined.

In our time, the individual who aspires to be a leader has to throw off traditional typecast roles: the wealthy entrepreneur or investor, the famous deal-maker, the tough chief executive, even the charismatic leader. These roles have been commoditized—they can be bought and sold in the marketplace. In important ways the real role is larger than these—the leader has to be in touch with, and act on, the moral currents that influence his colleagues. People do not want commoditized leadership, they want principles. They want leaders who will fight the war of ideas.

At the same time, even the most charismatic individual leader will most likely succeed as part of a team. The team members—the leaders and managers—have to be sensitive to the moral ideas of those around them and to the emotional needs that will turn these ideas into commitment and action. They must understand the moral implications of their strategy, and the strategic implications of their morals, and then be able to judge how to adjust and trade off the two to create alignment. They have to be prototypes for their colleagues. They have to tell their colleagues the moral identity stories that will win their hearts and minds and build a Community of Purpose. They have to live the parts that these stories create for them. And then they have to negotiate goals that turn these moral ideas into action, and be sufficiently flexible to adjust ideas and goals as the negotiations proceed.

To do all this requires more than ego, drive, intellect and experience. It requires a broader understanding of the moral issues and psychology that sway individuals. And it requires an intuitive or explicit understanding of the moral and cultural currents in the firm's environment.

What matters most is what people are inspired to do; and this depends on the ideas that drive them. Old assets and strengths can't be ignored, but new assets and strengths can be created when people are inspired to the necessary action. The difficult part? For me, it's not the framing of the strategy. It's the inspiration that turns strategy into action.

EPILOGUE

PURPOSE IN ACTION

In this book, I suggest that organizations can best succeed by adopting a philosophy. Personally, I respect philosophy most when it provides inspiration for making better decisions on a day-to-day basis. I suspect my readers feel the same; particularly when there are decisions to be made that relate to organizations and thus will have direct effects on hundreds, or perhaps hundreds of thousands, of people.

How then can we learn to apply a moral code and a fundamental Purpose to succeed even in the no-nonsense, dollars-and-cents realm of everyday business?

There are, I would suggest, three ways to put into practice the ideas that animate this book.

The first is just to sit with them and see how you feel about them. While I am far from an advocate of "New Age" metaphysics, I do believe that the best path from which to judge Purpose is the intuitive one. To discover your Purpose, you'll need to feel as deeply as you think—if you are uncomfortable with feelings or hostile to information you get from your gut, Purpose is going to be a problem for you.

So, if you can stand to do it, just sit with the ideas in this book and see if they feel right to you. If they ring true. If they energize and inspire you. If they give you a reason—or even the start of a reason—to go back to your work with a fresh sense of mission.

Another way to test the validity of these ideas is to think about the cases of companies and organizations you have known. About those that succeeded: What, if any, Purposes did they communicate to their employees, suppliers, customers and investors? Were they just "in it for the money"? And if not, what did they propose as a reason to get involved with them? About those that failed: What, in your view, was the cause of the decline? Did they make decisions based on expediency? And how did those decisions turn out?

At the end of this epilogue, I'll offer some case studies of companies where Purpose is on the front burner. But it is better to think first about the stories with which you have personal familiarity.

A third way to apply the ideas in this book is to embark on a deliberate exercise. What follows, therefore, is a series of self-administered diagnostics to help you explore the status of your Purpose and go forward most effectively.

Please note that Purpose is not the answer for every problem. I am not one of those self-proclaimed experts who have a single idea—a hammer—and see problems as simply needing a nail. While I like to think that the ideas contained in this book might lead to making the world a better place, I am not so egotistical as to think that Purpose is a panacea for every ill. Purpose is not an all-encompassing answer to a firm's problems. It is not something that can simply be "fixed" in isolation.

But make no mistake: For any firm that wants to prosper in the long run, Purpose is key. It can make a difference to decision makers at every level, from the kid who serves the burger correctly at an anonymous take-out window to the CEO who must choose between two bet-the-firm propositions.

Yes, a firm can exist—and, to a degree, succeed—without a Purpose, just as people can exist without a Purpose. Without a Purpose, though, life is just existence, a biological condition, a process with no goal save survival. Human civilization is the effort to transcend that meaningless, empty fate—starting with the self-betterment of the individual and ultimately leading to the creation of great civilizations. The instinct for that may be hard-wired; the path is not. And in choosing that path, we declare our Purpose.

And the best part of Purpose? It's that we never fully achieve it. There's always more, there's always better, there's always higher.

WHERE ARE YOU NOW?

The following eight questions represent a starting point for thinking about the Purpose of your current enterprise. You may not need this test; reflection alone may be enough. But to jump-start your reflection, questions like these would probably be helpful:

1. Customers are attracted to our products and services because:
   a. They are on the cutting edge and do things no other product or service can do.
   b. They are simply the best products and services in every respect: design, durability, and quality.
   c. They make people happy.
   d. They are the most powerful choice.
   e. None of the above.
2. Employees come to work for us, instead of other firms, because:
   a. They will have a chance to explore new avenues and invent new things.
   b. They will work on the most elegant products and services, and learn from world-class artisans.
   c. They will be treated with respect and be able to please customers.
   d. They will join the winning team, if they have what it takes.
   e. None of the above.
3. Investors and venture capitalists put their money into our firm, instead of others, because:

    a. They expect it to be a leader in new ideas and technologies.

    b. They know that there will always be a market for the very best.

    c. They recognize that there are great fortunes to be made in making people happy.

    d. This is the company that will dominate its niche.

    e. None of the above.

4. When people criticize our firm or suggest that we may be in trouble, they usually make their case on these grounds:

    a. We are too risk-prone and likely to overextend ourselves.

    b. Our prices are too high, and our market share too small.

    c. In the name of service, we don't play fair.

    d. We are frightening to deal with, as if we consider ourselves better than everyone else.

    e. None of the above.

5. When we reach our unfulfilled potential, it might look something like this:

    a. Leading the next wave of exploration, ahead of everyone else, returning with results that no one else has achieved, and selling enough of them to finance the next audacious leap.

    b. Producing a product or service so "insanely great" that everyone who sees it is transfixed.

    c. Being recognized as a source of happiness and well-being.

    d. Finding the world is significantly different than it would have been if we had never existed.

    e. None of the above.

6. Those who lead this firm (including myself, if I am a leader) have the following skills and priorities:

    a. The ability to bring a genuinely cutting-edge innovation to market.

    b. The ability to create and recognize elegance.

    c. The ability to make our customers truly happy.

    d. The ability to marshal superior intellect and intention.

    e. None of the above.

7. The best management system is the following:
    a. A system that allows innovators to make decisions themselves but holds them accountable to their choices.
    b. A system that sets up teams who can continually monitor and improve the quality of what they do.
    c. A system that focuses employees on service.
    d. A system that puts the best people in charge as leaders, with decisions reflecting their unique gifts and talents.
    e. None of the above.
8. When I leave my current job, this will be my personal most-desired legacy:
    a. I helped bring about new things.
    b. I helped create something beautiful.
    c. I helped make people happy.
    d. I helped the best people take charge.
    e. None of the above.

If you answered "a" to all, or nearly all, of these questions, your organization's Purpose is probably closest to "discovery."

If you answered "b," your organization's Purpose is probably closest to "excellence."

If you answered "c," your organization's Purpose is probably closest to "altruism."

If you answered "d," your organization's Purpose is probably closest to "heroism."

And if your answers ranged among all four, or if you answered "e," then you may not have any clear Purpose in your organization. Or it may not be one of these four. In which case, if you are seeking to galvanize your company and its success, Purpose may be a very good place to start.

APPLYING THE PURPOSE FRAMEWORK

How to apply the principles in this book depends on what type of company you are now. For example, if you already have a Purpose, recognized in the world at large, then that Purpose will set constraints for you and reveal opportunities. Here is a guide to those possibilities:

If your Purpose is Discovery: Take note of Intel. "Only the paranoid survive," said its CEO Andy Grove, not because he feared the world, but because he knew he could never rest. Indeed, Intel tried to get out from under this imperative by reinventing itself as a "heroic" company, master of the computer niche. So far, its reputation and profitability have suffered. Many "discovery"-oriented companies have tried to make a similar transition, and only a few have succeeded—like HP (which moved to altruism) and Nokia (which moved to excellence). Richard Branson operates with a continual discovery ethic in his Virgin companies: He continually seeks new challenges that will test his informal, customer-centric business model. The most successful Internet companies—eBay, Amazon, Google and Yahoo—have all been perennially capable of discovery. (Other ballyhooed Internet companies, like WebVan and Priceline, could not succeed because they adopted the Purpose of heroism.) The challenge for your strategy will occur as your company matures: Can you maintain the pace and uncertainty of discovery as you get larger (3M does); or, like Intel, HP and Nokia, will you seek to reinvent yourself?

If your Purpose is Excellence: Forget about cost leadership; you can never attain it because you are not selling commodities. Your profits depend on top-line performance. Apple prices its computers at a significant premium over Dell's, precisely because people know they are paying for a different standard of machine. Many companies, including Motorola and Deutsche Bank, have tried to combine cost leadership with a Purpose of excellence and failed. At the same time, you don't need a large organization; you can succeed with a small, innovative hierarchy. Warren Buffett's Berkshire Hathaway firm has only six employees; BMW has a very small, highly profitable organization by automotive standards. Your vulnerability is mediocrity; Apple, when Steve Jobs was not chief executive, suffered because the quality of its designs declined. J Sainsbury suffered when it was no longer perceived as the provider of the United Kingdom's freshest foods (Tesco overtook it by training its employees to remove any food they suspected of staleness from the shelves).

If your Purpose is Altruism: You are vulnerable to the extent you are perceived as hypocritical. When Wal-Mart or Marks & Spencer is seen as abusing employees, the business loses appeal. Telephone companies have a history of altruism, which is one of the reasons they suffered so badly in the scandals of the recent bubble. William Clay Ford's efforts to change Ford Motor Company's Purpose from effectiveness to altruism have not succeeded because he has not, to this date, walked the talk. He has not yet led the company to risk everything on the altruism of its professed environmentalism. (Toyota succeeds with its hybrid gasoline-electric Prius because it does make a full commitment, and because its environmentalism is more evident in its products.) Because competitive battles are so difficult for altruistic companies, you can expect, and should prepare for, fierce competition. Thus, like Wal-Mart and other successful altruistic companies, and like any effective foundation, you must maintain rigorous financial discipline to maintain the wherewithal to be altruistic.

If your Purpose is Heroism: Others accord you respect because of your strength and effectiveness, and you will never increase that through good works or craftsmanship. Microsoft's chairman, known for his drive to dominate his industry dating back to his dormitory days, started the Bill & Melinda Gates Foundation with his wife; the Ford Motor Company, founder of the auto assembly line, bought Jaguar, a car line distinguished by its elegant artisanship. But these attempts to broaden horizons have had no impact on the success of either company. Combativeness suits your Purpose; heroic companies, from GE to Microsoft to Procter & Gamble, are known for "taking no prisoners." Top leaders of heroic companies are most effective when they seek control: Jack Welch's line, "Control your destiny or someone else will," represents a heroic strategy. Thus, heroism requires scale, at least enough to dominate a niche. If you cannot ever be No. 1 or No. 2 in your market domain, as Mr. Welch once mandated for GE, then you will probably not be able to realize the benefits of this Purpose. You don't have to be there now, but you have to have a credible path for getting there.

DEVELOPING A PURPOSE

What if you do not have a clear Purpose already? Then the next question is: Why do you need one? In Chapter One, I listed six business situations that should push you to strengthen your Purpose. However, there is a seventh possible reason: You seek to be great.

Leaders pursuing greatness with any hope of getting there will inevitably recognize that they cannot be great in all possible ways. Some Purpose must be chosen. This, indeed, will probably be the first major challenge for a new leader.

Appendix One of this book describes how the firm I work for, Panthea, handles such challenges. But there are also generic steps that any leader may take to develop a clearer understanding of Purpose and to put that Purpose into action. These steps form an expanded version of table 11.2.

Step 1: Review Your Strategy

One of the starting points for discovering Purpose is the company strategy. Contrary to what some strategists believe, the strategy does not determine the Purpose. But it is a clear guide to the unconscious purpose—or predisposition—of the current leaders. So what is your strategy? Is it market domination? (That might suggest heroism.) First leader innovation? (That might suggest discovery.) Greater service at lower prices? (That might suggest altruism.) Or charging a premium price for premium goods and services? (That might suggest excellence.)

And if your strategy is not any of the above, how clear and focused is it?

Step 2: Draw Out the Implications

Now consider the implications that strategic options have on the Purpose and the Community of Purpose.

The implications for the Purpose are still in their infancy. Attempts to construct a positive Purpose from a commercial strategy are likely to produce rather trite results along the lines of, "We believe in customer service" or "We believe in excellence." This is the mistake that many businesses make when they draw up mission statements. To be sure, you may see some strong implications, which are mostly negative—that is, your strategy will suggest some Purposes that you cannot fulfill, at least not with a straight face. For example, if you are a commercial law firm aiming to establish yourself as one of the most aggressive in the business, you will have a problem with a Purpose about being fair to all, or about being as helpful as possible. Enron, with its exploitative inner strategies, tried hard in its heyday to convince the world that it had an altruistic Purpose. That just made the fall to the bottom all the more swift.

In every company there is a Community of Purpose—the people who will be charged with putting the Purpose into action. This will always include the top team, but how far it extends will vary, determined both by their moral ideas and by the requirements of strategy. Thus, for example, at ServiceMaster, the Christian ideas of the founder made it inevitable that the entire workforce should be considered part of the community—and the need to maintain the morale of those doing menial work, a consequence of the strategy, pulled in the same direction. Henry Ford's Nietzschean ideas meant that only a small elite close to him were ever part of the community—and the logic of assembly line production also pulled in the same way.

It is tempting to say that all employees should always be part of the community, but this is utopian. For example, in some professional service firms, or in universities, there is quite a sharp divide between professional staff and lower status workers, who occupy their own separate communities, and it is better to accept this than to pretend things are otherwise. The key question is, *On whose action does competitive advantage depend?*

Step 3: "Know Thyself": Understand Your Moral Ideas

As a leader of your company, you will be responsible for articulating and developing your company's Purpose. You will probably become a living symbol of that Purpose. How will you stand up in that role? To answer that question, leaders need to understand the moral intuitions and ideas that they hold themselves.

Think about the ultimate reasons for what you do—both the things you would like to do and the things you actually do. When thinking about this, try and avoid conventional reasons or codes that do not really grip you—concentrate on what gets to your gut. See if what gets to your gut relates to one or more of the traditions I have described—discovery, excellence, altruism or heroism.

This is not simply a matter of picking a single tradition. All the traditions may have some appeal.

The language through which you express your morality is often revealing. Readers might enjoy the following test:

Table E.1 Test Your Purpose

Rank these words (1 = best, 4 = worst) according to how well they express . . .			
. . . what you get personally out of business life			
1. Adventure	2. Fulfillment	3. Happiness	4. Achievement
. . . what you are aiming for in your business life			
1. Innovation	2. Excellence	3. General Good	4. Effectiveness
. . . what you think the most important personal qualities in business life are			
1. Consistency	2. Self-discipline	3. Empathy	4. Willpower

If you rate 1s highly, you tend to have an existentialist "Discovery" outlook; if you rate 2s highly, an Aristotelian "Excellence" outlook; if you rate 3s highly, a Humean "Altruism" outlook; and if you rate 4s highly, a Nietzschean "Heroism" outlook.

Step 4: Understand Your Company Traditions

Most companies evolve over time, so it is likely that any effective Purpose will feel consistent with the company's history and how its leaders and other employees have behaved in the past. But leaders can mine the company's past to see what moral resources are available to them.

This is not about digging up dead founders who no one cares about anymore, but about uncovering and strengthening the traditions that have guided previous behavior and that have the potential to continue to mean something. The company's history and myths can be researched, including heroes and prototypical personalities. In most companies, at least some employees will have a sense of the company's traditions, which can also be researched.

One of the interesting aspects of the IBM story is how its traditions were to some extent *re*discovered by Lou Gerstner in the 1990s. But what mattered were not the blue suits and the company songs, but the attention to customer problems and the spirit of enquiry. Similarly, Jeffrey Immelt, in discovering a Purpose of discovery for GE, went back to the company's technological origins. He started regularly visiting the original corporate laboratories, in Schenectady, NY—a part of the company that Jack Welch had never focused on much—and drew people who worked there into the strategic thinking of GE at large. People throughout the company, seeing where Immelt's attention was drawn, recognized that the strategic priorities of the company were about to change.

Step 5: Take a Purpose Inventory of the Top Team

Informal techniques are probably most appropriate for immediate colleagues. Managers can listen for the different moral vocabularies these colleagues use. They can also deliberately engage in conversations that reveal the language, and thus the possible sources, of their colleagues' moral preferences. The accompanying table consists of words and phrases associated with the four main traditions we have described. It is not a simple code converter, though: readers should look for larger patterns rather than simply ticking off words.

Leaders should beware of third-party reports of others' moral outlook—it is easy to impute particular moral views to others and then establish erroneous myths about them. Leaders should listen to the individuals themselves, or rely on the more formal testing described in the next step.

Table E.2 Moral Vocabularies

Existentialist Discovery	Aristotelian Excellence	Humean Altruism	Nietzschean Heroism
The Ethics of Choice Choice, Discovery, Individuality, Decision, Openness, Lack of Constraints, Responsibility for Self, Adventure, Excitement, Innovation, Learning, Freedom, Commitment, The Chosen Path, Quest, Consistency, Voyage, Subjective, Authentic	The Ethics of Virtue Virtue, Excellence, Quality, Courage, Restraint, Self-Discipline, Integrity, Pride, Good Temper, Friendliness, Truthfulness, Intelligence, Reasonableness, Shame, Honour, Proper, Character, Role, Citizenship, Community, Social Responsibility, Success, Fulfilment	The Ethics of Compassion Compassion, Altruism, Benevolence, Sympathy, Empathy, Emotion, Affection, Sentiment, Feelings, Relationships, Goodwill, Love, Charity, The General Good, Welfare, Utility, Well-Being, Happiness, Pleasure, Pain, Misery, Bargain, Useful, Profitable	The Ethics of Power Power, Heroism, Self-Mastery, Will, Achievement, Authority, The Elite, Nobility, Aristocracy, Courage, Pride, Firmness, Independence, Effectiveness, Efficiency, Leadership, Submission, Strength, Obedience, Competence, Potential, Potent, Productive

Sometimes characters in a popular movie can help reveal a person's sense of Purpose—even silly movies like the first *Pirates of the Caribbean*. The pirate Jack Sparrow (played by Johnny Depp) is clearly an adventurer, driven by discovery. His partner and foil, the blacksmith Will Turner (Orlando Bloom), is an avatar of excellence, holding to both craft and moral standards throughout the film. The governor's daughter, Elizabeth Swann (Keira Knightley), is altruistic—and ruthless in her pursuit of the greater good for everyone. And there are two representatives of heroism in the film: the evil mutineer Barbossa (Geoffrey Rush), who sought a treasure no mortal man was meant to have (and suffered accordingly), and the military leader of the colony, Commodore James Norrington (Jack Davenport), who gives up the love of his life in exchange for being the ultimate winner of the story.

Or consider the film *Casablanca*, with its four heroes: Rick Blaine, played by Humphrey Bogart, is holding tight to a small corner of excellence in a dismal world. Victor Lazlo, played by Paul Henreid, has the idealistic mien of a discovery-driven adventurer. Ilsa Lund, played by Ingrid Bergman, is the altruist of the film. And Captain Renault, played by Claude Rains? Look closely at his dialogue, and you will see a quiet but pervasive attitude that the strong should inherit the earth—and he wants to be among them. That, indeed, is arguably why he switches sides at the end.

Which of these characters resonate with you, and with the other members of your team, and why? Or if these stories don't resonate at all, choose examples that do—either from the stories in this book, or from other historical or fictional works.

The point is not to look for exact analogues but to use the characters, and people's feelings about them, to get a sense of which Purposes you and they would be most capable of enacting—and why.

Step 6: Take a Moral Inventory of the Community

The team also needs to have a feel for the moral ideas of at least a sample of the company's other employees and what these mean for action in the company.

There are various methods for doing this. I set out one such method here based on market segmentation techniques. The process consists of four steps:

1. Develop a first take on the company's Purpose and the implications this has for positive action.
2. Conduct a qualitative survey to establish how such desirable actions are encouraged or blocked by individuals' existing moral ideas, purposes and feelings, by their beliefs about the company, their work, themselves and life in general, and by factors external to them (company systems, customer behavior, colleagues, etc.). Also examine what other behavior patterns are encouraged by these ideas. Once possible patterns emerge, test these with a quantitative survey.
3. Segment the workforce. In other words, analyze this new data, and any existing data, by variables that can be used to

distinguish groups for different treatment. These variables may include demographics, role, length of service, performance, salary and so on. Then create segments around variables with a high correlation to those measured in step 2.

4. For each segment create a draft "employee portrait" covering the variables measured, showing what moral ideas and purposes exist, how these are expressed or thwarted in action at work, and how these differ from the first take used to initiate the process. Conduct further interviews and hold discussions to fill in and refine this portrait.

Be aware, however, that taking this moral inventory does not produce an answer to the question "What is our collective Purpose?" Indeed it may reveal multiple or even conflicting purposes in different parts of the organization.

Some strategic options will require that the company takes into account the moral preferences of external constituents, notably, of course, customers. Where this is the case a similar exercise to that just described can be undertaken.

Step 7: Identify a Purpose

Once all this data has been gathered from steps one to six, a creative leap often takes place. The company arrives at a single Purpose and strategy that both makes the most of the company's strengths and opportunities and fits the moral ideas of the top team and of a critical mass of other employees and outsiders.

This is not a casual decision. The strategy may need to be modified; some assets may need to be sold. Similarly, some people's moral ideas may be offended, and they may need to find work in a more congenial place. Depending on its extent, this may be an acceptable price to pay for a powerful Purpose. What is never an acceptable price is compromise and fudge—a Purpose that tries to accommodate all the contradictions to be found in any large organization and that therefore has no pull on anyone. The exercise will have been pointless if this is the output.

The phrase "need to find work in a more congenial place" may sound somewhat sinister, so let me explain: There is no need for 100 percent support for a Purpose. Rejection of a Purpose is not in itself grounds for dismissal. However, there are certain leadership roles, in the top team and elsewhere, where rejection of the Purpose by the incumbent will cause serious problems among colleagues. Where this happens, the individual involved needs to be redeployed, and if there is nowhere to redeploy him, then he or she will have to leave. There is no room for pacifists in an army that is desperately defending a city.

Occasionally it is not clear what changes are needed, or how to create a synthesis from the apparently contradictory demands of different groups of individuals and any viable strategic option. A single Purpose seems to require major—and dangerous—surgery. In these circumstances I recommend a series of carefully prepared, structured dialogues involving the top team and facilitated by an outside expert who can be trusted to help the group follow its agenda. The aim is to produce an acceptable synthesis, most likely involving a modification of strategy to accommodate moral ideas.

For example, if altruistic ideas are strong in the company and the traditional strategies are based on minimizing costs, the dialogue may prompt investigation into strategic positions based on investment in systems, branding and quality. Or if this is a company engaged in discovery, there may need to be serious consideration of research and development investment guidelines, how much to borrow, where to cut costs elsewhere, how to judge the risks in the light of the adventurer's imperative, and when, if ever, to cut off funding.

Step 8: Create Metrics and Models

No one takes corporate announcements of good intent seriously unless metrics to measure progress against these intentions are also introduced—and many large corporations have now done so. It may require quite a leap of imagination to create these metrics—much Purpose is difficult to quantify. To get around this companies can and do use surrogates—tangible things that are likely to be achieved if

Purpose is being followed. Identifying these surrogates is a key task, often requiring considerable care.

If progress can be measured in this way, then the top team's rewards can themselves be linked to the metrics. Of course Purpose is their purpose, and you might think it does not need material reinforcement. In practice everyone needs discipline. Linking rewards to Purpose in this way sends signals that the company is serious.

Step 9: Test Strategy and Purpose

Once metrics have been devised and tested, there needs to be a final stage of verification. The process is to develop models to test the effect of different courses of action on progress toward the Purpose.

For example if an energy company, say BP, wants to reduce global warming, it can develop models linking decisions likely to follow from its strategy to various factors contributing to or retarding warming. Then, various more-or-less likely scenarios can be run through the models. If this process indicates that managers would regularly have to choose between strengthening advantage and furthering the Purpose, then either the strategy or the Purpose would need revisiting. But if no obvious problems with the alignment emerge, then the models could be incorporated into the routine planning process and applied with the same rigor as discounted cash flow or other financial models designed to ensure profit maximization.

Not all companies and all Purposes need such rigorous tools. Professional service firms with a tradition of excellence can just continue to strive for excellence, at least while times are good. However, large complex businesses whose Purposes are not so obviously aligned need to embark on some such verification process. Fixing on a Purpose is a radical, although necessary, step and should never be taken lightly.

Step 10: Decide and Launch a Campaign to Make the Purpose Work

Finally the top team must endorse a Purpose and resolve to do what is necessary to make it work—buying and selling assets, redeploying people, introducing new decision-making processes and so on.

There is a brief description of a generic Campaign below, which complements the outline of the Panthea product in Appendix One. For those who are interested in learning more about Campaigns, this will be the subject of my next book.

A Campaign is a sequence of action designed to produce a clearly defined objective within a limited timescale and with limited resources.

Successful campaigns result from managing seven Ts:

Target: This should be precise, measurable and with a fixed date—for example to generate $x of revenue by y, or simply to launch a service by a given date. Everything you do subsequently should be geared to achieving the target, so get it wrong and the whole campaign goes wrong. Set a target the campaign team does not buy into and you will not achieve your goal.

Team: Who do you need on the team? More precisely, what skills do you need? What balance of personalities will work effectively together? What contacts do you need? And what interests need to be represented, or at least feel they are represented?

Theme: What will give the campaign its cohesion? The theme, perhaps encapsulated in a slogan, does not have to be precise in the way the target is, but it has to have an emotional resonance, linking the campaign to the larger Purpose of the organization and the people working for it. In this way it should build support beyond the team. At a later stage it can guide the branding of the service.

Trust: The theme will help build trust among others in the organization, but you will also need to take more active steps to win the confidence and support of key individuals and groups. You will have to identify these people, and the kinds of action you will need to take to win their trust.

Tactics: There are also people for whom trust is not enough. Tactics are defined in the dictionary as being concerned with an army's "actual contact with the enemy." Tactics involve being clear who the enemy might be, how they are likely to respond to what you are doing, and what you can do to wrong-foot them.

Tools: Most of the above has been about people. But you also need to consider the hard edged aspects of the campaign: What budget do you need? What services do you need to buy? What corporate facilities will help? What information do you need, and where are you going to get it from?

Time: Finally, you need to manage the timetable. In a campaign this is not so simple because the situation will be changing rapidly. You should design the timetable to create momentum—for example: What are the quick wins you can build on that will attract the support of those who only want to back winners?

FOUR PURPOSE-DRIVEN COMPANIES

The task of developing a sense of Purpose is hard to understand if it is taken out of the context of the specific situation of the firm. Here then are four stories of Purpose that are drawn from the present, from companies that are still developing their leadership agendas based on the Purposes they have chosen. These cases are of interest because they represent the common challenges and opportunities facing any enterprise in this area.

Deutsche Bank: Helping the World See Its Altruism

Deutsche Bank, with its headquarters in Germany, has traditionally been regarded as what its name suggests, a German bank, indeed *the* German bank. It was founded in 1870 "in particular to promote and facilitate trade between Germany" and other markets, and it played a key role in the imperial project, for example investing in railways in Turkey and Iraq and operating an Asian associate. By 1914 it claimed to be the largest bank in the world. That was a source of national pride—Germany's bank was both international in scope and patriotic at its core.

The bank lost most of its overseas assets after World War I, but continued to play a major role in Germany. Dismembered by the Allies after 1945, it reformed in 1957 and, driven by the same patriotic Purpose, reestablished itself as Germany's leading bank. Gradually it moved back into the international arena. In the 1970s it started to open branches and representative offices overseas, and in the late 1980s it started buying overseas operations.

This expansion was not entirely successful. Its acquisition of the British firm Morgan Grenfell in 1989 generated a sharp culture clash. For all its international aspirations, the bank itself remained German, with a patriotic Purpose that meant nothing to London investment bankers.

Change came in 2002 when a Swiss, Dr. Josef Ackermann, took over the helm and began transforming Deutsche Bank. Now it is a truly international entity—in a way that its Anglo-Saxon rivals cannot match. Its top four managers all have different passports. Its core group of managing directors holds 50 different passports.

And out of this mix has emerged a modernized Purpose. Deutsche Bank now consciously aims to serve its clients, to be helpful. And, consistent with this goal, Deutsche Bank was recently nominated the best bank to work for in the city of London.

However, the world at large does not yet know this and the bank is not making money as a result of it. Most observers will say that HSBC, for example, is a global bank and that Deutsche remains a German bank. They have repositioned themselves to be a global altruistic force, but they have not managed to make this known, or to exploit it successfully. Their transformation has therefore been misunderstood because it was undersold.

Ironically, this is a moment when banks can do more good, for more people, than probably ever before in human history. How can Deutsche Bank carve out an international identity for itself that attracts others to it as the bank that increases human wealth (and therefore happiness), bolstered by its track record within Germany? In my view, that is the challenge faced by its executive team.

Arab Bank: Creating a New Identity and Purpose

Like Deutsche Bank, Arab Bank is outgrowing its nationalistic origins. In this case, the original nation was Palestine, and more recently it has been Jordan. In 1911, Abdul Hameed Shoman emigrated from the village of Beit Hanina on the outskirts of Jerusalem to the United States. He had $32 in his pocket. Working in New York as a door-to-door salesman, he expanded his business and soon owned a successful textile enterprise.

When he returned to Palestine in 1929, Shoman had a new goal—to raise 15,000 Palestinian pounds and build an Arab financial institution that would play a key role in the region's economic advancement. In 1930, he launched Arab Bank, the first privately owned financial institution in the Arab World.

The bank's existence was put to the test in 1948 with the war in Palestine, when it lost its headquarters and more than 60 percent of its assets. Then a wave of nationalizations swept the Arab world, affecting 25 branches in Egypt, Syria, Iraq, Yemen, Sudan and Libya.

Abdul Hameed Shoman's vision took his enterprise beyond its roots in Jerusalem's Jaffa Gate to almost every Arab capital and beyond. By 1960, Arab Bank had more than 40 branches. In 1967, the bank—now incorporated in the Jordanian capital of Amman—was tested again, as Israel occupied the West Bank and Gaza. This time, Arab Bank lost all its branches there.

Despite the turmoil and political upheaval, Arab Bank never defaulted on a single payment—it honored all claims and commitments. For that alone, it earned a reputation for reliability and trustworthiness.

With Shoman's death in 1974, leadership passed to his sons Abdul Majeed, who became chairman, and Khalid, who became vice chairman.

By that time, Arab Bank was already well established in such international locations as Switzerland and Germany. Plans were underway for further expansion, based on the founder's dual vision of serving Arab individuals and businesses all over the world and building bridges of trade and investment with the West. This expansion was well-founded; Arab Bank's unparalleled Middle Eastern branch network, its international outreach and its solid reputation had established the bank as a powerhouse for the region's economic advancement.

Soon after the signing of the Palestinian-Israeli Oslo Peace Accords, Arab Bank was invited to return to the Palestinian Territories. It rapidly became the Territories' leading bank, and the
accredited bank for most of the international donor countries and
aid organizations.

Now the bank is led by Abdel Hamid Shoman, son of the late
Abdul Majeed. Arab Bank Group maintains a strong presence in 28
countries on five continents and is considered the largest financial institution in the Arab world. A truly international bank, it has reached
a new stage in its role of integrating the Middle East into the international community. At the same time, the bank must now compete
with international rivals, including HSBC and Barclays. How regional can they remain? And if they transcend their altruistic roots,
what other Purpose might they legitimately choose: Excellence (continuing their practices of high-quality lending and customer service)?
Heroism (becoming a financial force in the world, bolstered by their
unique position in the Middle East)? Or Discovery (finding an entirely new way to provide financial services in a globalizing world)?

Tesco: Being a Bigger and Better Altruist

Wal-Mart is the biggest retailer in the world. As we have seen elsewhere in this book, Wal-Mart would never have *become* so big and
profitable without its founder Sam Walton's strong Purpose—to
serve customers well. The Purpose helped make Wal-Mart the
world's retailing leader, a position that it still holds.

But now . . . here comes Tesco.

Tesco is now the third-largest retailer in the world. Like Wal-
Mart it started on the "pile-it-high-and-sell-it-cheap" model. It has
since repositioned itself, and while it is still focused on price leadership, it has a broader central proposition, summed up in its slogan
"Every little helps." This phrase is a longstanding British expression,
and Tesco's use of it is a deliberate way of saying, "Our Purpose is to
help the customer."

It appears that Tesco managers genuinely mean what they say. Sir
Terry Leahy, the chief executive, spends real time at peak periods on

the checkout line serving customers personally. Like Walton, Leahy is fanatical about information—in an earlier job he was responsible for the Tesco Club Card, the loyalty card that allowed Tesco to identify and respond to its customers' spending patterns in a way that no other retailer could then match.

Leahy's commitment sends a message to his employees: Tesco really cares about good service. Sam Walton created the "shop within a shop" concept, allowing very junior managers considerable autonomy to run departments. Tesco goes even further; it encourages shelf stackers to use their discretion—for example, they are told to remove stale food that they would not buy for themselves.

This requires contented staff—and here we clearly see the differences between Tesco and the Wal-Mart of today. Tesco recognizes the right of employees to belong to a union and has recently distributed stock bonuses to staff. Wal-Mart has resisted both practices. And while Wal-Mart appears willfully intransigent to those who oppose its relentless expansion in the United States, Tesco has recently launched an initiative to ensure that it is perceived to be a good citizen as well as a good retailer. This is not and should not be the company's moral purpose, although it can only help the company to remain true to its true Purpose: serving the customer. But how can they possibly stay true to this Purpose, keep their prices low, and expand—without getting overextended? That is the challenge facing any altruistic company.

Braun: Whose Excellence?

Founded by Max Braun in the 1920s, Braun became a leader in radios and small domestic electrical appliances. After World War II it was one of the beacons of hope guiding the reconstruction of West Germany, embodying as it did traditional German values of engineering excellence and the development of new technologies. And it still does. In its modern head offices near Frankfurt, there is a beautifully crafted elevator, designed by Braun's chief engineer.

Braun's signature is design. In the 1950s, Braun developed a distinctive approach to design, based on the Bauhaus view that good design was what *worked*. Surface prettiness was ultimately unimportant; reliability and functionality were what mattered.

The result was a highly productive creative tension between the designer-engineers, who wanted perfection, and the commercial managers, who wanted to get something into the shops. The strong values of the company—shared by all—ensured that this tension remained constructive.

In the 1960s the company was taken over by U.S.-owned Gillette, which pushed it to create electric razors and electric toothbrushes. To some extent its leading position in razors and toothbrushes masked a relative decline in the rest of its products. In recent years, Braun's position has been attacked both by low-cost manufacturers in the Far East and by design-led businesses, who responded to the increasing demand from consumers for "surface prettiness." Increasingly, consumers consider that style, rather than brand, is the signal of reliability and functionality.

Braun's first response was to move some manufacturing to the Far East, but its managers knew that this was not a completely adequate response. Now it is trying to reawaken the Braun tradition of excellence and to re-interpret what "Braun design" will mean in the twenty-first century.

At the same time, Gillette has recently been acquired by Procter & Gamble, one of the most successful heroic companies in the world. Can Braun find a way of operating consistent with its standards of excellence? Will that allow them to reconnect with old customers and build new markets? Or should their leaders rethink their Purpose, in line with their new corporate parent? Either direction contains challenges.

❦

What I have found in these four examples, and during a professional life of 30 years, is that what matters most to enduring advantage is what people are inspired to do, and this depends on the ideas that drive them. The critical success factor, and the starting point of great companies, is Purpose.

APPENDIX ONE

PANTHEA AND BOOZ ALLEN HAMILTON: OUR PROPOSITION

Readers of this book will notice that I am a senior partner of Panthea, a small but growing strategic leadership consultancy headquartered off Berkeley Square in London's Mayfair District. Panthea opened in January of 2005. I joined that June. The firm has been growing rapidly; it opened an office in New York in the summer of 2006, with more offices planned. As I write, Panthea has 15 partners, all of them leaders with proven track records at the top of consulting and industry. By having so many thought leaders working in the same firm, we do not just stimulate and learn from each other, we also provide a tremendous learning environment for junior consultants. Panthea, in turn, is partly owned by the global strategy and technology consulting firm Booz Allen Hamilton. Readers of this book may justifiably want to know how the concept of Purpose relates to Panthea's practice, or to its collaborative work with Booz Allen Hamilton.

Panthea defines strategic leadership as the process of "aligning direction, people and organization to deliver enduring success." Strategic leadership is based on the realization that successful leadership is more than just the leaders themselves. Leadership really matters. Strategic leadership—when direction, people and organization are aligned—is the most powerful lever to change performance and so help a firm win.

Today Panthea has ten tools, or products, that all interconnect, but that also stand independently; one of these relates directly to Purpose, and is called "Aligning Purpose and Strategy." I will not go into the other products in great detail, but I will explain them clearly enough so that readers will get a fuller sense of how Purpose and strategic leadership work hand-in-hand to produce real action and real results.

The ten current Panthea products are grouped under the headings of Direction, People and Organization. Even though these products are distinct, and can be used on their own, they combine to form a truly integrated proposition.

DIRECTION

1. The Leadership Agenda

Question clients often ask: How can I be more effective as a leader?

Panthea provides coaching, counsel and development support to CEOs and other leaders. This is especially the case for leaders who are in transition or who are facing unfamiliar and challenging situations.

2. Leadership Communications

Question clients often ask: How can I get my message across?

A firm may have a Purpose that has been agreed on across the top team, and it may have discovered this Purpose through a clear-sighted review of the strategy. But if the leader cannot get the new message across, then it is doomed to fail.

3. Aligning Purpose and Strategy

Question clients often ask: Where do we want to go?

Panthea helps leaders uncover shared values and a Purpose based on one of four moral ideas that have stood the test of time. This creates an enduring competitive advantage that motivates all the constituents of the firm, in particular employees and customers.

4. Rapid Strategy Review

Question clients often ask: What advantage do we need to win?

It is very important to point out that the Rapid Strategy Review is completely different from the in-depth Strategic Analysis performed by strategy consultancies like Booz Allen Hamilton, Monitor or McKinsey. Panthea's Rapid Strategy Review serves only to understand the existing strategy—not to offer new strategies—and more often than not takes place after a strategy firm, like Booz Allen Hamilton, has already done this work. The Rapid Strategy Review—as its name suggests—is a quick initial diagnostic that can assess whether there is a clear roadmap and whether it is actually being followed. It takes days or weeks, not months or years, as strategic engagements by strategy firms do.

The Rapid Strategy Review links in with Aligning Purpose and Strategy—reviewing the strategy so that it can then be aligned with the Purpose—but it also connects with other Panthea products. For example, an Italian client sought a Rapid Strategy Review before carrying out a Leadership Assessment of the top team. As it happens, in this case, and in all the cases to date for this product, we have relied on the input of our sister company, Booz Allen Hamilton, which has also effected this and most of Panthea's business introductions.

5. Campaigns

Question clients often ask: What are our immediate priorities?

For many leaders, the key problem that they face is not that they have too few strategic priorities, but that they have too many. Panthea's Campaigns product helps leaders focus on the key issues that have to be tackled right away. Panthea then provides support choosing the right team for the Campaign, and helps the team turn the proposed strategic objectives into meaningful action.

In larger Campaigns, especially those that go beyond the confines of a client firm and deal with important outside constituencies, Panthea's support extends to assistance with negotiation, public relations, market and regulatory analysis—and indeed anything that is needed to achieve success!

PEOPLE

6. Board Effectiveness

Question clients often ask: How well does my board perform?

Panthea undertakes board assessments and provides advice on effective working, optimal composition, and how to use the governance process to influence organizational performance.

7. Leadership Assessment and Development

Question clients often ask: What talent do I have and how should I develop it?

Panthea deploys a wide array of instruments to evaluate, benchmark and develop leaders. Panthea's partners include eminent psychologists and experts in psychometric testing. Our methods are highly sophisticated and flexible, and are designed to fit the needs of an individual client: We offer everything from a broad assessment of the potential of a graduate group to a highly detailed and sophisticated assessment of the strengths and weaknesses of a prospective CEO.

Development grows out of assessment. In a recent client project we have been working closely with the leading traders at a major financial services firm, first assessing them as individuals, and then using that understanding to improve their performance. Traders may not be at the top of an organization, but in some situations they can be true leaders of organizations.

8. Building the Top Team

Question clients often ask: Do I have the right top team?

Panthea evaluates, redesigns and facilitates teams to be aligned with a shared goal. We help to assemble teams that will work well together, and we assist in the processes of negotiation and integration.

ORGANIZATION

9. Organization Review

Question clients often ask: Is my organization fit for purpose?

Panthea conducts rigorous organizational reviews to provide leaders with an unvarnished picture of reality. We gather quantitative and qualitative data to uncover cultural attributes and capabilities.

10. Leadership Levels

Question clients often ask: Is accountability clear and streamlined?

Panthea helps leaders speed up decision making in an organization by ensuring that decisions are taken by the right person at the right level. Too often large organizations are rendered ineffective by the blurring of accountability, especially where there are more layers of management than are actually needed. Panthea's rigorous Leadership Levels product identifies exactly where accountability is blurred and hence enables firms to cut fat rather than muscle.

♨

When a client seeks broader strategic and technical expertise, we often act in partnership with Booz Allen Hamilton. Founded in 1914, Booz Allen Hamilton is one of the most effective and prestigious general management consulting firms in the world, with immense experience in both the public and private sector. It employs over 18,000 consultants in more than 90 offices, which are spread across the six inhabited continents. Booz Allen Hamilton is a part owner of and joint venture partner in Panthea, and it supports Panthea on a global basis; two Booz Allen Hamilton Senior Vice Presidents sit on Panthea's board.

More significantly, considerations of Purpose for multinational companies (and their suppliers) often require exceptionally broad expertise, drawing on experience with strategy, technology, operations and organizational change, in a wide variety of locations and backgrounds. The greatest challenge is to frame all this complexity in a way that allows senior executives to see the scope of change, the need for change, how their own leadership fits in, the necessary tasks for their own team and the changes required to make this work through the organization and beyond, into the supply chain and customer channels.

Purpose provides a vehicle for this. Once you understand what you are here to do, as an organization, it is much easier to see the kind of help and support you need. That is the gap that Panthea, often in partnership with Booz Allen, seeks to fill.

APPENDIX TWO

FIFTY KEY POINTS

The following are adaptations from the text, designed to give the reader a quick outline of the main argument.

1. Not all companies have a Purpose—but enduringly successful ones do.
2. Purpose is the game of champions. Only strong-minded men and women—adults with powerful intellects and real character and spines of steel—are suited for it.
3. Purpose is crucial for a firm's success: It is the primary source of achievement, and it reveals the underlying human dynamics of any human activity. It is also all that successful leaders want to talk about.
4. Moral concerns have immense utility. What help is Machiavelli when there's no one left to knife and there's nothing you stand for?
5. Competition has done us a lot of good in the last half century, but one question remains inadequately addressed: "What are we competing *for*?"
6. Purpose in companies is most effective when it draws on moral ideas that have stood the test of time. To build a business that lasts, one does well to draw on ideas that have lasted.
7. Purpose advances both competitiveness and morality: It is in an area of overlap between the two.

8. Purpose relates people to plans and it relates leaders to their colleagues.

9. Purpose cannot be chosen quickly or on an ad hoc basis; it has to be discovered.

10. Purpose's presence can transform a firm, and its loss can destroy an institution. As a result, it is worth more money than anything else.

11. Purpose is a paradox. It will boost profits—but will do so only if it is pursued for its own sake. It will boost morale, build the brand, help in assessing the strategy—but it can never be just a tool. It is this duality that makes it difficult to harness—and hence so valuable.

12. There are tell-tale situations that indicate a particular need for Purpose—problems with morale, strategy or reputation, and changes in leadership or structure that force a re-examination of identity or direction.

13. The first step to creating a shared Purpose is to understand the moral intuitions of colleagues; generally these have been influenced by the ethical traditions articulated by philosophers over the centuries.

14. The existentialist ethic of choice is associated with discovery and a love of the new. It put men on the moon, America on the map and dot coms in business.

15. The Aristotelian ethic of virtue is associated with excellence. It built the great cathedrals and most good professional firms.

16. The ethic of compassion developed by David Hume is associated with altruism and lies behind much politics and charity, but also businesses that exist to serve their customers.

17. The Nietzschean ethic of power is associated with heroism. It resulted in empires, the careers of many sports champions and some of the most spectacular growth companies.

18. There are other kinds of ethics, but they are generally less useful for modern business. These include patriotism, universalism, religion and the authority of the law.

19. At the most fundamental level, competition among companies is a matter of competing moral ideas. The winning ideas stimulate better innovations, attract and motivate the best people, and create better brands.

20. Purpose is not a mission, vision or value. It is not a tool, a vehicle for maximizing profit, a form of brand identity or a constraint.

21. Purpose is different from Reputation, Social Responsibility, Codes of Practice, Firm Principles, Corporate Governance and Long Term Thinking.

22. What mattered at Tom Watson's IBM was not the company songs and dark suits but Watson's Purpose, a quest for things "beyond our present conception" that required him and his colleagues to think of each situation afresh, as prescribed by the existentialists.

23. Warren Buffett is a textbook case of Aristotelian Purpose: a search for fulfillment by excellent performance of his role, involving exercise of personal virtues and reliance on comradeship.

24. Sam Walton's Purpose was to serve the customer—and this business mission was backed by his natural empathy. Over time this capacity to empathize—the root of Hume's ethics—gave his Purpose its moral character.

25. In 1909, Henry Ford set himself apart from other successful car manufacturers by his Nietzschean Purpose. It was his good fortune that this fitted the times—the world was hungry for a cheap automobile. In the 1920s Alfred Sloane's more customer-focused Purpose won the day.

26. Siegmund Warburg's Purpose was to create a Nietzschean elite that would display "fierce nobility and independence of judgment." Among this aristocracy is the banker, who gives his clients competitive advice that the city crowd had not thought of—or would not dare give, since this would break the rules of the club.

27. There are four main building blocks to morale: extrinsic rewards such as bonuses and praise, enjoyment of the task itself, membership in a community and Purpose.

28. Rewards affect rational decision making but also have an effect on emotions: They send feedback on performance, send signals about status and the future and influence perceived standing within the firm.

29. Enjoyment of a task can be stimulated by goals and by task design, but only up to a point. Hence the need for the other building blocks.

30. Community requires there to be genuine respect for individual employees among senior managers. This can make the company a meaningful community even when the work itself is mundane.

31. Purpose makes employees feel their work is worthwhile and so maintains morale and energy levels.

32. The most effective organizations maintain a balance: Too much community relative to Purpose and there will be a fall-off of creativity, a lack of flexibility, risk aversion and even unethical behavior; too little community and there will be stress, lack of coordination and even fragmentation.

33. Purpose reduces risk aversion and fear, and helps innovators see beyond current convention.

34. Purpose can encourage leaders to make those radical decisions—decisions others would not make—that change the basis of competition in their industries and create dominance for the firm.

35. Strategic positioning creates the possibility of monopoly profits and thus advantage because the array of activities required to deliver it is

difficult to imitate, especially if the activities are mutually supportive and closely coordinated.

36. For the most part firms can achieve profitable positions because of their distinctive strengths and their ability to coordinate these strengths. Relationships are key to a firm developing distinctive strengths.

37. Purpose underpins trust between individuals, both within and beyond the firm, and makes individuals more sensitive to each other's requirements, thus helping to build relationships.

38. Purpose helps behavior support the strategic position because it is a consistent guide for making decisions, it will have influenced the choice of position itself and it provides consistency over time.

39. Leadership is the ultimate advantage. When it is present, it makes all other advantages possible.

40. There are four components of leadership: First devise a direction or outline plan; then create collective support; then negotiate individual cooperation; then set up systems to maintain momentum. This can be expressed as Think, Inspire, Mobilize, Empower: the TIME framework.

41. The TIME framework proposes an analytical approach to leadership, which allows for action. One can use it to assess individuals and to assemble leadership teams. There is nothing that can be done to improve leadership without effective assessment.

42. The TIME framework connects leadership, at least linguistically, to the notion of time. Time is vitally important for leadership.

43. Thinking is the starting point of change. A creative leap requires time: Ideas have to ripen, associations have to be revealed.

44. Thinking about Purpose should include some of the following questions: What strategic positions fit our assets and other strengths? What Community of Purpose does this imply? What can we learn from the heritage and heroes of the firm?

45. Inspiration is an act of transmission, generating ideas and passion and commitment from the community around us.

46. Some leaders inspire by provoking a sense of dependency among their colleagues. The best leaders inspire by acting as a prototype for their colleagues, and this contributes to both community and Purpose.

47. Some of the ways of inspiring a Community of Purpose are: creating a top team of leaders who are "one of us," spending time on the "front line" and telling identity stories that project the group's Purpose and aspirations.

48. Mobilization is not a top-down, bureaucratic process. It's a delicate negotiation in which big-picture ideas are injected into day-to-day tasks.

49. Empowering is about structures—incentives, decision rights, information flows and work processes. All of these can be designed in ways that help realize and develop a coherent Purpose.

50. What matters most to enduring advantage is what people are inspired to do, and this depends on the ideas that drive them. The critical success factor is Purpose.

NOTES

CHAPTER 2

1. Philip Selznick, *Leadership in Administration* (1957).
2. Richard Pascale and Anthony Athos, *The Art of Japanese Management* (1981).
3. James Collins and Jerry Porras, *Built to Last* (1994).
4. Richard Ellsworth, *Leading with Purpose* (2002).
5. Collins and Porras (1994).
6. The 4.5 years figure is from E. Sullivan, "The Changing Role of Careers," *Journal of Management* (1999).
7. Survey commissioned by the Commission on Standards in Public Life and reported in *The Independent*, September 9, 2004. Of those asked, 24 percent would trust people in large companies to tell the truth, and 68 percent would not.
8. A *Business Week*/Harris poll, June 2002, quoted in Ira Jackson and Jane Nelson, *Profits with Principles* (2004).
9. World Economic Forum, "Trust in Companies: Executive Summary" (2003), quoted in Jackson and Nelson (2004).
10. Goran Lindahl quoted by Christopher Bartlett and Samantha Ghosal, "Changing the Role of Top Management beyond Strategy to Purpose," in *Harvard Business Review* (1994).
11. A point made by Costas Markides in his contribution to *Best Practice*, from Perseus Books (2003).
12. Masaru Ibuka, quoted in Collins and Porras (1994).
13. This is as paraphrased by Mary Warnock, *Existentialist Ethics* (1967).
14. Warnock (1967) paraphrasing Jean Paul Sartre, *Being and Nothingness* (1943).
15. Jean Paul Sartre, *Existentialism and Humanism* (1946).
16. The fact that wittiness is on the list highlights the difference between Aristotelian virtue and Christian virtue. It appears on Aristotle's list because wittiness is an aspect of character that is also a form

of excellence, whereas for Christians virtue is more like the embodiment of some abstract normative principle ("be charitable" and so on).

17. Martha Nichols, "Does New Age Business Have a Message for Managers," in *Harvard Business Review* (1994).

18. Strictly speaking, Hume (better known as an epistemologist than a moralist) would have denied that there was an ultimate "reason" for actions, since happiness is an emotion and emotion is not rational, but we can use the word "reason" as a convenience provided we do not take it too literally.

19. This quote is from David Hume's *Treatise of Human Nature* (1739). All subsequent quotes are from his *An Enquiry Concerning the Principles of Morals* (1751).

20. Sam Walton and John Huey, *Made in America—My Story* (1992).

21. Friedrich Nietzsche, *On the Genealogy of Morals* (1887).

22. This is the famous Protestant work ethic described by Max Weber in *The Protestant Ethic and the Spirit of Capitalism* (1930).

23. William Pollard, *Soul of the Firm* (1996).

24. Religion is clearly also still an important influence on politics in some parts of the world, notably in the United States. Confucian and Asian philosophies matter greatly in the East; this book has a traditional European/American bias.

25. Hans Kung, *The Catholic Church* (2001).

26. Kenneth Andrews, *The Concept of Corporate Strategy* (1971).

27. Rakesh Khurana, "The Curse of the Superstar CEO," *Harvard Business Review* (2002).

CHAPTER 3

1. Milton Friedman, "The Social Responsibility of Business Is to Increase Its Profits," *New York Times Magazine* (September 13, 1970).

2. Ralph Larsen in *European Corporate Responsibility Report* (2001) quoted in Ira Jackson and Jane Nelson, *Profits with Principles* (2004).

3. On the other hand, a more pragmatic view of the decision was given by Jim Burke, the then chief executive, in a lecture at Harvard Business School shortly after the affair. It is often difficult to disentangle profit maximizing and "ethical" motives for a decision, and a chief executive lecturing at a business school in the mid-1980s may well have chosen to emphasize profits and downplay ethics.

4. Michael Rion, in Donald Jones (ed.), *Doing Ethics in Business: New Ventures in Management Development* (1982). The Cummings Corporate Responsibility director pointed out that such training was needed because of "the reality of management discretion and influence." In other words, there is often no obvious answer to a dilemma—it may be difficult to make a decision as drastic as the Tylenol one.

5. Tom Chappell, *Managing Upside Down* (1999).
6. Newspaper interview, *The Guardian*, July 5, 2003. Fitzgerald actually referred to Corporate Social Responsibility, which is often used as a synonym for good citizenship.
7. Michael Porter and Mark Kramer, "The Competitive Advantage of Corporate Philanthropy," *Harvard Business Review* (2002).
8. McDonald's statement quoted in Robert Grant, *Contemporary Strategy Analysis* (4th edition, 2002). General Electric and Goldman Sachs are quoted in Hugh Davidson, *The Committed Enterprise* (2002).
9. Wamer Bennis and Bert Nanus, *Leaders: The Strategies for Taking Charge* (1985).
10. Peter Jenson quoted in Davidson (2002).
11. Stephen Demeritt, Vice-chairman of General Mills, quoted in Davidson (2002).
12. John Browne, Statement in *BP in China: Partnership for Progress* (2000).

CHAPTER 4

1. These quotes, and others in the chapter, unless indicated otherwise, are from Kevin Maney, *The Maverick and His Machine* (2003).
2. Turnover, profit and employment figures for IBM throughout this chapter are from the IBM website.
3. Thomas J. Watson Jr. and Peter Petre, *Father, Son and Co.: My Life at IBM and Beyond* (2003).
4. This is actually a simplification. Watson was driven by customer demands in the late forties, but he was also spurred on by the desire to trump Harvard, which in 1944 developed what was then the most advanced electro-mechanical computer, with IBM sponsorship. Harvard issued a press release about the machine without giving IBM sufficient credit, in Watson's view, and to make matters worse, they did this the day before Watson was due to take part in a joint launch ceremony.
5. Mary Wamock, *Existentialist Ethics* (1967).

CHAPTER 5

1. Berkshire Hathaway annual report 2002.
2. These quotes, and the others in this chapter, from Buffet himself, are from Lawrence Cunningham, *The Essays of Warren Buffet: Lessons for Corporate America* (2001). The remaining quotes, unless otherwise indicated, are from Roger Lowenstein, *Buffett: The Making of an American Capitalist* (1995).
3. The quotes from Aristotle are from the *Guderian Ethics* and the *Nicomachean Ethics*. I recommend the Penguin edition, *The Ethics of Aristotle* (1976).

4. The phrase "Après moi, le déluge" is believed to derive from the end of the reign of Louis XV, King of France (1715–74), whose fiscal policies led to the French Revolution in 1789. It translates as, "After me, comes the flood."

CHAPTER 6

1. These quotes, and the other quotes about Walton and Wal-Mart, are from Sandra Vance and Roy Scott, *Wal-Mart: A History of Sam Walton's Retail Phenomenon* (1994). The quotes from Walton himself are from Sam Walton and John Huey, *Made in America: My Story* (1992).
2. C. K. Prahalad, *The Fortune at the Bottom of the Pyramid* (2005).
3. David Hume, *Treatise of Human Nature* (1739).
4. This figure is from Walton and Huey (1992), but the consolidation is well documented.

CHAPTER 7

1. This quote and all quotes regarding Henry Ford, unless otherwise stated, are taken from the Allan Nevins three-volume history, *Ford, the Times, the Man, the Company* (1954), *Ford, Expansion and Challenge* (1957), *Ford, Decline and Rebirth* (1962).
2. This and other quotes from Nietzsche in this chapter are from Friedrich Nietzsche, *Beyond Good and Evil* (1886).
3. Ford was quite ruthless with other shareholders: As we have seen, he walked out of the Henry Ford Company, he got rid of Malcomson by setting up a second company to cream off profits on parts manufacture, and he bought out the shareholders in 1920 by threatening to walk out of the Ford Motor Company and start afresh.
4. Quoted by Nevins (1957) from Ford's ghostwritten *My Life and Work*.
5. These quotes, and all others concerning Warburg, are from Ron Chernow, *The Warburgs* (1993).
6. Siegmund Warburg, *An Anthology for Searchers* (unpublished, quoted by Chernow, 1993).

CHAPTER 8

1. Karl von Clausewitz, *On War* (1833).
2. Towers Perrin and Gang & Gang Research, "Working Today: Exploring Employees' Emotional Connections to Their Jobs" (2003). This is based on a survey of 1,100 employees conducted in September 2002 that showed a statistically significant correlation between positive emotional attitudes toward work at the time of the survey and total shareholder returns over the previous five years. The 1986 survey is re-

ported in Frederick Schuster, *The Schuster Report* (1986). The management measures were partly about rewards, partly about goals and feedback, partly about work scheduling and organizational development. The 1994 survey is reported in M. Husselid, "The Impact of Human Resource Management Practices on Productivity and Company Financial Performance," *Academy of Management Journal* (June 1995).

3. E. Chambers, "The War for Talent," *McKinsey Quarterly* (1998).

4. Reggie Van Lee, Lisa Fabish and Nancy McGraw, "The Value of Corporate Values," *strategy+business* (Summer 2005).

5. *Fortune* (May 27, 2002). A fund investing each year in the best companies to work for would have achieved total shareholder returns of 10.7 percent, as against 5.7 percent in the Standard & Poors index. A Maryland fund management company, Knowledge Asset Management, has since 2001 set up three portfolios of companies that spend aggressively on employee development. All three portfolios outperformed the market in 2003 by between 17 percent and 35 percent (of the market return). Source: *Harvard Business Review* (March 2004).

6. In January 1998 the Standard & Poors 1,500 was worth c. $9.2 trillion. The extra return amounts to 5 percent of this, i.e., $460 billion, hence my headline figure (stocks excluded from the 1,500 were valued at at least $800 billion in 1998, making up the extra $40 billion).

7. A review in 2000 of 78 studies since 1970 of positive reinforcement in the workplace showed that 93 percent of these demonstrated the effectiveness of positive reinforcement. See evidence quoted in chapter 1 of L. Porter, G. Bigley and R. Steers, *Motivation and Work Behavior* (2003). Of course many performance-related pay schemes are poorly designed, and do not take into account the attitudes of the individuals involved or what kind of behavior is really desired (for example, individual incentives are created when what is wanted is better teamwork). The poor design of such schemes does not undermine the general point about positive reinforcement.

8. A survey of 4,000 U.S. employees conducted by Deloitte & Touche in 2002 showed that for 50 percent of workers, small pay rises had a negative effect on morale.

9. This theory was originally advanced by J. S. Adams in "Toward an understanding of inequity," *Journal of Abnormal and Social Psychology* (1967). The prediction is that workers who feel that their efforts are inequitably rewarded *as compared with relevant others* will feel distress, and will try to deal with this by (a) reducing their efforts, (b) leaving, (c) trying to get their rewards increased, (d) trying to get the rewards of the comparison group reduced, (e) changing the comparison group or (f) going into denial. The theory does not predict which of these behaviors will occur—in other words, the theory is clear that inequity results in low morale (distress), but is not clear about what

impact on performance this will have. Research since then has supported the theory (reviewed in R. Mowdray and K. Colwell, "Employee Reactions to Unfair Outcomes in the Workplace," in Porter, Bigley and Steers [2003]).

10. "The Best European Companies to Work For," *Fortune Europe* (February 2002).

11. Quoted in Lynda Gratton, *The Democratic Enterprise* (2003).

12. Czikszentmihalyi, *Flow: The Psychology of Optimal Experience* (1990).

13. For the evidence on community see the research reviewed in Michael Pratt, "Social Identity Dynamics in Modern Organizations," in Michael Hogg and Deborah Terry (eds.), *Social Identity Processes in Organizational Contexts* (2001).

14. The traditional sense of obligation is described by Christopher Meek in "Ganbatte: Understanding the Japanese Employer," in Porter, Bigley and Steers (2003).

15. The 2 percent figure is from *Training* magazine (1992), quoted in Richard Ellsworth, *Leading with Purpose* (2002).

16. Abraham Maslow, *The Farther Reaches of Human Nature* (1971).

17. Anna Kretz, a GM manager, quoted in Jeffrey Pfeffer and Robert Sutton, *The Knowing-Doing Gap: How Smart Companies Turn Knowledge into Action* (1999).

18. James Collins and Jerry Porras, *Built to Last* (1994).

19. Bernard Burnes, *Managing Change* (3rd edition, 2000).

CHAPTER 9

1. Schumpeter, "The Creative Response in Economic History," in Richard Clemence (ed.), *Essays on Entrepreneurs, Innovations, Business Cycles and the Evolution of Capitalism* (1951).

2. Tony Eccles, *Succeeding with Change: Implementing Action-Driven Strategies* (1994).

3. Michael Porter and Scott Stern, "National Innovative Capacity," in *The World Economic Forum Global Competitiveness Report* (2002).

4. Barry Jaruzelski, Kevin Dehoff and Rakesh Bordia, "Money Isn't Everything," *strategy+business* (Winter 2005).

5. Akio Morita, quoted in James Collins and Jerry Porras, *Built to Last* (1994).

6. Daniel Vasella, "Make It Meaningful," *Harvard Business Review* (August 2002).

7. The limits to competition in established markets can become particularly rigid where there is a complex or long value chain: New entrants have to grapple with well-established patterns of supply and distribution, while existing players can become quite comfortable with relationships that were probably fashioned around their strengths. As we

saw, Walton as well as Ford had to struggle with this. This, of course, is why the Internet was so liberating in industries as diverse as travel, personal computers and personal finance.

8. Masaru Ibuka, quoted in Collins and Porras (1994).
9. "When Boeing [non-executive] director Crawford Greenwalt asked a member of senior management about the projected return on investment of the proposed 747, the manager told him they had run some studies, but couldn't recall the results. Greenwalt buried his head in his hands in response." Collins and Porras (1994).

CHAPTER 10

1. Michael Porter, "What Is Strategy?" *Harvard Business Review* (1996).
2. Gary Hamel and C. K. Prahalad, "Strategic Intent," *Harvard Business Review* (1990).
3. H. Mintzberg describes strategy formulation as this organizational learning process in "The Design School," *Strategic Management Journal* (1990).
4. John Kay, *Foundations of Corporate Success* (1993).
5. Porter (1996).

CHAPTER 11

1. Tony Eccles, *Succeeding with Change: Implementing Action-Driven Strategies* (1994).
2. A. Haslam and M. Platow, "Your Wish Is Our Command," in Michael Hogg and Deborah Terry (eds.), *Social Identity Processes in Organizational Contexts* (2001).
3. Daniel Goleman, *Emotional Intelligence* (1995).
4. Larry Bossidy and Ram Charan, *Execution* (2002).
5. John Gardner, *On Leadership* (1990).
6. "Leadership at the Turn of the Century," in John Kotter, *What Leaders Really Do* (1999).
7. These words are drawn from a list in Robert Eccles and Nitin Nohria, *Beyond the Hype: Rediscovering the Essence of Management* (1992). As they say, "words may come and go, but action is always the managerial imperative." Perhaps the most overused phrase of all in business is "change management."
8. Bossidy and Charan (2002).
9. Private conversation (2004).
10. In reality many businesses are led by a team even if the CEO is the figure who makes the headlines.
11. "I believe passionately that maintaining the status quo is not an option. It is simply unacceptable that 16% of the world enjoys 80% of its

wealth while a fifth of humanity survives on less than one dollar a day . . . the failure of governments to reach any substantive agreement on market liberalisation or reduction in subsidies at Cancun's WTO meeting is a bitter disappointment and, quite frankly, morally unacceptable. It is outrageous that rich countries' farm subsidies are greater than Africa's gross domestic product and indefensible that the EU and the U.S. government should continue to defend such trade distorting practices." Niall Fitzgerald, Speech at London Business School, October 2, 2003.

12. Ira Jackson and Jane Nelson, *Profits with Principles* (2004).

13. Jackson and Nelson (2004).

14. John Kotter, *Leading Change* (1996).

15. Kets de Vries, *The Leadership Mystique* (2001).

16. John Viney, *Drive* (1999).

17. Michael Hogg, "Social Identification, Group Prototypicality and Emergent Leadership," in Michael Hogg and Deborah Terry (eds.), *Social Identity Processes in Organizational Contexts* (2001).

18. Those tempted by charisma should remember that leaders cannot work miracles; until the word became debased, "charisma" was a property of those who could.

19. Research by Haslam, Brown, McGarty and Reynolds cited in Hogg and Terry (2001).

20. Peter Drucker, *The Practice of Management* (1954).

21. Howard Gardner, *Leading Minds* (1995).

22. Rollo May, *The Cry for Myth* (1991). Archbishop Rowan Williams in his 2002 Dimbleby lecture says that "you can only tell the story of your own life, it seems, when it isn't just your story."

23. See Patrick Geary's *The Myth of Nations* (2002) for an interesting account of the development of national myths.

24. Aspirations, as described here, combine with beliefs and capabilities to shape what groups and individuals can and will do.

25. Howard Gardner, *Leading Minds* (1995).

26. The quotes are made up, of course, but they reflect the characters involved.

27. W. Chan Kim and Renee Mauborgne, "Tipping Point Leadership," *Harvard Business Review* (2003).

28. The research on the effectiveness of goals is summarized in chapter 2 of I. Robinson et al., *Motivation* (1985, 2nd edition 1992).

CRITICAL BIBLIOGRAPHY

For those who are interested in the subjects covered in this book, I have found the following articles and books helpful.

PART ONE: WHAT IS PURPOSE?

Purpose in Organizations

Philip Selznick's *Leadership in Administration* (1957) is an outstanding and unjustly neglected classic. Selznick observed business with the perspective of a sociologist, and he understood the company as an institution—a novelty in his time. He made the important distinction between "organizations," which were "technical instruments judged on engineering premises," and "institutions," which were "the receptacles of group idealism," and explained that it was the role of the leader to turn an organization into an institution.

William Guth and Renato Tagiuri in "Personal Values and Corporate Strategy," *Harvard Business Review* (September 1965), were among the first to argue for the importance of personal values in the development of corporate strategy. They wrote, "Are there new strategic alternatives which might effect a closer match between economic opportunity for the company and the other-than-economic values which they or their associates possess?" They were not concerned with the greater social good, but with the requirement that "corporate strategy inspire personal commitment" at the same time as the organization remains viable.

W. Ouchi, "Markets, Bureaucracies and Clans," *Administrative Science Quarterly* 25 (1980). In this seminal article, Ouchi introduced the idea that organizations could be controlled through shared values—and that this represented a third form of control, along with markets and bureaucracies.

Tom Peters and Robert Waterman, *In Search of Excellence* (1982). At a moment in history when it looked like expediency was the only winning strategy for business, Tom Peters and Robert Waterman came along and proposed an alternative purpose, which they called "excellence." The examples tended to focus on discovery and heroism as well, but it was such a basically strong idea that it resonated with a large number of people. This tremendous book has been somewhat superseded by Collins and Porras (1994), who write in a similar vein, but it is still well worth reading.

Robert Jackall, "Moral Mazes: Bureaucracy and Managerial Work," *Harvard Business Review* (1983). This is a distinctly hard-edged view of the bureaucratic ethic. Jackall describes the political activity and attitudes required for survival in a modern corporation, which are quite incompatible with any personal or corporate Purpose.

E. H. Schein, *Organizational Culture and Leadership* (1985, 2nd edition 1992). Schein is probably the leading expert on corporate culture, and this is a sophisticated account of what it is and the extent to which it can and cannot be influenced by deliberate management.

Charles Perrow's *Complex Organizations: A Critical Essay* (3rd edition 1986) is a useful antidote to the enthusiasms of Selznick, Barnard, Peters and Waterman, and Porras and Collins. He defends bureaucracy as the best form of organization we know, castigates the "beyond bureaucracy" school as writers of science fiction and points out that most people do *not* find fulfillment through their employing organization—and that if they do, it is strictly on the organization's own terms.

Gerard Langeler, "The Vision Trap," *Harvard Business Review* (March 1992). This is an entertaining account of how excessively grandiose visions might be inspiring for a while, but can distract managers from the pragmatic decisions needed to run an effective business (for example, encouraging perfectionism among software designers often results in endless delays).

James Collins and Jerry Porras, *Built to Last* (1994). An undoubted classic that adopts a rigorous approach to the question, What makes for a lastingly successful, visionary company?

The authors investigated the eighteen businesses founded before 1950 that received the most mentions as "visionary" in a survey of CEOs. For each of these companies, they identified a similar "comparison" company that was also successful but mentioned less often in the survey. The visionary companies outperformed the stock market as a whole by a factor of over 15 between 1926 and 1990, while the comparison companies outperformed by a factor of over 2.5. By comparing each pair, the authors drew the following conclusions:

1. At visionary companies, the leader's role is to create (and re-create) the company, the machinery that allows people to work together effectively; it is not to have a great idea, or to inspire.
2. These leaders tend to be homegrown.

3. Visionary companies' underlying values and purposes vary to a great extent, but in all cases go beyond profit, are widely and firmly believed in and do not change over time.
4. These values are combined with a constant drive for improvement and change in less fundamental aspects of the business, and are mobilized by a series of stretch targets and by mechanisms that stimulate discontent with the present.
5. Employees of visionary companies believe in their employers' ideologies, to the point that they can appear brainwashed.
6. Visionary companies evolve by trial and error: They are open to new ideas and experimentation and then pursue those avenues that work.

In the paperback edition (1998), Collins and Porras added a short section on purpose. There is a particularly interesting sentence on page 224 in which they admit, "In our hardcover edition . . . we did not give enough attention to purpose as distinct from core values and we under-emphasized its importance."

Christopher Bartlett and Sumantra Ghoshal, "Changing the Role of Top Management: Beyond Strategy to Purpose," *Harvard Business Review* (1994). This groundbreaking article explains just why top management's role is changing from strategy to purpose.

William Pollard is the former chairman of The ServiceMaster Company. His book *The Soul of the Firm* (1996) is a good case study of leadership driven by religious Purpose. The foreword to the book summarizes its message: "Leadership in the firm has a responsibility to the ethical, professional, and personal development of every individual in the organization." This responsibility is based on a belief that "all of us are created in the image and likeness of God" and "respect for the dignity and worth of every individual."

Jon Katzenbach's *Peak Performance* (2000). An important book that describes five different paths companies can use to achieve emotional energy and commitment in the frontline workforce. They are "Mission, Values and Pride," "Process and Metrics," "Entrepreneurial Spirit," "Individual Achievement" and "Recognition and Celebration." His team looked at 20 large businesses and two U.S. government agencies. Both of the agencies but only one of the businesses, 3M, used "Mission, Values and Pride" as its sole path to peak performance. Like Porras and Collins, he argues that "it is not the content or appropriateness of 3M's mission and values that makes the company so effective" but its "relentless consistency" in promoting these. Nonetheless, the approach will work only when there is a rich history that employees are proud of, the purpose of the organization is noble in the eyes of the employees and the leadership is driven by values. Of the other 19 companies, five make use of the "Mission, Values and Pride" path in combination with other paths.

Richard Ellsworth's *Leading with Purpose* (2002) is principally an argument for putting customers before shareholders. There is evidence that this is often in the long-term interests of shareholders—because it creates loyal customers and motivated employees. In the long run, economies in which such views predominate will benefit at the expense of those in which they do not.

Patrick Lencioni in "Make Your Values Mean Something," *Harvard Business Review* (July 2002), argues, contrary to my position, that values must be created by the CEO and a handful of key people and then pushed hard, using all the human resource systems (recruitment, rewards, communication, dismissals and so on). A more democratic approach, he says, is in danger of diluting the organization's strategy. I urge the reader to consider Lencioni's case, especially as his point of view is different from mine.

Art Kleiner, *Who Really Matters: The Core Group Theory of Power, Privilege and Success* (2003). An interesting and entertaining account of a well-known phenomenon: Organizations exist to serve the interests and purposes of a core group. It would be nice if these organizations included a moral (Kleiner says noble) purpose, but, he argues, the time frame for feedback on Purpose is long, which undermines attempts to pursue it—look at how Browne backpeddled after the share price fell following the launch of the Beyond Petroleum brand. Nonmembers of the core group should recognize that they have a cold-hearted but possibly mutually rewarding deal with the company and should not get too emotionally involved. As always, Kleiner is offering wise advice that the practitioner can ignore only at his or her own risk.

Gerry Johnson and Kevan Scholes's well-known textbook *Exploring Corporate Strategy* (7th edition, 2003) has a useful section on the purpose of business. They present four stereotypical ethical "stances" adopted by businesses: (1) Our duty is to maximize short-term shareholder gain—it is the responsibility of markets and governments to constrain us so that this results in optimum outcomes for society; (2) our duty is to maximize long-term shareholder gain, and this requires good relations with other stakeholders (the position is presented by Badaracco and others—see below under "Ethics and Business: The Management Literature"); it remains the duty of markets and governments to constrain us, but there is less to constrain; (3) our duty is to maximize the welfare of all our stakeholders—shareholders are only one group—and judgment is required as to how to achieve the right balance; (4) our duty is to further our mission, which is defined in terms of changing society in some way.

Economics versus Ethics

Both Purpose and the role of relationships are neglected in the standard "neo-classical" economics taught in universities, although there has always been recognition among academics outside this tradition that individuals' decisions are influenced by ethics, that the social context does affect outcomes and that an adequate theory will need to take these things into account. Adam Smith is the pre-eminent example. He argued in *The Wealth of Nations* (1776) that the self-interest of each resulted in the wealth of all (the working of the invisible hand), but he was not a prophet of unbridled self-interest or amorality in business. The invisible hand works best when there are common standards of behavior in society, supported by a combination of self-restraint and Humean fellow feeling. The market is sustained by society, which is sustained by ethics. More on the ethical side of his theory is to be found in his earlier book, *The Theory of Moral Sentiments* (1759).

The other classical economist with an ethical bent was of course Karl Marx. I leave aside the well-known failures of his analysis—notably his failure to appreciate how capitalism could expand its markets and so create prosperity for all. More relevant to this discussion is his insistence on the essentially communal nature of man, and that work was "life's prime want"—in other words, an end in itself as well as a means of survival. Neither of these ideas found adequate expression under raw nineteenth-century capitalism, but of course they can under the advanced capitalism of Purpose. Fortunately it is not necessary to abandon markets to achieve this. For a very quick summary and assessment of his work see Jonathan Wolff's *Why Read Marx Today* (2002), and for a one-volume collection see David McLellan (ed.), *Karl Marx: Selected Writings* (2000).

The divorce between economics and ethics took place in the late nineteenth century. The two main villains are generally thought to be William Jevons and Leon Walras, geniuses both who independently developed theories describing "general equilibrium" in the economy. They are the founders of "neo-classical" economics, and their work, subsequently refined, forms the basis for modern textbook economics. They were both trained as physical scientists, and Walras was also an engineer. They both applied the mathematical techniques that had been so successful in nineteenth-century science and engineering to the problems that had been described by Adam Smith and others, and created very powerful, internally consistent models that, within limits, have proven to have considerable predictive power. However, in order to describe human behavior algebraically they had to eliminate complexities about ethical motivation and social and institutional context. They also eliminated discussion about what outcomes were ethically desirable.

Perhaps the most famous rejection of their theory was that made by J. M. Keynes, most comprehensively in *The General Theory of Employment, Interest and Money* (1936). I am not concerned here with his technical arguments about the demand for money, but cite the following as examples of his more rounded description of the economy: "If human nature felt no temptation to take a chance, no satisfaction (profit apart) in constructing a factory, a railway, a mine or a farm, there might not be much investment merely as a result of cold calculation"; and, "if the animal spirits are dimmed and the spontaneous optimism falters, leaving us to depend on nothing but a mathematical expectation, enterprise will fade and die."

Recently there has been increased interest in re-establishing links between ethics and economics, and Amartya Sen's splendid short book *On Ethics and Economics* (1987) is a manifesto for this program. He points out that behavior is driven by the need to cooperate as well as by individual goals, that in any case these individual goals can be driven by ethics as well as self-interest and that even self-interested goals are not all about material consumption. Sen also describes Adam Smith's combination of ethics and economics and the subsequent divorce. Other books similarly sympathetic to "ethical economics" include Joan Robinson's *Economic Philosophy* (1962) and Paul Ormerod's *The Death of Economics* (1994).

James Buchanan in *Ethics and Economic Progress* (1994) also supports the re-integration of ethics and economics, but from the right rather than the left. He argues that what he calls "puritan" ethics—work hard, save—increase the size of the economy. It is therefore in everyone's economic interest to help establish such ethics—to "pay the preacher," as he puts it. Of course some might say he puts the cart before the horse—after all, ethical decisions should precede economic ones—but at least the argument demonstrates an interaction of the two types of decision making.

Moral Philosophy

I have drawn heavily on Alasdair MacIntyre's *After Virtue* (1981). This is one of the best and most influential books of modern moral philosophy. MacIntyre's starting point is the prevailing view among modern moral philosophers that ethical statements are simply an expression of emotion or preference and lack any real authority. This lack of authority dates back to the scientific revolution of the seventeenth century, which undermined the authority of the Church and tradition, and thus of the morality dependent on them. The resulting vacuum prompted a project, lasting from the eighteenth to the twentieth century, to find an alternative basis for authority, a project that ultimately failed. Various candidates were put forward—reason, sentiment, utility, human rights—but all have been effectively undermined by critics.

During the nineteenth century both Kierkegaard and Nietzsche in their different ways recognized the hopelessness of the project, both insisting that the individual had to create his or her own moral authority. However, they did not show that this more traditional, Aristotelian morality was bound to fail in the same way. Unlike many subsequent philosophers, Aristotle does not justify virtues on the basis of some prior justification of rules, principles or goals, which can always be questioned. Rather, they are justified as leading to success, the good life for man, or human fulfillment, within a specific community. MacIntyre then sets out his own scheme based on this philosophy.

Modern life consists of a number of practices, for example professional activities, games, social forms, hobbies and so on. Each of these practices has associated virtues, that is, behaviors that lead to fulfillment or success within those practices. But morality is concerned with life as a whole, so the question arises: What is fulfillment or success in *life as a whole* as opposed to within the individual practices? The unity of a life is rather like the unity of a story, and this gives us a clue: Life is in fact a kind of quest, that most traditional of stories. It is a quest not for some specific thing but for fulfillment, the good for man.

This may sound circular, but it is not circular in an unproductive way, because the individual has something to start the quest with, namely the goods or fulfillments available within the specific practices. He or she then orders and balances these practices, searching for a larger fulfillment built on these, which is appropriate to the individual and the community he or she is part of. Thus, in addition to virtues that encourage success within practices, there are more general virtues that encourage success in this quest. (Those attracted by Peter Senge's ideal of personal mastery will no doubt be attracted by MacIntyre's ideas, too.)

MacIntyre is interesting but quite hard going, and certainly not suitable as an introduction to moral philosophy. For those looking for an introduction I recommend John Mackie's *Ethics: Inventing Right and Wrong* (1977), Bernard Williams's *Morality: An Introduction to Ethics* (1972) and a collection of essays: Joel Feinberg, *Moral Concepts* (1969). For those wanting a more general introduction to philosophy I recommend Roger Scruton's *Modern Philosophy: An Introduction and Survey* (1994) and Bertrand Russell's classics *A History of Western Philosophy* (1945) and *The Problems of Philosophy* (1912). These are extremely lucid and that rare thing—opinionated—introductions by leaders in the field. Scruton's book contains a superb bibliography.

Existentialism is described in Mary Warnock's *Existentialist Ethics* (1967), a short and brilliantly lucid account of the subject. She is sympathetic but sensibly skeptical toward the existentialist position.

Kierkegaard's most famous work is *Either/Or* (1843), a collection of essays, diary entries and letters assembled by a fictitious editor in the course of which Kierkegaard asks the reader to choose between the "aesthetic" and the "moral" way of life. Kierkegaard's philosophy was a reaction to Hegel's philosophy, which was in turn a reaction to the ethical problems caused by the collapse of traditional authority and community during the Enlightenment and the scientific revolution of the seventeenth and eighteenth centuries. According to Hegel, man was isolated and there was no basis for determining what he should do; if he followed his instincts alone he would be involved either in frustrating struggle or in the lassitude that accompanies lack of real Purpose. Hegel, building on the work of Kant, therefore elevated objective reason and the state into the tools that would release man from this unsatisfactory set of alternatives.

Kierkegaard was repelled by what he saw as the excessively systematic style of Hegel's solution, which failed to take into account what it was really like to be a human being, and, as Kierkegaard saw it, made "everyone an observer" rather than an actor in life. He therefore proposed a different response to the problem: People should focus on what it was for *them* to be alive. In contrast to the grandiose schemes of "objective" science and philosophy, he emphasized the importance of subjectivity.

For those who want to read later existential texts, the best bets are probably Jean-Paul Sartre's essay "Existentialism and Humanism" (1946) and his novel *Nausea* (1938).

Aristotle's moral philosophy is set out in the lecture notes that became the *Eudemian Ethics* (edited by Eudemus) and the *Nicomachean Ethics* (named after his son Nicomachus), both written in the fourth century B.C. The latter is the better known and one of the most influential works on the subject. Despite this, readers brought up on contemporary ideas of "happiness" and "welfare" can easily misunderstand Aristotle's central concept of happiness ("eudaimonia"), perhaps better translated as fulfillment, flourishing or success, and may be taken aback by his contention that an individual should aim for his own fulfillment, not the greatest happiness for the greatest number. But Aristotle is less concerned with how to be "good" in a nineteenth-century moralistic way than with how to live well, that is, how to be fully human. The Penguin edition—*The Ethics of Aristotle* (1976)—has a good introduction. MacIntyre's *After Virtue* (q.v.) is an interesting attempt to apply Aristotelian ideas to modern life.

Hume's two main relevant works are *Treatise of Human Nature* (1739) and *An Enquiry Concerning the Principles of Morals* (1751). Other works in this tradition are Adam Smith's *The Theory of Moral Sentiments* (q.v.), which forms an important counterbalance to his *Wealth of Nations* (q.v.), and John Stuart Mill's *Utilitarianism* (1861), which attempts to justify the pursuit of the general happiness as the supreme good. Modern philosophers are highly critical of Mill—for a modern discussion of utilitarianism, see J. Smart and B. Williams, *Utilitarianism, For and Against* (1973)—but his view of morality remains dominant in both Anglo-Saxon public policy and, to a lesser extent, private life.

Friedrich Nietzsche's main works are *Beyond Good and Evil* (1886), *On the Genealogy of Morals* (1887), *The Gay Science* (1887) and *The Will to Power* (1901), all available in modern translation. Nietzsche wrote in a deliberately iconoclastic and shocking style. He did not produce systematic philosophy— indeed, he did not see himself as a philosopher but as a philologist—and at first sight much of his writing appears like ranting. However, his predictions about the twentieth century proved horrifyingly accurate. Readers who find the texts impenetrable may want to limit themselves to the apothegms— one-liners—in *Beyond Good and Evil*. For better or worse, Nietzschean morality has tended to be dominant in the executive suite. It has also influenced political thinkers such as Leo Strauss, whose *The City and Man* (1977) has in turn been highly influential among the neo-conservatives in the George W. Bush administration, notably Paul Wolfowitz.

Kant is not an easy read, and those who are interested might start with the relevant chapters of one of the introductory texts recommended above, or with Roger Scruton's *Kant: A Very Short Introduction* (2001). For those who want to read the original text, the two main ethical works are *Groundwork of the Metaphysic of Morals* (1785) and *Critique of Practical Reason* (1788). Norman Bowie (1995), described in the next section on ethics and business, is an interesting if idealistic attempt to apply Kantian ideas to business.

Karl Deutsch's *Nationalism and Social Communication* (1953) is excellent. It explains the mechanics behind the ideals—for example, nationalism could not have become a significant force before the arrival of cheap printing and circulation of newspapers.

The classic work on the impact of *religious* Purpose on business is Max Weber's *The Protestant Ethic and the Spirit of Capitalism* (1904, English translation 1930), which argued that there was a link between Calvinism and the drive for material success that fueled the development of capitalism. Subsequent research has produced empirical support for some of Weber's conclusions, but most of them are widely disputed.

The tradition of authority in the Catholic Church is captured in Hans Kung's *The Catholic Church* (2001), a critical and riveting history. For those who wish to read, or dip into, the original texts, St. Augustine's *Confessions* (398) and *City of God* (426) are widely available in modern translations and are quite readable. However, I do not imagine many readers will want to complete the five volumes of St. Thomas Aquinas's *Summa Theologica* (1272)—the expression of a unified, dominant theological and moral system that no one could attempt to compile today.

Ethics and Business: The Management Literature

In general I am not enthusiastic about the management literature in this area. My experience of consulting with large companies is that all too often it does not deal with the real issues senior managers face, and often the ethics it attempts is trite. Nonetheless there is some good work, and here, for those interested, is a sample.

Douglas Sherwin in "The Ethical Roots of the Business System," *Harvard Business Review* (November 1983), argues that business is a system in which shareholders, employees and other stakeholders are all components, and that managers must manage with this in mind. This requires that they are guided by values, which in turn reflect society's ideas about what a business is for.

Edward Freeman and Daniel Gilbert in *Corporate Strategy and the Search for Ethics* (1988) argue that "almost all questions of corporate strategy are questions of ethics" and that "corporate strategy must return to the individual values of corporate members *before it is formulated* . . . addressing the problem as one of 'implementation' or 'culture' simply tries to fix (in vain) the wrong problem." They discuss the different kinds of objectives a company might have and they probe the ethical basis of "the excellence revolution" that was sweeping the United States in the 1980s. They believe this is "respect for the individual [that] lies beneath the surface of the concern for customer and quality, and is . . . the key to understanding the incredible commitment and performance that are the results."

Joseph Badaracco, "Business Ethics: Four Spheres of Executive Responsibility," *California Management Review* (April 1992). Badaracco is a world expert on business ethics, and he argues in this article that managers should make moral judgments using standards provided by Aristotle, Mill, Jefferson and Machiavelli. These standards cannot be weighed against each other in a straightforward way; managers should use them flexibly rather than simply attempting to apply a set of general rules to particular circumstances.

Robert Solomon's *Ethics and Excellence* (1992) is an exhortation to managers to adopt Aristotelian ethics in business and includes a summary of what this might mean. He quite correctly places particular emphasis on the importance of community. To be virtuous, "according to Aristotle one has to think of oneself as a member of the larger community . . . and strive to excel, to bring out what is best in ourselves and our shared enterprise." The communal nature of the virtues means there is no sharp split in what is good for the community and what is good for the individual: "What is best in us involves our virtues, which are in turn defined by that larger community, and there is therefore no ultimate split or antagonism between individual self-interest and the greater public good."

Martha Nichols in "Does New Age Business Have a Message for Managers?" *Harvard Business Review* (1994) describes the limitations and potential interest of the "New Age" model, as exemplified by The Body Shop, Tom's of Maine, Ben & Jerry's and so on.

Norman Bowie, *Business Ethics: A Kantian Perspective* (1995). Chapter 3, "The Firm as a Moral Community," is the most interesting in the book and explores the implication of Kant's injunction to treat all humans as ends, not means. Managers can follow this injunction only if they operate on the basis that the organization is a vehicle for achieving the shared ends of its participants and as such becomes valued in itself. It becomes, to use John Rawls's distinction (*A Theory of Justice*, 1971), a "social union" as opposed to a "private society," this last being an organization that is not valued in itself and in which participants have noncomplementary objectives.

Ryuzaburo Kaku's "The Path of Kyosei," *Harvard Business Review* (July 1997) is an interesting account of the Japanese model of corporate citizenship by the ex-chairman of Canon.

Tom Morris's popular *If Aristotle Ran General Motors* (1997) contains, in his own words, "a good dose of ancient wisdom mixed with some contemporary philosophizing about human motivation and human excellence." It is a striking example of the feel-good genre.

Tom Chappell's *Managing Upside Down* (1999) is a firsthand account of trying to manage an "ethical" business—Tom's of Maine—and some of the dilemmas this creates. Of course this kind of private business is not a model for publicly held businesses, but Chapell's account of the dilemmas he faced is honest and interesting

Hess, Rogovsky and Dunfee, "The Next Wave of Corporate Community Involvement: Corporate Social Initiatives," *California Management Review* (January 2002). This is a good example of the "why ethics pay" literature. As they put it: "Moral desires expressed by stakeholders are embodied in capital, consumer and labor markets," with the result that managers must "respond to and anticipate" these desires. "A failure to do so may have a significant negative impact on shareholder wealth."

Diane Coutu, "How Resilience Works," *Harvard Business Review* (2002). Coutu argues that strong values enable organizations (and people) to find meaning in adversity, increasing their resilience.

Roger Martin, "The Virtue Matrix: Calculating the Return on Corporate Responsibility," *Harvard Business Review* (2002). Ethical "leaders" go beyond what is generally considered decent behavior in their business communities; they practice this virtue for its own sake, but this may produce commercial returns. These cannot be guaranteed—there may even be losses—but in principle the risk involved is no different than any other business risk and does not involve betting the firm. Martin goes on to suggest that business leaders can put pressure on their peers to adopt similar policies. In this way, the virtue that was at the strategic frontier becomes standard practice in the business community, increasing the social benefit that the original initiative brings about.

For a good example of the cynical approach to business ethics, read the article by two McKinsey consultants, David Cogman and Jeremy Oppenheim, "Controversy Incorporated," *McKinsey Quarterly* (2002). The authors argue that companies can use their social assets (partly created by corporate social responsibility activities) to allow them to engage in controversial activities.

The importance of an ongoing dialogue on ethical issues is illustrated in a story told in Edmondson and Cha, "When Company Values Backfire," *Harvard Business Review* (November 2002). An advertising agency owner promoted a set of well-meaning, benevolent values at his agency. However, the staff wove their own ideology into the values and felt that he was not living up to them—and became extremely disaffected. There were no feedback mechanisms to nip the problem in the bud.

Michael Porter and Mark Kramer, "The Competitive Advantage of Corporate Philanthropy," *Harvard Business Review* (December 2002). This is one of the most sophisticated articles in a field that generally has a rather cynical feel. The authors' argument is that well-targeted philanthropy can change a company's competitive conditions to its advantage.

Lynn Paine's *Value Shift* (2003) reports that U.S. business leaders attach increasing importance to appealing to all stakeholders and to strong corporate ethics, although generally for instrumental reasons—that is, to reduce the risk of scandal, improve employee morale, help build reputation and create trust, so reducing transaction costs. She grapples with this question of whether ethics are a means to an end or an end in themselves. Paine's practical prescriptions are similar to Badaracco's (q.v.); she suggests that applying ethics is not about following codes but involves asking four kinds of question: (1) Will this action serve a useful purpose? (2) Is this action consistent with relevant principles? (3) Does this action respect the legitimate claims of the people likely to be affected? (4) Do we have the power to take this action?

For an up-to-date survey of what major corporations (mainly U.S. corporations) are doing to achieve profits with principles, see Ira Jackson and Jane Nelson's book of the same name (2004). The book is packed with examples, which the authors use to illustrate seven principles of ethical business.

PART TWO: GREAT STORIES OF PURPOSE

Kevin Maney's *The Maverick and His Machine* (2003) is strongly recommended to anyone who wishes to know more about Watson or IBM. The book gives an excellent sense of Watson the man and the development of the company. My only complaint is the title: Watson was not interested in convention, so from the outside he might have seemed like a maverick, but this word belittles the strong Purpose that drove him. Nor was he really interested in machines. The story is continued in Thomas J. Watson Jr. and Peter Petre's *Father, Son and Co.: My Life at IBM and Beyond* (1990). This is a remarkably frank account of Watson Jr.'s stormy relationship with his father—and indeed just about everyone else he dealt with.

Roger Lowenstein's biography *Buffett: The Making of an American Capitalist* (1995) is excellent. The Berkshire Hathaway annual reports, including Buffett's letters to shareholders, make good reading and are available on the Web. The letters are organized thematically in *The Essays of Warren Buffett: Lessons for Corporate America*, edited and introduced by Lawrence Cunningham (2001). Robert Hagstrom's *The Essential Buffett* (2001) is one of several books drawing lessons from Buffett's career—but I would recommend reading the master's own letters first.

Sam Walton's *Made in America: My Story*, written with John Huey (1992), is a gripping read. Even if you do not care for the folksy style, and do not take Walton's homilies at face value, the book makes you feel privy to an astonishing story. It is probably best read in conjunction with more dispassionate accounts. Sandra Vance and Roy Scott's *Wal-Mart: A History of Sam Walton's Retail Phenomenon* (1994) is solid and useful. Also useful are two Harvard Business School case studies: *Wal-Mart Stores' Discount Operations* (1986, revised 1989) and *Wal-Mart Stores Inc.* (1994, revised 2002). For those who want an up-to-date account of Wal-Mart since Walton's death, there is Robert Slater's *The Wal-Mart Decade* (2003), written with the active support of the company's PR department.

The outstanding book about Henry Ford and his company is Allan Nevins's three-volume history of the Ford Motor Company: *Ford, the Times, the Man, the Company* (1954), *Ford, Expansion and Challenge* (1957), *Ford, Decline and Rebirth* (1962). It combines telling details about individuals with just the right amount of economic data. Also useful is the one-volume history of the company by Douglas Brinkley, which takes the story to the present day: *Wheels for the World* (2003).

Ron Chernow's *The Warburgs* (1993) is a comprehensive and very well-researched history of the family since the late nineteenth century. It is better on family dynamics than on business dynamics, however, and those interested in Siegmund can also read Jacques Attali's *A Man of Influence* (1986), which goes into more detail about his business career. It should be said that Attali's book has been heavily criticized for inaccuracies by those who knew Siegmund, and, perhaps because materials about the subject were so hard to come by, the book is filled out with political and economic history that is not strictly relevant.

PART THREE:
HOW PURPOSE BUILDS GREATNESS

Introductions to Psychology and Its Main Schools

Different theories of morale all draw heavily on different theories of psychology. Among the textbooks introducing psychology, I can recommend D. P. Schultz and S. E. Schultz, *A History of Modern Psychology* (7th edition, 2000) and B. R. Hergenhahn, *An Introduction to the History of Psychology* (4th edition, 2001). The Schultzes start the story in the late nineteenth century and are particularly strong on behaviorism, gestalt and psychoanalysis, with a somewhat cursory summary of humanistic psychology (Maslow) and cognitive psychology. Hergenhahn begins the story with the pre-Socratics, but about half of the book (300 pages) covers the same ground as the Schultzes, and gives slightly more space to modern trends in cognitive psychology and psychobiology.

Psychoanalysis was developed as a therapeutic tool by Sigmund Freud in the late nineteenth century. For those who want to read some of Freud's own work, I recommend his *Introductory Lectures on Psychoanalysis*. For a commentary, read Richard Wollheim, *Freud* (1991).

Behaviorism was partly a reaction to psychoanalysis and other nineteenth-century schools that depended heavily on introspection. A new generation of self-consciously scientific psychologists (e.g., John Watson) declared that purely mental phenomena, such as beliefs, decisions and willpower, were unknowable, while later B. F. Skinner in *Science and Human Behavior* (1954) continued to insist that mental concepts had no explanatory value and therefore were redundant in a science of behavior. This science could, however, measure correlations between stimuli and reactions, then build and test predictions. Naturally this perspective tended to encourage an industrial psychology in which workers were seen as cogs in the productive machine.

Meanwhile another school developed that also tried to create testable theories but that did allow for mental concepts. The Gestalt psychologists were particularly interested in how we come to know the world as we do; they postulated that we do not build our picture of the world up from the details, but start with various gestalts, or whole pictures, which we then fill in with the details. This had implications not just for how we learn about the world but also for how we are motivated—not primarily by extrinsic rewards but by a gestalt of the task and of one's self. Kurt Lewin, author of *Field Theory in Social Science* (1951), worked in this tradition.

Cognitive psychology grew out of Gestalt and was originally primarily concerned with knowledge and beliefs. In the 1950s the advent of artificial intelligence gave it a great boost by helping psychologists conceive of the effects of mental events as parts of systems with other, directly observable parts. In other words, there was no need for introspection: It was possible to rely entirely on experimental and survey evidence, but at the same time to model the effects of beliefs, attitudes and so on. Psychology could be both "mental" and "scientific." This approach has become dominant in modern academia and therapy, and now extends beyond theories of perception and knowledge to all aspects of social and mental life.

Since the beginning of the twentieth century there has been an alternative tradition, variously called Jungian, humanist or existentialist. Its protagonists thought it more important to capture the profundities of human experience than to rely on verifiable data. Carl Jung, one of its leading figures, was originally an associate of Freud, but whereas Freud saw human culture as a sublimation of more basic drives, Jung studied it to find clues about man's higher nature. For a quick summary of his work, I recommend Anthony Storr's *Jung* (1973). Similar interests drove existentialist philosopher Martin Heidegger, who wrote about how human beings deal with death, and later Abraham Maslow (see below under "Motivation and Morale"). Also interesting is Victor Frankl, *Man's Search for Meaning: An Introduction to Logotherapy* (1962). Frankl is a psychotherapist who survived the Holocaust and whose approach to therapy was influenced by that experience.

Motivation and Morale

Abraham Maslow, concerned with how man can achieve fulfillment, authored the famous theory of the hierarchy of needs: physiological, security, belonging, esteem and self-esteem, and self actualization. See his *Motivation and Personality* (1954). A good introduction to Maslow is a collection of his writings called *The Maslow Business Reader* (ed. Deborah Stephens, 2000), while the ideas he developed toward the end of his life are included in the posthumously published *The Farther Reaches of Human Nature* (1971).

Douglas McGregor's *The Human Side of Enterprise* (1960) famously sets out two theories managers might have of human nature and motivation, theory X and theory Y. Theory X—the conventional manager's wisdom at the time McGregor wrote—portrays the average worker as lazy and therefore in need of coercion, control and direction if he is to do anything productive. This is less unpleasant than it might sound since, according to the theory, the worker prefers to be told what to do and prefers security to responsibility. Theory Y by contrast holds that work is as natural as play, and that workers can become committed to corporate objectives if suitably treated; if they do, they will direct and control their own work effectively. Under the right conditions many of them will seek responsibility and will exercise creativity and ingenuity—capacities that are much underutilized. Perhaps theory Y is now the conventional manager's wisdom—at least in theory. Although some of the content is a bit dated, the book is entertainingly written and worth reading—a lot of modern business books are just a rehash of what McGregor wrote.

Edward Deci and Richard Ryan are leading academic theorists of motivation, of which they distinguish five types: extrinsic, in which individuals are motivated by rewards distinct from the work itself; intrinsic, in which individuals are motivated by pure enjoyment of the work; and three intermediate categories in which individuals are motivated by the *outcome* of the work, even though the work itself may be boring and unrewarding. These three categories are distinguished by the reason that the outcome motivates. First, the individual may give himself a psychic reward for achieving the outcome, perhaps because it is associated with success. This is similar to the role the super-ego plays in Freud's theory (Deci and Ryan call it "introjection"). Second, the individual may value the outcome because he thinks that is what social values dictate ("identification"). And third, the individual may value the outcome as part of an integrated value system that helps define his personal identity ("integration"). In this last case he does not "simply do what [he] thinks the social values dictate, [he] behaves, feels and thinks in a way that is congruent with the social values because [he] has accepted them as [his] own." Deci and Ryan present a far more sophisticated system than most cognitive psychologists, based on years of empirical work in a variety of settings—educational, work, community—though it is by no means easy reading. The main work is *Intrin-*

sic Motivation and Self-determination in Human Behavior (1985), but the work is summarized in their article in Porter, Bigley and Steers (2003)—see below.

Mihaly Csikszentmihalyi's *Flow: The Psychology of Optimal Experience* (1990) and more recent *Creativity* (1996) and *Good Business* (2003) present a sanguine picture of life at work. His identification and popularization of flow has been extremely useful.

For a popular account of the evidence from neurological research on the power of emotion over reason, see Antonio Damasio, *Descartes' Error: Emotion, Reason and the Human Brain* (1994).

I can recommend two academic works on commitment and community at work: J. Meyer and N. Allen, *Commitment in the Workplace* (1997), which offers a good overview of the research in this area; and Michael Hogg and Deborah Terry (eds.), *Social Identity Processes in Organizational Contexts* (2001), which is a collection of stimulating and relevant papers.

Oliver James's *Britain on the Couch* (1998) charts the danger of an excessively meritocratic value system. This system creates constant need for approval, not just in work but in all areas of life, so that even successful people feel that they are not quite making it and fall prey to depression. The book is stimulating and challenging, raising important issues for managers as well as politicians.

Kenneth Thomas's *Intrinsic Motivation at Work* (2000) is partly based on Deci and Ryan's theories (see above) and is readable and useful, with practical suggestions on managing motivation.

Paul Lawrence and Nitin Nohria's *Driven* (2002) is an attempt to explain human nature in terms of four drives, based on a mixture of published neurological research and an interpretation of evolutionary theory. The four drives are to learn, to acquire, to bond and to defend.

L. Porter, G. Bigley and R Steers, *Motivation and Work Behavior* (7th edition, 2003) is a good textbook, consisting of a series of reprinted academic papers grouped by theme and an introductory section outlining the history and current state of the subject. Particularly useful articles are Edward Deci and Richard Ryan, "Self-determination Theory and the Facilitation of Intrinsic Motivation, Social Development and Well-Being"; Steven Kerr, "On the Folly of Rewarding A, While Hoping for B"; R. Mowdray and K. Colwell, "Employee Reactions to Unfair Outcomes in the Workplace"; Teresa Amabile, "Motivating Creativity in Organizations: On Doing What You Love and Loving What You Do"; and Christopher Meek, "Ganbatte: Understanding the Japanese Employee."

I note here one absence: adequate databases. I have cited a number of research surveys in chapter 8, and there are plenty of studies measuring, for example, attrition rates or loosely defined forms of morale. However, to the best of my knowledge there are no databases linking Purpose, morale, action and performance. We need a new generation of metrics.

Action and Management

Chester Barnard, author of *The Functions of the Executive* (1938), was president of New Jersey Bell Telephone Company and was one of the first management writers to discuss morality and purpose as sources of energy for the firm. As he put it, "It is impossible by definition that formal organizations can act without the moral element." His account of purpose, however, was essentially of a manipulative tool, to help implement the rational decisions made by management. His book was and is extremely influential.

There are two classics on how decisions are taken in the firm. In *Organizations* (1958), J. G. March and H. A. Simon introduced the idea that managers were subject to bounded rationality: They wish to be rational but are hampered by limited information processing capacity, and hence they are more influenced by the practices and assumptions of the organization they work for. In March and Simon's view, the typical firm limits the range of responses of its managers—what does not fit into the worldview is ignored. R. M. Cyert and J. G. March developed these ideas in *A Behavioral Theory of the Firm* (1963), presenting a semiformal theory of the firm, based on the problems of decision making March and Simon had begun to describe. The firm is not omniscient but rather is an "adaptively rational system." These books are important because they show that the alternative to decisions influenced by Purpose is not some rational optimization of outcomes, but some other form of internal tradition.

John Hunt's *Managing People at Work* (1979, 3rd edition 1992) is an excellent summary of much of the research on people at work, teams, leaders and organizations. Hunt defines leadership as "the capacity to mobilize in competition or conflict a potential need in a follower," although this takes the form of the leader giving "meaning to possibilities" in the follower.

Jeffrey Pfeffer and Robert Sutton in *The Knowing-Doing Gap: How Smart Companies Turn Knowledge into Action* (1999) present an excellent account of why managers do not act on the knowledge they have—using some vivid examples from well-known companies.

Hugh Davidson, *The Committed Enterprise* (2002), presents a very straightforward account of how to achieve "the committed enterprise." Its main value is in its quotes from the United Kingdom as well as from U.S. business leaders and its case studies.

Perseus Books, *Best Practice* (2003), is a collection of articles, some of which contain a lot of management consultant's sales hype, but there are also some interesting and relevant contributions. These include pieces by Rosabeth Moss Kanter, Tom Brown, Richard Leider, Christopher Bartlett, Ken Murrell, Meredith Belbin, Jean-Claude Larréché, Costas Markides, Allan Kennedy, Jeffrey Pfeffer and Robert Sutton, Warren Bennis, Jim Kouzes and Annette Simmons.

Innovation

I have not been especially inspired by the innovation literature. There are, however, a few classics.

Joseph Schumpeter is famous for the emphasis he placed on the role of the entrepreneur in driving change and innovation in the economy, and thus re-introducing the human element into the model. The collection *Essays on Entrepreneurs, Innovations, Business Cycles and the Evolution of Capitalism*, edited by Richard Clemence (1951), gives a good flavor of his work. It is not technical and is highly stimulating. "The Creative Response in Economic History" has become a classic, and his article on "Capitalism" for the *Encyclopaedia Britannica* is a marvelous if somewhat dated synthesis.

T. Burns and G. Stalker's *The Management of Innovation* (1961) remains a key text on innovation. They identified two ideal types of organizations (in a study of small- and medium-sized Scottish firms): the mechanistic and the organic. The mechanistic firm is the traditional bureaucracy. In the perfectly organic firm, by contrast, there is continual redefinition of individual tasks through interaction with others, a network structure of control, based on presumed community of interest, authority attaching more to expertise than to position, lateral communication of advice rather than vertical communication of instructions, and commitment to the firm's tasks rather than to simple organizational loyalty. They found that organic companies are more successfully innovative than mechanistic ones.

Rosabeth Moss Kanter's *Change Masters: Innovation and Entrepreneurship in the American Organization* (1983) is in effect research and advice on how the large corporation can achieve the "organic" form described by Burns and Stalker in *The Management of Innovation* (see above). This is not natural for large corporations—and a whole set of additional managerial skills is required.

A readable account of creativity is given in Anthony Storr's *The Dynamics of Creation* (1972), although he is principally concerned with the individual artist or scientist, not the team member working in a corporation.

Robert Coram, *Boyd: The Fighter Pilot Who Changed the Art of War* (2002). Boyd was a pilot who was fascinated by the mental processes necessary to be an effective aviator and innovator. He intuited the two-stage nature of innovation: first, analysis of what we are familiar with into components, and then resynthesis into something new that deals with our situation better.

On creativity, the works of Teresa Amabile are useful. See her article on "Motivating Creativity in Organizations" in Porter, Bigley and Steers (see above on "Motivation and Morale"). For more detail see her *Creativity in Context: Update to the Social Psychology of Creativity* (1997). She makes the point that creativity involves being able to resist the temptation to jump to an algorithmic approach and often requires a great deal of trial and error.

Strategy and Advantage

Alfred Chandler's *The Visible Hand: The Managerial Revolution in American Business* (1962) is a massive study of the managerial revolution at the beginning of the twentieth century that created huge and enduring competitive advantages for large American companies. A particular set of technological advances created the conditions in which the classic large company structure became dominant. My argument is that different social forms now underpin advantage—after all, the technological conditions have also changed.

Kenneth Andrews's *The Concept of Corporate Strategy* (1971, 3rd edition 1987) is a short classic that I strongly recommend. He argued that a successful, actionable strategy will always fit the preferences of the chief executive and the values of key managers, as well as having some appeal for all employees. The implication is that those making strategic decisions should always consider values: Andrews explicitly makes the case for "the moral component of corporate strategy."

Chris Argyris and Donald Schön's *Organizational Learning* (1978) is a must-read book, if somewhat hard going. Building on the work of Simon and March and of Cyert and March (see above), the authors describe three levels of organizational learning. At level one, most managers keep their heads down—and problems are dealt with without any changes to the policies and objectives. At level two, the organization is capable of altering policies and objectives in response to its problems. Most organizations find it difficult to get to level two, which is essentially what Mintzberg describes as the strategy process. At the third level, the organization responds by improving the learning system itself. Argyris was an important influence on Peter Senge (q.v.).

Michael Porter in *Competitive Strategy* (1980) and *Competitive Advantage* (1985) has successfully imported microeconomics into management, and I, like many other writers, owe much to him. In addition, his *The Competitive Advantage of Nations* (1990) is a tremendous account of the value of social capital outside the firm. Perhaps the most lucid exposition of his view of strategy is his *Harvard Business Review* article, "What is Strategy?" reprinted in *On Competition* (1998). It is notable that Porter does not discuss people in his books. There is therefore no discussion of Purpose, or any serious discussion of human leadership for that matter. This is to his credit: He does not produce engineering solutions to human problems.

Karl Weick, "Substitutes for Strategy," in D. Teece (ed.), *The Competitive Challenge* (1987), argues that strategy is primarily a motivational tool. "True believers impose their view on the world and fulfil their own prophecies. Note that this makes strategy more of a motivational problem than a cognitive forecasting problem." He tells the story of the Hungarians lost in the Alps who used a map of the Pyrenees to find their way and thus save their lives. "Strategic plans are a lot like maps. They animate people and they orient people."

Gary Hamel and C. K. Prahalad pointed out in "Strategic Intent," *Harvard Business Review* (March 1989), that the companies that had risen to global leadership in the 1970s and 1980s had started out with ambitions—"strategic intents"—that were not limited by their current size or "capabilities." They advanced toward these goals by setting intermediate targets around which staff rallied. In "The Core Competencies of the Corporation," *Harvard Business Review* (May 1990), they argue that the critical success factor in many businesses is the ability to integrate different technologies into a single, distinctive technological "competency" that forms a platform for existing, planned and unforeseen products. This is likely to require integrating resources across the corporation, and it is important that the limited, market-focused horizons of the SBU do not get in the way. In "Strategy as Stretch and Leverage," *Harvard Business Review* (1993), the authors build on these ideas, emphasizing how the gap between existing resources and aspirations needs to be wide enough to leverage those resources in the most competitive way.

H. Mintzberg, "The Design School," *Strategic Management Journal* (1990). In this important article, Mintzberg criticizes the "design school" of strategy (Andrews, Bower, Christiansen, Hamermesh) for its apparent insistence that strategy is intentional, rational, done at the top, based on a few simple ideas (since otherwise it cannot be done at the top), explicit, distinctive, fully formed when it emerges and separate from implementation. This works only when the environment is both relatively simple and relatively stable. For most organizations, strategy formulation is learning from action, and if they conceptualize it as something distinct from implementation, they are bound to fail. Mintzberg's views are set out in greater detail in *The Rise and Fall of Strategic Planning* (1994).

J. Barney in "Firm Resources and Sustained Competitive Advantage," *Journal of Management* 17 (1991), defines resources as anything the firm controls that allows it to conceive of and implement its strategies. Resources create advantage when they are valuable, rare and difficult to substitute for or imitate (because of history, causal ambiguity and social complexity). To sustain advantage a company must have resources that are immobile and diverse.

John Kay, *Foundations of Corporate Success* (1993). This is a very good analysis of why successful companies are successful. Kay analyzes the sources of advantage and places them into four categories: "architecture," reputation, innovation and strategic assets. Of these the most significant or fundamental is "architecture"—a network of "relational contracts" in and around the firm. Relational contracts are mutual understandings, or relationships of trust, and are by their nature long term. It is always possible to score short-term gains by undermining relational contracts.

Robert Grant, *Contemporary Strategy Analysis* (4th edition, 2002) is an excellent textbook for those who want an easy primer on competitive advantage.

Relationships

Erving Goffman is perhaps unique—a sociologist who writes in an entertaining way. He writes about everyday encounters and what is really going on when they take place. From my point of view, the emphasis he places in *Encounters* (1961) on games as a prototype for much social activity is particularly relevant: Games have boundaries, and anything outside the boundary is irrelevant to the conduct of the game. A good game allows deployment of skill and engagement of emotion, but not encroachment of external anxieties. This creates a kind of "euphoria" that is part of the attraction of games. A shared purpose, I might add, creates the boundary of a game.

Perry Anderson's *Passages from Antiquity to Feudalism* (1974) is a masterful economic history of ancient and mediaeval Europe. Anderson uses a Marxist conceptual framework, but this supports rather than obscures the subtlety and clarity of his analysis. This book is highly recommended for those interested in how economic advantage was manifest in other eras.

In *The Anatomy of Relationships* (1985), Michael Argyle and Monika Henderson describe some of the key features of human relationships. For example, they point out that relationships are like games in so far as they have goals (sources of satisfaction, rewards), typical activities, roles, settings and rules. Rewards from relationships themselves, as opposed to their purely instrumental effects, tend to be confined to intimate relations in the West, but extend to work relations in the East, where ritualized exchanges of gifts and reciprocal obligation are formalized. There are many other relevant observations in this book: For example, groups of friends occur spontaneously when networks become very dense; we like people who share our values even if their personality is very different, and above all we like people who like us.

David Landes's *The Wealth and Poverty of Nations* (1998) is a historical account of why some countries have become rich and some remained poor. It combines global scope with fascinating detail. One small but typical example: Landes describes how the invention of spectacles boosted the late medieval economy by allowing skilled craftsmen to continue doing detailed work beyond the age of 40. Overall, he reminds us of the importance of geography, and of the interplay between geography and the human spirit, although he refrains from any grand synthesis. It is an excellent source for those wanting a historical perspective on comparative and competitive advantage.

I have also found Michael Jensen, *Foundations of Organizational Strategy* (2000), useful if only to mark out the opposite of what I believe: It presents with admirable internal consistency a certain kind of economist's view of organization. The following gives a flavor: "I believe it is productive to define an organization as a legal entity that serves as a nexus for a complex set of contracts (written and unwritten) among disparate individuals . . . the behavior of the organization is like the equilibrium behavior of a market. We do not often characterise the steel market or the wheat market as having preferences and motives or making choices."

D. Cohen and L. Prusak, *In Good Company: How Social Capital Makes Organizations Work* (2000). This is a lucid account of the importance of social capital in organizations. For a collection of some of the important contributions to the theory of social capital, see E. Lesser (ed.), *Knowledge and Social Capital* (2000).

Leadership

Henry Kissinger's *A World Restored* (1973), describing European diplomacy between 1812 and 1822, is interesting on three levels—as history, as an analysis of the interplay of power and legitimacy and as an insight into the thinking of this famous diplomat. It is the interplay of power and legitimacy that concerns me—since this is required for the effective alignment of strategy and Purpose, and at its most effective creates enduring advantage.

James Kouzes and Barry Posner's *The Leadership Challenge* (1987) identifies five elements of leadership—challenging the status quo, inspiring a shared vision, enabling others to act, setting an example and encouragement, through positive feedback and celebration. Challenging the status quo involves taking risks and encouraging others to innovate and take risks. Setting an example is particularly important, and leaders need to make themselves visible—"walk the talk"—and then make a point of interacting in the right way and asking the right questions: These send strong signals about what is valued.

Peter Senge's *The Fifth Discipline* (1990) is a classic that outlines the five disciplines that companies need to maximize learning, and hence be successful. Two of these are relevant to Purpose. First, there is "personal mastery," that is, "approaching one's life as a creative work." This involves assessing both what one really wants *and* where one really is; the gap between the two generates creative tension, a constant goad to learning and action. Second, there is shared vision or purpose. Individuals with personal mastery are not blind followers, so shared vision arises out of a dialogue, not the kind of brainwashing described by Collins and Porras (q.v.). The other three disciplines are "mental models"—those pictures of the world that guide our actions; "learning in teams"; and the "systems thinking" that pulls the other disciplines together. Senge is not always an easy read but is worth the effort.

Robert Eccles and Nitin Nohria in *Beyond the Hype: Rediscovering the Essence of Management* (1992) correctly put the spotlight on action, to be contrasted with the various panaceas offered to managers. They emphasize the importance of personal identity and rhetoric in generating effective action, and go on to point out that the key lessons for managers have changed little over the years—most business books say the same things again and again and again. The authors, both of whom have been chairmen of the Department of Organizational Behavior at Harvard Business School, are in a position to know.

Bill Drath and Chuck Palus in *Making Common Sense: Leadership as Meaning-Making in a Community of Practice* (1993) argue that people do things because they make sense, they have a meaning, that is they exist within a larger frame. Leaders are those who can express this kind of meaning on behalf of a community and thus influence what members of the community do.

Tony Eccles, *Succeeding with Change: Implementing Action-Driven Strategies* (1994). This is a practical but quite complex guide to implementation—

a somewhat more down-to-earth, U.K.-based version of Kotter's *Leading Change* (q.v.). There are plenty of examples and an interesting section on the use of managerial power. Eccles is skeptical about the involvement of employees in decision making, perhaps because in 1981 he wrote a book about Britain's largest worker cooperative *(Under New Management)*.

Howard Gardner's *Leading Minds* (1995) is an excellent, well-researched account of twentieth-century leaders in different walks of life. Gardner is a psychologist, but his interest is less in the personal style of the leaders and the influence they have on others face to face than in their power to influence at a distance, through both words and actions. He concentrates on the stories, particularly the identity stories that leaders tell their followers. Each chapter is devoted to one of the leaders. The book is an especially good read since all of the profiled leaders are interesting figures (e.g., Ghandi, anthropologist Margaret Mead, scientist Robert Oppenheimer, Pope John XXIII, Margaret Thatcher).

Daniel Goleman's *Emotional Intelligence* (1995) presents in accessible form modern research on what has always been a vital component of successful management.

John Kotter has produced several books on leadership. In *Leading Change* (1996), he sets out eight stages in the effective leadership of change. These are creating urgency, creating a coalition, developing vision and strategy, communicating the vision, empowering employees to implement the strategy, generating some quick wins, keeping up the momentum and changing the culture to "anchor" the change. The book is punchy, clear and easy to absorb, and I agree with the broad thrust of his message: Change involves a number of stages, and it is tempting to skip some of these, but you do so at your peril. Kotter's *What Leaders Really Do* (1999) is a collection of articles dating back to the 1970s; the early work in particular is both entertaining and insightful.

Ronald Heifetz and Donald Laurie, "The Work of Leadership," *Harvard Business Review* (January 1997). This influential article rejects the conception of leadership as "grand knowing and salesmanship"—the idea that the core of leadership is having a vision and then persuading people to share it. Instead the goal is to help people throughout the organization to take responsibility and adapt to the environment.

I have been influenced by Russell Ackoff. See for example *Re-creating the Corporation* (1999) or *Ackoff's Best* (1999). Ackoff began his academic career as a philosopher and then switched to operations research, an unusual combination that perhaps explains his ability to look at the big picture as well as the detail. He describes the organization as a system and the implications this has for management and leadership.

William Isaacs's *Dialogue and the Art of Thinking Together* (1999) is a difficult book but displays valuable intellectual integrity. It explains how collective inspiration can be produced by "thinking together," and describes the processes involved—a more arduous but more effective alternative than traditional tell and sell.

Peter Drucker is the supreme business commentator of the second half of the twentieth century, a kind of one-man *Harvard Business Review,* and I, like most writers on management, owe much to his insights. They are scattered in a huge volume of work, and for those who are not already familiar with this, I recommend a recent anthology, *The Essential Drucker* (2001). His "classics" include *The Practice of Management* (1954) and *Management, Tasks, Responsibilities, Practices* (1974).

James Collins's *Good to Great* (2001) was written partly because Collins's earlier book with Jerry Porras, *Built to Last* (q.v.), gave some readers the mistaken impression that if your firm was not born a great company, it had little chance of becoming great. Collins and his team identified eleven companies that had been transformed from good to great at different times between 1964 and 1999. He concluded that the companies shared the following features: low-key, almost self-effacing leaders who first formed a top team that worked effectively together and only then developed a strategy; a team that was able to accept the awful reality of where they were while still maintaining their confidence that they would achieve their objectives; a clearly defined business concept, involving an activity they could be best in the world at and that they cared about passionately, and a clearly understood model of how that activity would generate profits; a culture of discipline, which made hierarchy and bureaucracy redundant; careful and innovative use of technology, and no attempts to make sudden leaps—rather, steady progress until a critical point is reached, when things take off.

Manfred Kets de Vries is a professor at Insead University with training in psychoanalysis, management and economics. *The Leadership Mystique* (2001) is subtitled "a user's manual for the human enterprise" and contains a good account of leadership failure as well as success from a psychoanalytical perspective.

Jack Welch, *Jack* (2001). This is a highly entertaining and readable account of Jack Welch's career. It's a perfect case study of the leader as superhero.

Larry Bossidy and Ram Charan's *Execution* (2002) is a book by a CEO and a consultant about how to manage a large company. Their practical prescriptions can be boiled down to a quite simple list:

• Engage in vigorous dialogue with your colleagues—make sure meetings involve a real exchange of views.

- Involve those who have to follow the plans in the strategic and operational planning process.
- Understand the business so that you can ask penetrating questions.
- Make sure specific people are accountable for specific tasks—do not let meetings end without clear allocation of responsibilities.
- Hold people accountable for what they have promised—engage in relentless follow-through, and do not tolerate repeated failure: Fire people when you have to.
- Make sure the right people are in the right jobs—pay very close attention to the recruitment and promotion process.

Rakesh Khurana, "The Curse of the Superstar CEO," *Harvard Business Review* (September 2002). For anyone who believes in the charismatic leader, this makes particularly interesting reading.

W. Chan Kim and Renee Mauborgne, "Tipping Point Leadership," *Harvard Business Review* (April 2003). This account of how New York police chief William Bratton cut crime rates is an excellent case study.

Other Writers on Leadership

Despite the thousands of studies on leadership that have been produced in the last 40 years, we agree with Owain Franks and Richard Rawlinson, who in the article "The Theory of Leadership and the Leadership of Theory," published in *European Business Forum "Leadership"* (2004), wrote that there was as yet no well-established and widely applied theory of leadership comparable to the theories that guide marketing and strategy.

Nonetheless the somewhat fragmented literature has been well summarized in John van Maurik's survey *Writers on Leadership* (2001). Van Maurik covers the work of no fewer than 38 writers, some of whose work I have described elsewhere in this bibliography. I have not drawn significantly on the work of the others, but I provide a quick resumé here of those who have something to say relevant to subjects covered in this book, should readers wish to follow up on them. They fall into three groups: those primarily concerned with boss-subordinate or team leader–team relationships, those primarily concerned with the personal development and skills of the leader and those primarily concerned with the effects leaders have on organizations (or other wider groups).

Relationships. The first group includes R. Tannenbaum and W. H. Schmidt, who, in "How to Choose a Leadership Pattern," *Harvard Business Review* (1958), defined a continuum from authoritarian to delegative management styles (compare McGregor [q.v.] writing at about the same time), and R. R. Blake and J. S. Mouton, who in 1964 suggested a two-dimensional space for mapping management styles—concern for tasks and concern for relationships. Both pairs of writers also emphasized the need for style and situation to fit. Ken Blanchard made the same point in the 1970s and again suggested two dimensions of management style, in this case level of discretion allowed and level of support offered to subordinates. In the 1980s increased attention was paid to the working of teams, and John Adair in *Effective Leadership* (1983) expanded on Blake and Mouton to suggest that team leaders need to be concerned not just with tasks and relationships but with tasks, individual needs and team needs. Later John Whitmore in *Need, Greed or Freedom* (1997) combined this kind of thinking with Maslow to argue that team member needs evolve: from a need to be included, to a need to make a mark, to a need for meaning and purpose. Team leadership styles must evolve accordingly from authoritarian to a "coaching" style—the style of the "questioning coach" advocated by another writer on teams and leadership, Rupert Eales-White (*The Power of Persuasion*, 1992).

Development. The second group includes Warren Bennis, author of *Leaders: The Strategies for Taking Charge* (1985, with Burt Nanus) and *On Becoming a Leader* (1998), who emphasizes the importance of a strong sense of purpose and of "self-invention," and also offers some political tips. Stephen Covey (*Seven Habits of Highly Effective People*, 1989) echoes Bennis's interest in purpose, and the independence it implies, but sees this as merely a platform for successful relationships (or more generally what he calls "interdependence"). Robert Kelley (*How to Be a Star at Work: Nine Breakthrough Strategies You Need to Succeed*, 1998) produces an overlapping set of successful habits. He points out that in current conditions a good leader and a good follower have much in common, including independence of mind, and that good leaders need good followers. Maurik himself has developed a sophisticated system of leadership skills in *The Portable Leader* (1997) and *The Effective Strategist* (1999).

Leaders and organizations. The third group includes Hunt, Kotter, Kets de Vries, Kouzes and Posner, Gardner, Collins and Porras, Senge, Drath and Palus, and Hamel and Prahalad, for whom see separate entries. Roger Harrison (*The Collected Papers of Roger Harrison*, 1995) argues that successful change involves both "action tactics" and "healing tactics"—in effect disrupting and then re-creating the social system. The leader contributes to both of these primarily through symbolic acts—by being an example (cf. Kouzes and Posner, and Gardner). According to R. J. Marshak ("Managing the Metaphors of Change," in *Organizational Dynamics*, 1993), an important part of this symbolism is the language the leader uses—and he contrasts the kinds of phrases and descriptions appropriate to three levels of change (what he calls developmental, transitional and transformational). John Burdett (*Managing in the Age of Discontinuity*, 1993) follows Senge in emphasizing the importance of creative tension in change, and offers advice on how to achieve this. J. M. Stewart ("Future State Visioning—A Powerful Leadership Process," in *Long-Range Planning*, 1993) emphasizes the importance of a vision (echoing Hamel and Prahalad) and recommends a process for developing an effective one.

Also useful is the *Harvard Business Review* (December 2001), which includes an interesting reading list of some classics on leadership

Three Classics Relevant Today

Thucydides's *The Peloponnesian War* (transl. Steven Lattimore, 1998) is a classic text on strategy, leadership and Purpose. Thucydides is important for several reasons. He pointed out the hopelessness of trying to reconcile different systems of morality—in his case the systems of political morality of Athens and Sparta. He writes about the Peloponnesian War, which can be seen as a war of ideas. His characters are constantly appealing to moral ideas in their orations. They are also constantly involved in what modern leadership writers would call "contingency" and "transformation" leadership efforts. Thucydides was the first to study both leaders and their oratory. His Funeral Oration attributed to Pericles has been the model of many later leadership speeches, including Lincoln's Gettysburg Address. In it he answers the questions, What are we fighting for? Where will we fight? How will we win? What do we need to do this? What kind of people are needed?

Niccolo Machiavelli's *The Prince* (transl. George Bull, 1961) repays reading. It is very short and full of striking thoughts about the dynamics of power, some of which on reflection might be as relevant today as when they were made in sixteenth-century Italy. He was, famously, a realist—a bureaucrat who lost his job, not a theoretician, and the interest is to see how his observations apply to modern situations. Antony Jay's *Management and Machiavelli* (1967) is an excellent, well-written book doing just that.

Karl von Clausewitz was another practitioner of leadership, and his *On War*, originally published in 1833, is a masterpiece. Unfinished when he died, it is very long and cries out for a good editor; the business reader will want to be selective. However, this greatest exponent of military strategy offers exceptional insights into the power of a higher purpose that guides strategy, and he speaks explicitly of the superiority of moral factors. His thought is often misunderstood: He shares with Adam Smith the distinction of being more quoted than read. The Everyman edition (1993) contains an excellent commentary by Bernard Brodie, which helps the reader find his way around this lengthy work.

INDEX